D1420692

QE2
BRITAIN'S
GREATEST
LINER

BRUCE PETER
PHILIP DAWSON
IAN JOHNSTON

WITH FOREWORD BY
HRH THE DUKE OF EDINBURGH

CUNARD

Published by:

Ferry Publications, PO Box 33, Ramsey, Isle of Man IM99 4LP

Tel: +44 (0) 1624 898446   Fax: +44 (0) 1624 898449

E-mail: ferrypubs@manx.net   Website: www.ferrypubs.co.uk

CONTENTS

ACKNOWLEDGEMENTS

THE authors wish to express their thanks to Miles Cowsill and John Hendy for their support and enthusiasm for this publication. The authors and publishers would especially like to thank His Royal Highness The Duke of Edinburgh for agreeing to write the foreword, Caroline Heard, David Parsons and Anthony Cooke for reading and editing the manuscript, John Peter for preparing the illustrations, Eric Flounders and Michael Gallagher of Cunard, Dot Tilbury and Maxine Cannon of the Isle of Man Post, Robert Lloyd for the special painting, Andrew Lowe of Signature Design and Jo Clark of Printer Trento.

In addition, the following have assisted greatly with the research and the provision of images:

Dickie Bannenberg, Beaupre Bannenberg, Brian Beardsmore, Tony Benn, Klas Brogren, David Buri, Michael Cango, Sherban Cantacuzino, Carola Casson-Zogolovitch, Duncan Chappell, Ian Collard,

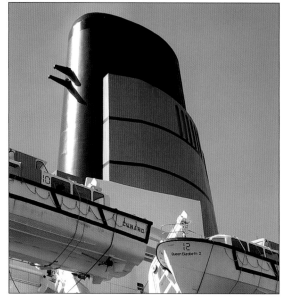

*The **Queen Elizabeth 2**'s funnel during her 2007 Round Britain cruise. (Lauren Gradwell)*

Hall Coons, James Cousins, Richard Danielson, Gary Davis of Maritime Photographic, Maurizio Eliseo, Colin Forbes, Professor Richard Frewer, Keith Gladhill, Dr Ann Glen, Jim Gordon, Professor Thom Gorst, Lauren Gradwell, Richard Gray, Elain Harwood, Ann Haynes, Tony Heaton, Nicholas Hills, Alan Irvine, Kate Irvine, Trevor Jones, Tom Kameen, Andrew Kilk, Juliet Kinchin, Peter Knego, Peter C. Kohler, John Lang, Mike Louagie, Philip Masaad, John McNeece, Christopher Marsden, William Mayes, Colin Meill, Justin Merrigan, Dr Catherine Moriarty, Dr Ken Neil, Philip Neumann of Fotoflite, Iain Pattie, Dr Jane Pavitt, Stephen Payne, Josette Reeves, Lady Reilly, Roisin Reilly, Andrew Richardson, Tony Rive, Theodore W. Scull, Colin Smith, David L. Smith, Graham Smith, The Earl of Snowdon, David Trevor-Jones, Dr Ken Neil, Gordon Turner, Tage Wandborg and Dr Lesley Whitworth.

© Ferry Publications 2008
Published by Lily Publications Ltd on behalf of Ferry Publications
Produced and designed by Lily Publications Ltd
Printed in Italy

FOREWORD

BY HRH THE DUKE OF EDINBURGH

Queen Elizabeth 2 will go down in history as the last trans-Atlantic passenger liner to be built in this country, but for everyone alive at the time, she will be particularly remembered for her part in the Falklands War.

I had the opportunity to visit her in 1967 while she was being completed at John Brown's famous shipyard in Glasgow. Two years later I accompanied the Queen to Southampton to see her off on her maiden voyage. Much has changed since those days. In 1969 there were regular passenger liner services from London, Liverpool and Southampton to ports all over the world. Since then, they have all been superseded by airliners. But that was not to be the end of the QE2.

The authors of this book deserve to be congratulated on putting together this record of the design and construction of this remarkable ship, and the story of her fascinating career from passenger liner, to troopship and ultimately to a cruise liner.

HRH The Duke of Edinburgh

HM The Queen and HRH The Duke of Edinburgh attend the launching ceremony of the **Queen Elizabeth 2** *on 20 September 1967. (Gallagher collection)*

INTRODUCTION

The brand-new **Queen Elizabeth 2** *lifts her safety valve, sending plumes of steam into the air, during her sea trials in November 1968. The liner's sleek lines and*

THE *Queen Elizabeth 2* was a beautiful child of the 1960s – representing much more than mere luxury and exclusivity. The liner emerged during a brief window in time when the world was changing rapidly and, momentarily, anything seemed possible. Cunard took a supreme risk to build a ship the like of which had not been seen before. Aesthetically, technologically, in layout and planning – and even the lifestyle on board – the QE2 reflected the last word in progressive thinking. How could this failing liner company, hitherto associated with all that was stale and stuffy about the British establishment, come to commission such an advanced modernist liner?

When the QE2 was under development, a great deal was at stake. This was, after all, the final national flagship, funded with a Government loan to rescue both Cunard and the struggling British shipbuilding industry. Furthermore, the QE2 was designed and built primarily as a showcase of modern British identity – although commercial success was expected too. Every passenger ship built subsequently has been designed only with the latter aim in mind. No succeeding ship has therefore caught the imagination like the QE2 because no ship since has embodied the hopes and fears of a nation in the same way. From her pre-launch days, when her incomplete hull and superstructure towered majestically over Clydebank, the liner was an icon.

Not only did the world's media report on every development during the lengthy design gestation and construction process, but also the architectural press devoted journal issues to celebrating what was considered to be a great British achievement. The photographs in the special editions of *The Architectural Review* and *Design* dedicated to the QE2 fixate on dynamic shapes and forms, dramatic colour palettes, state-of-the-art technology, award-winning bespoke furnishings and the most felicitously-resolved design details, the quality of which none of today's cruise ships could aspire to emulate. Even *The*

Motor Ship reported regularly and at length on the steam-powered QE2's progress.

Now, over four decades later, the QE2 has aura as well – the accumulation of memories and associations brought about through decades of constant service, always in the public eye. There were the fearsome Atlantic storms, the enormous swells sliced through by her graceful bow, the heroic rescues of souls from other stricken ships, the brave service in the Falklands War, the remarkable metamorphosis from steam to diesel power, the world cruises, tropical ports and celebrity passengers – but there were also embarrassing mechanical breakdowns, 'disastrous' refits, a severe grounding and other dramas which made the headlines. For the newsmen and for the public, the QE2 continued to matter.

More generally, the liner's changing ownership, operation, crewing and clientele have reflected social shifts and revolutions in business culture during the past half-century. When a new flagship was first conceived in the 1950s, Cunard were very much an 'establishment' company which had been in existence since the mid-nineteenth century. Then, only a couple of years after the QE2 entered service, they became part of the conglomerate Trafalgar House – an upstart firm whose aggressive business methods

graceful curves were the epitome of modernist naval architecture and industrial design. (Gallagher collection)

were more in tune with the coming era of free market capitalism. Later, in the 1990s, Cunard passed to Carnival – a global corporation, ultimately headquartered in Miami and owning an international portfolio of cruise line brands. Simultaneously, the QE2 changed, via successive refits, from being a modernist liner, conceived around the idea of egalitarian open space and relaxation, into a post-modern 'retro' ship, evoking a mythical 1930s 'golden age' of liner travel and reconfigured to maximise onboard revenue streams. The crew, meanwhile, changed from being British and unionised to 'international' contract labour, with only some British officers and hotel staff remaining. The passenger demographic has also altered and, in recent years, the QE2 has become much more accessible to wider cross-sections of society than she once was.

No passenger ship – apart from the ill-fated, but omnipresent, *Titanic* – has had as much written about her as the QE2. Back in 1969, Neil Potter and Jack Frost, shipping correspondents for *The Daily Telegraph* newspaper, published an 'official' account of the QE2's design and construction, but a potentially more interesting architectural study by Sir Hugh Casson and Sherban Cantacuzino failed to

materialise, although both wrote shorter critiques of the ship for *The Architectural Review*. Later on, numerous liner historians and even the ship's Captain, Ronald Warwick, not to mention Carol Thatcher, have written about the QE2. What more is there still to be said? Well, the continuing absence of an architectural study of the ship's origins, construction and subsequent design evolution means that there remains plenty of scope for adding new perspectives.

The lack of appreciation for the QE2 as an icon of British modernism has also negatively impacted upon perceptions of the significance of her designers. While historians have reappraised the work of numerous progressive British architects working on *terra firma*, those who designed the QE2 remain marginalised in existing accounts of post-war design. Yet, for James Gardner, Dennis Lennon, their assistants and collaborators, the liner was their *magnum opus* – a uniquely bold and brilliant proclamation of faith in the future. Moreover, her spotless paintwork and expanses of scrubbed teak decking were much more uplifting than the drab grey concrete urban architecture of the same era. That the QE2 survived in pristine and unaltered condition for only three years was unfortunate; that her innovative underlying planning enabled her to serve as a flagship liner and cruise ship for over forty is an achievement worth celebrating.

This book brings together the enthusiasm and diverse expertise of three life-long admirers of the QE2 – and a great deal of new primary scholarship. Indeed, many people and organisations have generously given their time and assistance to help assemble the complex and fragmented jigsaw of the QE2's design, operational and cultural history.

Bruce Peter - Philip Dawson - Ian Johnston
November 2008

(*J.E.K. Smith*)

CHAPTER I

CUNARD AND THE CLYDE

QE2
BRITAIN'S
GREATEST
LINER

ON 21 September 2007 the QE2 made a brief and nostalgic visit to the River Clyde as part of her round-Britain cruise. It prompted huge interest from the media, not to mention a stunning tribute by the Red Arrows who performed a half-hour aerial spectacular over her as she lay alongside at Greenock. When the QE2 sailed later that evening, she was accompanied by a veritable flotilla of yachts, motor launches and assorted other craft. Emotions were running high – she was, after all, 'Scotland's ship', launched on the Clyde exactly forty years ago to the day. To many, the QE2 is a poignant reminder of the once great capabilities of shipbuilding and engineering on Clydeside, tempered by the sadness that these achievements are unlikely to be repeated. She is the last of her kind and follows other iconic twentieth century Cunarders such as the *Lusitania*, the *Aquitania*, the *Queen Mary* and the *Queen Elizabeth*. All of these ships were the products of just one yard, John Brown & Co Ltd of Clydebank.

Perhaps less well known by those who turned out to see her is that the QE2 is part of a relationship between Cunard and the Clyde that had lasted for over 120 years. While many people came on that September day to see the QE2, the world's most famous liner, others, fewer in number perhaps, came to see a ship that represents the last part of that magnificent history and a Britain that no longer exists.

With the retiral of the QE2 from Cunard service in 2008, a backward glance at her construction reveals a Britain whose industry was in a fight for survival. This was no more so than in shipbuilding where a meteoric collapse into statistical irrelevance was in its first phase. At that time, the business did not have the answers to the many pressures that foreign competition imposed on it across labour, management and investment issues. For those closest to it, it was inconceivable that an industry that had been in existence for generations, associated with such world-renowned products, should be facing extinction. Yet a seismic shift that would change the fundamental nature of Britain as a manufacturing nation was under way. The John Brown shipyard at Clydebank, for a time probably the most well known yard in the world, was in a parlous financial state. While the QE2 was under construction, the parent company had decided to divest themselves of their loss-making shipyard.

Two-and-a-half years after the QE2 departed, shipbuilding at Clydebank ceased. That it did so in rancour and disbelief makes the point that there is no good way for an industry so deeply embedded in the national consciousness – such as shipbuilding – to end. That the QE2 is a beautiful and well-built ship, redolent of the very best in British design, is a bitter-sweet paradox.

This was in stark contrast to the challenge of new opportunities and the excitement of steam-driven technology that must have confronted Samuel Cunard when he first set about creating the great enterprise that would bear his name. The Clyde, too, was emerging as the world's leader in marine engineering and shipbuilding developments; the inventiveness and skills of the yards along its banks would change the pattern of seaborne trade for ever.

The relationship between Cunard and the Clyde began in January 1839, when Samuel Cunard came to the UK from Halifax in Nova Scotia to submit to the Admiralty his bid to run the Royal Mails across the Atlantic. When the Admiralty indicated its willingness to accept his proposal, Cunard was advised to visit Robert Napier in Glasgow, renowned as the designer and builder of reliable steam engines, to discuss the ships that would deliver Cunard's proposed service. Napier wisely encouraged Cunard to consider ships of greater power and size than intended to ensure his ships were able to meet the demanding conditions likely to apply on the North Atlantic in the light of severe Admiralty penalties for delays and cancelled sailings. As such ships were more costly than Cunard was able to afford, he was now presented with the additional task of raising the necessary funds. The solution, brokered by Robert Napier, was an introduction to George Burns and David McIver, two successful Glasgow shipowners. After further deliberations over the power, size and number of ships to be built, agreement was reached in July 1839 in Glasgow to invest in the British & North American Royal Mail Steam Packet Company, as Cunard's firm was to be known. Four ships would be required, all of which were to be built on the Clyde.

By this time, Glasgow and the Clyde had emerged as the leading centre for the production of marine steam engines, still a very new technology. The first four Cunarders – the *Britannia*, the *Acadia*, the

*Top: The **Campania** of 1882 was a thoroughly modern and fast steamer whose sleek profile was dominated by two magnificent funnels. (Smith collection)*

*Centre left: The pioneering Cunarder **Britannia** is depicted arriving at Halifax on 17 July 1840. (Gallagher collection)*

*Above: A splendid low-angle view of the **Carmania** belching coal-smoke whilst on sea trials in 1905. (Smith collection)*

*Left: The magnificent four-stacker **Lusitania** of 1907 was one of Cunard's most prestigious liners of the Edwardian era and a fine example of Clyde shipbuilding when the river was at its zenith. (Smith collection)*

11

Above: The **Queen Mary** *is fitted out at Clydebank in 1935. (Smith collection)*

Top left: The powerful tug-tender **Romsey** *was brought to the Clyde from Southampton specially to help guide the giant* **Queen Mary** *down-river on 24 March 1936. (A. Ernest Glen, Bruce Peter collection)*

Left: The brand-new **Queen Mary** *begins to gather speed for the first time in the Firth of Clyde off Greenock. (A. Ernest Glen, Bruce Peter collection)*

Below: With her hull topsides freshly painted in Cunard livery, the **Queen Elizabeth** *is readied for launching at John Brown's shipyard during the summer of 1938. (Smith collection)*

Caledonia and the *Columbia* – were constructed at John Wood & Co's Port Glasgow shipyard, while the engines were manufactured by Napier at his works in Glasgow.

While other vessels would leave the slipways at Port Glasgow, Napier decided to enter into shipbuilding on his own account and, by 1841, he had acquired a modest shipyard at Govan. It was from this yard that many paddle-driven Cunard vessels were constructed, including the *Persia* in 1856 and the *Scotia* in 1861, the second largest paddle ship in the world after the *Great Eastern*.

Napier's pre-eminence as a marine engineer and iron shipbuilder ensured a constant flow of young men through his works, eager to learn and become prominent engineers and shipbuilders in their own right. Two such men were the brothers James and George Thomson, who worked for Napier at his Lancefield Foundry in Glasgow. In 1847 the Thomson brothers left Napier's employment to found their own business, James & George Thomson, in the Anderston district of the city, where they began constructing steam engines. Their works was given the name Clyde Bank Foundry. In 1851 they added shipbuilding to their activities at Govan with their first ship, the tender *Jackal*, built for Cunard. In winning this small contract, they were probably assisted by a third brother, Robert, who had become Cunard's first Superintendent Engineer.

It is with this business established by the Thomson brothers in 1847 that a direct link is made to John Brown & Co, the builders of the QE2. The business flourished and a series of large, well-appointed steamships – including the *Jura* (1854), the *Russia* (1867) and the *Abyssinia* (1870) – left the ways to join the growing Cunard fleet. However, as the River Clyde and Glasgow grew both as a centre of commerce and industry and as a port, their shipyard was acquired by compulsory purchase order to make way for port expansion. An alternative site was found on the north bank of the river, about seven miles downstream from Glasgow. The location was little more than farmland but it was here, in 1871, that a new shipyard was laid out, taking with it the name Clyde Bank. It was from this yard, ninety-six years later, that the QE2 would be launched.

A small town grew rapidly around the shipyard, eventually being named Clydebank after the yard to which it owed its existence. Here, the Thomsons built a series of liners, each generally bigger and faster than the one before – including the *Bothnia* (1874), the *Gallia* (1879), the *Servia* (1881) and the *Aurania* (1883).

Elsewhere on the Clyde, another shipyard had rapidly become established as one of the most significant anywhere, based largely on the excellence of its machinery. The man behind this yard was John Elder who, in 1854, had famously demonstrated his compound steam engine which delivered a 30% reduction in coal consumption over existing engines. The advantages to shipowners were obvious. By 1860 his yard was probably the most advanced privately-owned ship and engine builder anywhere at the time and, indeed, it began to overtake Napier as the Clyde's most prestigious shipbuilder. Elder's works, later named The Fairfield Shipbuilding & Engineering Co Ltd, constructed a series of record-breaking Atlantic liners for various shipping companies. Where, previously, Cunard had placed their orders with Thomson at Clydebank, they now turned to Fairfield who produced the Blue Riband-winning *Umbria* (1884) and the *Etruria* (1885), to be followed a decade later by the *Campania* and the *Lucania* (both 1893).

At the end of the nineteenth century, the Sheffield forgemasters John Brown & Co Ltd, seeking to expand their business into shipbuilding, acquired the Clydebank yard for little less than £1 million. Under its new management and designation of John Brown & Co, the Clydebank yard was poised again to become Cunard's most important builder of very large liners up to the QE2.

First came the 20,000grt *Caronia* and *Carmania* (both 1905), the latter fitted with steam turbines to test this new technology against the quadruple-expansion reciprocating machinery fitted in her sister. Next was the 32,500grt *Lusitania* (1907), along with her Tyne-built sister *Mauretania*, built to wrest the Blue Riband and supremacy on the North Atlantic from North German Lloyd. In 1910, with White Star's Olympic Class ships under construction and Hamburg-Amerika's planned trio of even larger ships, Cunard's response was the 45,647grt *Aquitania* (1914). John Brown's output was by no means restricted to merchant vessels, however. In the years preceding – and during – the First World War, the yard constructed a series of large and fast battle cruisers

*Painted in war-time grey, the newly-built **Queen Elizabeth** is manoeuvred down the Clyde in February 1940. (Smith collection)*

*A remarkable view aft from the bridge wing of the **Queen Elizabeth** on the River Clyde. (Smith collection)*

for the Royal Navy, including the largest of them all: the *Hood*, launched in 1918.

The prolonged depression of the 1920s did not prevent a resurgence of competition on the prestigious North Atlantic route as Italian, German and French shipping lines made preparations to build bigger and faster ships. The coveted Blue Riband and national prestige served as important drivers in this contest and, by the latter 1920s, Cunard also became involved in the design of new ships. There were two reasons why they were essential: the age of Cunard's existing vessels and foreign competition. Cunard's trio of large North Atlantic liners then operating the weekly service to New York – the *Mauretania*, the *Berengaria* (originally the German *Imperator* of 1913) and the *Aquitania* – were growing old. North German Lloyd, meanwhile, were completing the 50,000grt *Bremen* (1929) and the *Europa* (1930) and the Compagnie Générale Transatlantique were known to be considering a ship much larger than the 43,000grt *Ile de France*. This ship would become the *Normandie* (1935). In Italy, plans were in place to build two express liners which eventually materialised as the *Conte di Savoia* and the *Rex* (both 1932).

In July 1929 the *Bremen* brought the *Mauretania*'s remarkable 20-year retention of the Blue Riband to a close, with a westward run at an average speed of 27.83 knots.[1] Both the *Bremen* and the *Europa* made a great impact on the North Atlantic route and attracted large numbers of American passengers away from Cunard, thanks to their advanced design and great speed.

Cunard's response was the *Queen Mary* (1936), followed by the *Queen Elizabeth* (1940). From an early

stage in the development of these ships, Cunard consulted with Clydebank and it is likely, given the long-standing relationship that existed between shipyard and owner, that John Brown was intended from the outset as the eventual builder. The *Queen Mary* was laid down in December 1930, but the deepening global financial crisis that followed the 1929 Wall Street Crash engulfed Cunard, forcing them to suspend the contract after one year. In fact, it was not until April 1934 that work recommenced.

Such was the national importance of this ship, however, that resumption of work on her symbolised that Britain was back in business and that the worst of the Depression was over. Nevertheless, the British shipbuilding industry that emerged after the end of the Depression was smaller, through closures, while many skilled jobs had gone as men emigrated or endeavoured to find work in steadier employment. It was the first serious contraction of the UK industry in its history.

In December 1936, just nine months after the departure of the *Queen Mary* from Clydebank, the *Queen Elizabeth,* her slightly larger sister, was laid down. While other British shipyards had tendered for both *Queens*, there is no doubt that Cunard had the highest confidence in the people and facilities at the John Brown yard. Demonstration of the excellence of the quality of marine engineering at Clydebank, for example, came in February 1940 when the *Queen Elizabeth*, painted in wartime grey, left the shipyard in secrecy to prepare for a fast crossing to New York and safety, lest she be bombed by the Luftwaffe at Southampton. There had been no time to conduct machinery trials of any sort, apart from static dock tests. With all of the systems complexity of the world's largest and – probably – fastest ship, she crossed the Atlantic without mishap, reflecting credit of the highest order on the engineering staff at Clydebank. Cunard's Chairman, Sir Percy Bates, said of this event 'that the supreme confidence on the part of the men who built the liner and those who had to run her as to the satisfactory state of her machinery was one of the highest testimonials ever paid to British shipbuilding'[2]

During the Second World War, John Brown became preoccupied with the construction of warships for the Royal Navy, as it had done over twenty years earlier. At the end of this conflict, both Cunard and John Brown prepared to enter into a long period of prosperity. As soon as they had finished their wartime careers, the *Queen Mary* and the *Queen Elizabeth* were reconditioned and restored to the North Atlantic service. It was agreed that work on the *Queen Mary* would be undertaken at Southampton, to which large numbers of men from the fitting-out trades were despatched from Clydebank. The *Queen Elizabeth*, however, was mainly reconditioned off Greenock at the Tail of the Bank, about ten miles down-river from Clydebank, with final fitting out being completed in Southampton.

New construction began with the passenger and refrigerated cargo liner *Media* (1946). She was followed by the *Caronia* (1949), designed for the cruise market, and a series of intermediate liners – the *Saxonia*, the *Ivernia*, the *Carinthia* and the *Sylvania* (all built between 1954 and 1957) – for the Liverpool to Montreal service.

By the mid-1950s the challenge facing Britain as the world's shipbuilder took statistical form when Japan and then Germany overtook Britain in shipbuilding output. New attitudes and new approaches in ship construction were emerging as these countries rebuilt their industrial infrastructures. By the end of the 1950s, these statistics assumed an altogether more serious relevance as orders taken on a profitable basis began to elude many British builders. At Clydebank, John Brown's perspective was focused on two very important potential contracts. The first was for one of the large fleet aircraft carriers which the Royal Navy wished to build, while the other was for the new Cunarder to replace the *Queen Mary*, then

reaching the end of her active life. These contracts were seen not just as traditional John Brown products but essential in an increasingly tough shipbuilding environment. In the event, the aircraft carrier project never materialised and was finally killed off by the Government in the 1966 White Paper on Defence. Early in 1959, however, the first positive steps towards the new Cunarder were made when Cunard's Chairman, Sir Fred Bates, telephoned Sir James

*With Arran in the background, the 1948 cruise liner **Caronia** undergoes sea trials on the Measured Mile. (Smith collection)*

McNeill, Clydebank's Managing Director, to say that they were going to proceed with a replacement for the *Queen Mary*.

As with the *Queen Mary*, which had started on the drawing board over thirty years previously, Cunard asked John Brown for preliminary designs and costings for the new ship. That Cunard should approach just one shipyard, in an otherwise open market, to discuss a contract which would quite literally be of national importance for a ship that would be built, in part, with Government funds, speaks volumes for the high regard in which Cunard held the Clydebank shipbuilders. On 9 April, the story made headlines in the national press, according to which talks were in progress between Cunard, the Government and John Brown over a new ship to replace the *Queen Mary*.[3]

CHAPTER 2

NARRATIVES OF MODERNITY AND MODERNISM

ROM the time when the *Lusitania* and the *Mauretania* brought the greater speeds and other technical advancements of steam turbine propulsion to the North Atlantic in 1907, Cunard also started engaging experienced land-based architects and specialist contractors to design the interiors of their principal liners. This followed the lead already taken by Hamburg-Amerika Line in commissioning Charles Mewès (1860-1914) to design the First Class interiors of their own 1904-delivered *Amerika* in the same luxuriant revivalist Beaux Arts styles as he had adopted for the Paris Ritz Hotel in 1898. James Miller (1860-1947), who had designed pavilions for the 1901 Glasgow International Exhibition, and Harold A. Peto (1854-1933), a then retired prominent London-based architect, were chosen to design the First Class public

Empire hardwoods abound in the **Queen Mary**'s *First Class Lounge. (Bruce Peter collection)*

rooms and some of the private suites aboard the *Lusitania* and the *Mauretania* respectively.[4] Interiors for the later *Aquitania* were designed by Arthur J. Davis (1878-1951), who was then the London member of an international design partnership with Charles Mewès in Paris and Alphonse Bischoff in Cologne, specialising in shipboard and hotel design. The ocean-going style of the period was generally French Beaux Arts, as found in the best hotels and most elite private homes and clubs on both sides of the Atlantic, where it was intended to reflect an opulent *haute bourgeois* impression of that era's *bon vivant* and, to some degree, a reassuring sense of homely comfort and luxury to those perhaps still wary of going to sea.

Cunard's steady progression to larger and more modern liners had been curtailed following the *Aquitania*'s completion in 1914 as the *status quo* of world shipping was upset by the First World War and the circumstances of its aftermath. While North German Lloyd and the companies that were brought together under state auspices to form the Italian Line also progressed to new record-breaking Atlantic liners in the early 1930s, the ultimate dream of building the thousand-foot liner became more attainable as the inevitable next step in asserting supremacy in the continuing spiral of North Atlantic competition.

The first Queens

By the time the *Queen Mary* and the *Queen Elizabeth* were designed in the 1930s, public taste had changed in favour of the *moderne* styles showcased at the 1925 *Exposition Internationale des Arts Décoratifs et Industriels Modernes* in Paris. This was brought to sea – and, by this means, to the United States – through the interior design of ships such as French Line's *Ile de France* (1927) and Swedish American's *Kungsholm* (1928). The style was taken up in the latest New York landmarks, such as the Chrysler Building, Rockefeller Plaza (which included its famous Radio City Music Hall and The Round Room restaurant) as well as countless other department store, hotel and private house interiors across America and elsewhere. Cunard returned to Arthur Davis and brought in architect Benjamin W. Morris, of the New York partnership Morris & Connor, to design the interiors of the *Queen Mary*, then known only by her yard number, 534. In 1928 Morris had designed an Art Deco opera house façade for what was eventually to materialise as the Radio City Music Hall – but he was already known to Cunard for having designed their New York Offices.[5]

During the rather long gestation period of the *Queen Mary*'s planning and building, perceptions of ocean-going style had shifted from the decorative modernity of the *Ile de France* and the modern romanticism of the *Kungsholm* to the impressive 'grand vistas' of the *Normandie*'s daring axial plan. Questions were being asked at home about why the latest British ships, and Cunard's vaunted new 534 in particular, showed no signs of adopting similar ingenuity and imagination in the design of the passenger facilities.

Above left: The First Class Dining Saloon of the 1939 **Mauretania**. *(Bruce Peter collection)*

Above: The First Class Smoking Saloon on the **Queen Elizabeth**. *(Bruce Peter collection)*

Left: A First Class cabin on the **Queen Elizabeth**: *Art Deco meets the Festival of Britain. (Bruce Peter collection)*

Below left: The Mayflower Room on the **Franconia**. *(Bruce Peter collection)*

Below right: The **Sylvania**'s *rather eclectic First Class Lounge in 1950s Regency style. (Bruce Peter collection)*

Besides, increasing numbers of travellers wanted to know why they had to book aboard foreign ships to experience the latest trends in ocean-going hospitality and service.

Meanwhile, there were a number of significant examples of progressive architecture appearing on *terra firma* in Britain. For example, several prestigious London hotels were built or refurbished in the manner of the Paris *Exposition*. Claridges and The Savoy (1927), both the work of Basil Ionides, The Strand Palace (1930) by Oliver Bernard and The Dorchester (1931) by Sir Owen Williams all asserted thoroughly modern hospitality architecture. Moreover, the BBC Broadcasting House, with interiors by Serge Chermayeff, Wells Coates, Raymond McGrath and others, as well as the re-branding of London Transport under Frank Pick, had shown that contemporary design was compatible with forward-looking national institutions. At the seaside, meanwhile, Oliver Hill's Midland Hotel at Morecambe (1933), Joseph Emberton's Fun House at Blackpool Pleasure Beach (1934) and Eric Mendelsohn and Serge Chermayeff's De La Warr Pavilion at Bexhill-on-Sea (1935) also generated much excitement about the idea of modernism, which appeared to be slick, glamorous and daring.

A critical essay published in the *Architects' Journal's* 25 January 1934 issue pointed out that new ships flying the French, German and Swedish flags could offer accommodation and service of the highest standards in well-bred modern surroundings that were unpretentious and straightforward, though tasteful and entirely comfortable. The recent redecorating of a 182-metre Tourist Class gallery aboard Cunard's *Berengaria* in ersatz Tudor style, with half-timbered walls and wrought iron work, was fiercely derided as an example of what seemed to be chronically wrong with Britain's shipboard architecture. The essay's author, Baird Dennison, went on to implore that 'Even if the new Cunarder *must* have an outlandish name ending in 'ia' (and how wearisome those obscure Roman provinces are becoming) let it be something nearer *Contemporania*... Fly the pennant of our brave new world from her mizzen, not the pseudo antique's.'[6] Although Cunard distanced itself from the Modern Movement per se, the Line's Chairman, Sir Percy Bates, was also keen to ensure that the new

flagship should reflect the tastes of the great numbers of Americans who would inevitably patronise her in service.

While the Cunard ship was to be representative of all that was best in British technical achievement, art and culture, Cunard were dubious about going so far as to adopt anything perceived as too *moderne* or trendy. Indeed, interior designers of both the *Queen Mary* and the subsequent *Queen Elizabeth* were asked to avoid using large amounts of marble, glass and other heavy materials that had gone into the *Normandie's* public interiors in favour of lighter wood veneers so as to keep the centre of gravity as low as possible and minimise the possibilities of excessive rolling at sea. Some ideas from the French ship's layout and more open planning were, however, incorporated in the *Queen Elizabeth*, thanks to the greater amount of uninterrupted internal space resulting from her two-funnelled layout.[7]

Within the *Queen Mary's* more structurally conventional hull and superstructure, and above her powerful triple-expansion steam turbine machinery, her passenger accommodation and public facilities were an eclectic melange of *moderne* and traditional British hotelier styling that seemed to express Cunard's own established identity, but left many disappointed by the lack of the *Normandie's* refreshing sense of excitement. The marginally larger *Queen Elizabeth*, which only entered commercial service in 1946 following her wartime military deployment, featured a similar interior design scheme in a slightly more austere rendition, co-ordinated by George Grey Wornum (1888-1957) who had designed the new Royal Institute of British Architects headquarters in London's Portland Place.

The *Architect and Building News'* critic wrote positively of the romance of the *Queen Mary* lying in the contrast between the frightening inhumanity of the steel hull, cutting its way through inhospitable seas, and the cozy intimate interior warmth, within which all facets of everyday human life are lived to the strains of the ship's orchestra and against the background of animated colour and cocktail-hour conversation. While the craftsmanship and finish, the soft lighting and luxurious furnishings were praised, he concluded, nonetheless, that the great variety of decoration and artwork created an overall effect of 'mild and expensive vulgarity.' Be that as it may, Cunard and their passengers were obviously satisfied and the *Queen Mary* became a benchmark for the design of all subsequent Cunarders until the *Caronia* of 1948. Indeed, the ship retained much of her original interior design until withdrawal from service in 1967.

By the 1950s, when Cunard's senior management and technical staff first began to ponder their next generation of trans-Atlantic liners, the company had built up a reputation for solid dependability. Cunarders were known for their reliability and highly-polished onboard service – not for their avant-garde design. Unlike its trans-Atlantic rivals, Cunard was profitable and, in an era of post-war rationing and austerity, anything which earned dollars was beyond criticism.

Moreover, in British establishment circles, modernism was treated with suspicion. No wonder – following the October 1917 Revolution, the Soviet Union had embraced the Modern Movement to symbolise its new Communist regime – and many of the most prominent modernist designers in Britain were foreign émigrés of socialist persuasion. They – and their British followers – believed passionately that the role of the architect was not simply to design buildings to the satisfaction of their clients but, instead, to use all available means to encourage social and cultural revolution. This, they hoped, would bring about a new kind of egalitarian society, in which modern design and planning would eradicate the hierarchies and inequalities of the past. In such a scenario, of course, neither the aristocracy nor the *bourgeoisie* would be able to show off their social status through the deployment of grand historical design styles and, instead, everyone would live amid surroundings of contemporary design and with a similar, unpretentious quality of construction and finish. Not surprisingly, in Britain, modernist ideology and aesthetics sat most uncomfortably in the context of the nation's architectural inheritance from the past – and, indeed, the *laissez-faire* cultural context of the 1930s present.

In contrast, the *moderne* look, found on the *Queen Mary* and the *Queen Elizabeth*, was merely a fashionable modern decorative design style with no social or political dimensions whatsoever – a fact which only served to infuriate those aligned with modernism who

viewed it as being a positive danger to their reformist agenda. Although in the early 1930s the two aesthetics often were virtually indistinguishable in appearance, in theory progressive architects and designers were forced to align themselves either with one camp or the other. This depended upon whether they viewed their practice as being subservient to the needs of commerce or allied to high culture and, thus, with a moral mandate to take the lead in bringing about social reform.

Aspiring modernists looked to passenger ship design for inspiration as liners were technologically-charged and highly-serviced mega-structures which appeared to offer potential as models for futuristic architectural developments on *terra firma*. While Le Corbusier *et al* admired the 'new architectural forms; elements both vast and intimate, but on man's scale; freedom from the 'styles' that stifle us; good contrast between solids and voids, powerful masses and slender masts...'[8] of the exterior of Cunard's *Aquitania*, paradoxically the layout of vessels of this type reflected already deeply-entrenched social hierarchies. The aristocracy and the *haute bourgeoisie* travelled amid the spacious and opulent surroundings of First Class, while the mid-market occupied less ostentatious Cabin Class and those less wealthy still travelled in spartan Third Class. Even so, by the inter-war era, ocean liners had become powerful symbols of modernism and of modernity and the hope remained that – one day soon – the external aesthetics and hidden technologies of these vessels would be married to social programmes to benefit the many, not only the few.

Come the Second World War, the Government began to use modernist imagery in propaganda posters – most famously Abraham Games' 'Your Britain: Fight For It Now' series, which depicted futuristic, white buildings emerging from the ruins of wartime blitzkrieg. In one poster, Finsbury Health Centre by Berthold Lubetkin was shown and, in another, the Kensal House flats – a model residential development at Ladbroke Grove by E. Maxwell Fry. The idea was to use these buildings to show the British people that their country was paternalistic and genuinely concerned for their health and well-being. After victory, the posters implied, the Government would ensure that ill-health and slum housing would be consigned to the past and that everybody would enjoy

21

*Top: What modern industrial design could achieve: the **Canberra** shows off her futuristic lines. The liner's exterior appearance benefited greatly from the close working relationship between her naval architect, John West, and the Casson-Conder architecture and design firm. (Bruce Peter collection)*

Above: The Festival Pleasure Gardens at Battersea, designed by James Gardner in a tongue-in-cheek Regency style. (Bruce Peter collection)

*Above left: To illustrate the desirability of involving industrial designers in modern passenger ship design, this artist's impression, prepared by John Brown & Co when the yard tendered unsuccessfully to build the **Canberra**, shows a rather messy and old-fashioned silhouette. (Smith collection)*

Left: A general view of the main Festival of Britain South Bank site, showing the Royal Festival Hall, Dome of Discovery and Skylon. (Bruce Peter collection)

the benefits of a bright, modernist future.

These aims were in line with those of Clement Attlee's post-war Labour Government, which won a landslide victory in the 1945 General Election and so had a clear mandate for social reform. Unfortunately, Britain was essentially bankrupt and, while the Marshall Plan underwrote the rebuilding of the shattered economies of mainland Europe, Britain had to fend for itself. In these circumstances, exporting manufactured goods to the USA became a vital source of income and, in relation to this aim, the rebuilding of the British merchant fleet was a top priority.

Cunard were relatively fortunate in that their most prestigious liners –the *Queen Mary*, the *Queen Elizabeth*, the second *Mauretania* and the *Aquitania* – had survived the war unscathed. Indeed, having been pressed into service as a troopship upon delivery in 1939, the *Queen Elizabeth* would be entering civilian service for the first time in 1946 after being fitted out, to all intents and purposes, a brand-new liner, but very much in the 1930s *moderne* style. Cunard's crack ships sailed faster than torpedoes and so were difficult for hostile submarines successfully to target. Consequently, their intermediate liners and cargo vessels took the brunt of enemy action. As well as replacing these less prestigious ships, Cunard also took the radical decision to construct a purpose-built cruise liner, the *Caronia*, for delivery in 1948. The reason was to target wealthy Americans with luxury voyages and, as with the *Queen Mary* and *Queen Elizabeth*, the order went to the John Brown shipyard at Clydebank.

In terms of design, the *Caronia* was remarkably similar to Cunard's pre-war liners; there was felt to be no need to change a successful formula. Most other British shipping lines also developed their post-war construction programmes from where they had left off in 1939. Even in the pre-war era, however, Britain's position as the world's leading maritime nation had been increasingly threatened by upstarts such as Italy, the Scandinavian countries and, especially, America. These emerging forces in liner shipping made more enthusiastic usage of progressive design, rather than simply maintaining the *status quo*. The Italian trans-Atlantic liner *Conte di Savoia* may have been destroyed by wartime aerial bombardment, but her radically modern interiors by Gustavo Pulitzer Finali continued to resonate. The Danes, meanwhile, had long been

enthusiastic users of motor propulsion and, by the latter 1930s, had begun to combine Burmeister & Wain diesel engine power with streamlined superstructures and modernist interior design – as seen in DFDS' *Kronprins Olav* and *Kronprins Frederik* of 1937 and 1946. America took the most decisive lead, however. Having refused to take part in the 1925 Paris *Exposition*, claiming merely to copy its high-end design from Europe, by 1939 America had become a style leader in its own right, thanks largely to the work of its professional industrial designers such as Raymond Loewy and Henry Dreyfuss. In addition, after a devastating fire had destroyed the liner *Morro Castle* in 1933 with substantial loss of life, America had introduced a very tough new regulation to govern fire safety on all US-flagged ships. 'Method 1', as the ruling was known, mandated an entirely fire-proof construction using modern materials, such as Marinite and aluminium alloy. To the American Government, a traditional liner, filled with lustrous woodwork, was not only old-fashioned but also positively dangerous.

Furthermore, during the Second World War, America had applied Fordist production methods to shipbuilding in its 'Liberty' programme, in which substantial cargo vessels were manufactured in their thousands, with construction times reduced from years to as little as seven weeks from keel-laying to delivery. Prefabrication and assembly techniques of this kind were practically unknown in British shipyards. Such advanced thinking about ship design and manufacture influenced the post-war rebuilding of yards in Germany, Italy and Japan which quickly became serious threats to British hegemony in shipbuilding.

Attlee's Government was undoubtedly aware that Britain was falling behind on many fronts – industrially, economically and in terms of social provision – and so a series of exhibitions was staged in the immediate post-war era to promote modern British design. Firstly, in 1946, 'Britain Can Make It' was staged in the empty galleries of London's Victoria & Albert Museum. With rationing still in effect and many of the items being shown either pre-production prototypes, or made only for export, the show was derisively popularly dubbed as 'Britain Can't Have It.' This event was a precursor to the Festival of Britain in 1951 – a nationwide event whose centrepiece was the South Bank of the River Thames in Central London.

The Festival's London site was, to some degree, modelled on the Stockholm Exhibition of 1930, likewise promoting the contemporary socialist-biased values of the Welfare State in such things as comprehensive education, affordable new housing and the scientific and technological advancement of domestic life. The exhibition's principal architects had been proponents of modernism in the 1930s and of the humanistic values it embodied. Hugh Casson was responsible for co-ordinating the People of Britain exhibit, a friendly and 'homey' perspective of the nation's populace in various walks of life at work, home and leisure. Misha Black handled the Land of Britain exhibits, presenting the United Kingdom's agricultural, industrial, scientific and technical achievements. James Gardner, who had designed the 'Britain Can Make It' exhibition in 1946, was responsible for the Festival Pleasure Gardens amusement park at nearby Battersea.[9]

The Sea and Ships Pavilion, designed by Basil Spence, was one of the most prominent in the Land of Britain section and its architecture was revolutionary. Spence wanted to achieve something of the atmosphere of a shipyard and so, under a 'high-tech' floating roof, he created an open-plan, multi-level exhibit with scaled-down cut-away replicas of typical British merchant ships.[10] Nearby, the Dome of Discovery and the Skylon were equally radical structures. The former was a gigantic aluminium-clad 'flying saucer', floating on stilts and housing scientific displays, and the latter was an illuminated 'space needle' sculpture, held aloft by tensioned wires and abstractly hinting at the forthcoming age of space exploration.

The Festival of Britain cost a great deal to stage and, not surprisingly, the event was controversial as those on the right of politics, who found a ready outlet in Lord Beaverbrook's reactionary tabloid papers, did not think that money should be 'wasted' promoting what they perceived to be 'failing' Labour policies of nationalisation and the Welfare State. When Winston Churchill's Conservatives won the 1951 Election, they ensured that the Festival site was quickly demolished and only the Royal Festival Hall was left as a permanent legacy of the event. Even today, after more than half a century, that great concert venue continues to delight on account of its strikingly fresh and spacious modernity and its beautifully-crafted fittings and details.

Short-lived as the Festival of Britain was, many facets of the exhibition had a profound effect upon post-war British design. Indeed, the following year, James Gardner was commissioned to produce the decorations and displays for the Coronation – an event much more in keeping with Conservatives' vision of Britain but, nonetheless, requiring to be packaged in a modern aesthetic suitable for a new Elizabethan era. The forthcoming Royal Yacht, *Britannia*, was to be a symbol of the new monarchy and, fresh from his Festival of Britain success, Hugh Casson was given responsibility for the interior design which was carried out in conjunction with J. Patrick McBride of McInnes Gardner in Glasgow. The style selected was predictably traditional, though with an attractive sense of understatement.

The young HM Queen Elizabeth II and her consort, HRH Prince Philip, The Duke of Edinburgh, were regarded with awe and fascination. On the one hand, they were glamorous and photogenic but, on the other, they appeared to be just another couple bringing up young children, like so many other families in Britain. This 'baby boom' generation, born in the latter 1940s and early 1950s, would all come of age together, creating a wave of youth culture that swept first through Britain's schools, then its universities, work-places and leisure environments. This critical mass of teenagers, coupled with a new consumerism, helped to bring about a distinct 'pop' culture in music, fashion, language, consumer goods, interior design and design for transport. Few aspects of British culture were unaffected – and not even Cunard could escape the shock of the new.

Ultimately the nation's shipowners, along with their own design and technical departments, would look to the Festival of Britain's principal architects, their colleagues and associates for the way ahead. Hugh Casson, Misha Black and James Gardner became the acceptable face of modernism, so far as the British establishment was concerned. These men were anything but proselytizing Marxist revolutionaries but, rather, sensible, pipe-smoking English 'chaps' who could be depended upon to deliver large and complex projects in a satisfactorily up-to-date aesthetic. Through their high-profile public commissions and

*Left: The First Class Hallway on the **Kronprins Frederik** by Kay Fisker was characterised by graceful curves and immaculate detailing. (Bruce Peter collection)*

*Above: The First Class Smoking Saloon on the **Kronprinsesse Ingrid**, reflecting the streamlined shape of the superstructure. (Bruce Peter collection)*

*Below: The Princess Lounge on the **Oriana**, designed by Design Research Unit, had a dramatic ceiling treatment and free-standing mural panels by John Piper at either end. (Bruce Peter collection)*

leading roles in the Council of Industrial Design, they dominated the British design scene in the latter 1950s and throughout the 1960s.

Just after the Second World War, the Orient Line's Chairman, Sir Colin Anderson – who was also President of the Design and Industries Association, a pro-modernist lobby group of progressive designers and industrialists – made a trip to North America to see what could be learned from the new hotels and advances in railway sleeping car designs emerging there. Anderson was accompanied by the architect and interior designer Brian O'Rorke, who had previously drawn up the interiors of Orient Line's *Orion* (1935), and the Line's Chief Naval Architect, Charles F. Morris. At the time of her inauguration, the *Orion* had been widely admired by forward-looking architectural critics and her uncluttered interiors thereafter set the terms of reference for Orient Line's policies on passenger ship architecture. O'Rorke was subsequently commissioned to design interiors for the *Orcades*, completed in 1948 as the Line's first large post-war passenger liner, as well as the larger *Oronsay* and *Orsova* of the early 1950s. Other British lines tended to be less advanced in the architectural design of their first new post-war ships.

Yet, the four-ship *Saxonia* class of intermediate North Atlantic liners, built for Cunard between 1954 and 1957 for the Liverpool to Montreal service, seemed to be a step backwards, even from the architecture of the pre-war *Queens*. In official Cunard publicity material, their design approach was explained as 'recreating the past in terms of the present by using modern methods of construction to interpret some of the gems of historical interior design and construction.' What this really amounted to was retaining the traditional arrangement of public spaces, with their Victorian and Edwardian era decorative frills and embellishments replaced by a veritable cornucopia of forms, colours, textures, patterns and motifs, supposedly representing someone's conceptions of modern British design.[11]

With the exception of Orient Line, which had maintained a systematic approach to passenger ship architecture since the *Orion*, most British shipping lines appeared to be satisfied that whatever identity they had already built up through service experience would suffice to carry them forward for as long as they wished to transport passengers. Furthermore, by the 1960s there were many factions in the industry that foresaw a more lucrative future in cargo operations and would have been content to abandon passenger service altogether.

By comparison, long-range air travel was emerging as a virtually new phenomenon, faced with the challenge of setting rather than modernising its image and standards of service. BOAC (British Overseas Airways Corporation) foresaw that the creation of a distinctive design identity was crucial to their role of developing modern air travel and progressively promoting it as the new means of fast, safe and reliable travel to a post-war society with greater disposable income and more free time to travel and enjoy their prosperity. In 1946 the airline's Chairman, Viscount Knollys, established a BOAC Design Committee, with Kenneth Holmes, Principal of the Leicester College of Art, as its Creative Director. The Committee was mandated to assert a design identity appreciable by everyone coming into contact with its facilities, services and representatives. The policy was also aimed at fulfilling the Council of Industrial Design's objectives of creating world-wide goodwill through promoting British industrial production and goods, including aircraft and other equipment and facilities. The airline's corporate identity covered everything from the graphic design of timetables, brochures, menu cards and other printed items, including luggage tags, matchbook covers and playing cards, to the interior design of airliner cabins.[12]

As long-established as railway travel was, British Railways also foresaw the need to assert a strong corporate identity as part of their massive Modernisation Plan, introduced in 1958. A Design Panel was created to assist the railway in its conversion from steam to diesel traction and the introduction of new rolling stock – and to assert modern standards of comfort, service and corporate identity in an industry whose world-wide direction was being set by the examples of Trans European Express (TEE) and the new Roma Termini railway station in Italy. Leading British architectural firms, including Casson-Conder, Misha Black's Design Research Unit (DRU), Ward & Austin and others were commissioned to design everything from locomotives and passenger coaches to graphic items and ferries operated by the railway. The

*Above: A cabin on Orient Line's 1960 **Oriana**, designed by Design Research Unit. The space is elegant and simple in appearance with full-length curtains, bold fabric designs and neatly-resolved details. (Bruce Peter collection)*

*Above right: Bulky but businesslike, the **Oriana** was possibly unique in expressing the volumes of the upperworks in true constructivist style, rather than the streamlined approach usually favoured by progressive passenger ship designers in the 1960s. (Bruce Peter collection)*

*Right: The **Ohrmazd**, built by Burntisland Shipyard for Pakistani owners and delivered behind schedule in 1968, was styled externally by Design Research Unit. The resemblance of the two-tone smoke-stacks to the QE2's eventual funnel design is striking. (Ambrose Greenway collection)*

*The Tourist Class Peacock Room (below) and the First Class Meridian Room on P&O's **Canberra** demonstrate Casson-Conder's bright, airy approach to modern British liner interior design. (Bruce Peter collection)*

famous 'double arrow' symbol, created by DRU, was subsequently introduced as the logo of British Rail and of Sealink, as their ferry division was later to become known.

Since 1948, ferries connecting Britain's rail services across the Irish Sea, and with Europe via the English Channel and North Sea, had been designed essentially as mini ocean liners. This aesthetic was retained as drive-through car decks were introduced on the Dover-Boulogne service aboard the *Lord Warden* in 1951. The *Maid of Kent* joined the *Lord Warden* and her French-owned counterparts on the same route in early

firm's later shipboard work also included accommodation aboard the Blue Funnel Line's *Centaur* and some of the Tourist Class interiors of the *Oriana*.[14]

DRU, meanwhile, designed the owner's, passenger and crew accommodation, wheelhouse, service areas and superstructure of the East & West Steamship Company of Karachi's cargo/passenger liner *Ohrmazd*, as well as taking the lead role in drawing up the *Oriana*'s interiors, assisted by Brian O'Rorke and Ward & Austin. Sir Hugh Casson later served as co-ordinating architect for the *Canberra* and was involved, both directly and indirectly, in the design of the *Queen*

British Railways' **Maid of Kent** *was the first railway vessel to benefit from the input of specialist industrial designers, in this case Ward & Austin. (Ferry Publications collection)*

1959 as the first ship completed under the railway's Modernisation Plan. The traditional lines of the ship's exterior belied the modernity of the attractive Ward & Austin-designed interiors, praised by the architectural press as having an appropriately workmanlike but graceful style, with clean lines, simple forms and solid colours in soft tones. The hard-wearing and easily serviceable finishes and interior fittings throughout the passenger accommodation were carefully chosen and co-ordinated to be as attractive as they were functional.[13]

The *Maid of Kent* became the prototype for other British Rail and Sealink ferries built throughout the 1960s for various routes, as well as being a reference for the larger ships of the decade to follow. Ward & Austin's involvement in these included the design of custom-made furnishings and fittings, restaurant tableware and a complete system for standardised cabin fabrication throughout British Rail's fleets. The

Elizabeth 2. These forthcoming liners – and their foreign competitors – would be among the finest yet seen, reflecting modernism's ascent as the new orthodoxy for 1960s art, design and architecture.

In the latter 1950s, the two principal British lines in the Australia trade, Orient Line and P&O, joined forces, each ordering a new flagship for the Southampton to Sydney route via Suez. First to enter service was Orient Line's *Oriana*, delivered in 1960. This remarkable vessel caused a mild sensation by breaking the record for the fastest passage to Australia, taking just under four weeks to reach Sydney on her maiden voyage. Built by Vickers at Barrow-in-Furness, the liner had a powerful-looking hull with soaring lines and a slender entry at the waterline. However, this was surmounted by a most unusual, almost constructivist, superstructure treatment, in which the various volumes – containing public rooms, promenades, officers' quarters, the navigation bridge and air conditioning plant – were expressed individually and piled up amidships with a small funnel at the summit. From any angle, the *Oriana* was utterly unique and certainly memorable, but hardly beautiful in the traditional sense. Instead, the liner's grace lay within as she had a very effective and distinctive layout and some exquisite public spaces. Misha Black's Design Research Unit drew up most of the First Class interiors, as well as creating a uniform graphic identity for the entire ship. Many cabins, on the lower decks, were arranged around internal 'courtyards', so that even those deep within the hull had a window, looking onto a communal space, illuminated by natural daylight. The public rooms were also bright and airy, with high ceilings, uncluttered surfaces and numerous contemporary art installations.[15]

P&O's *Canberra*, designed by the naval architect John West, working in conjunction with Casson-Conder, was equally spacious – but with a very sleek and streamlined silhouette, featuring twin funnels located towards the stern and a superstructure formed of a series of receding layers, piling up towards the bridge structure, just forward of amidships. As with the *Oriana*, much of the *Canberra*'s upperworks was fabricated from aluminum alloy to save weight. Inboard, the *Canberra* had many striking public rooms – indeed Casson-Conder's interiors were a *tour de force* of British modernism at its very best. For example, the Club Bonito and Bonito Pool formed a single indoor/outdoor space which acted as a lido by day but became a ballroom after dark. Moving forward, the main public rooms in each class were open-plan and those in First Class were connected by a dramatic spiral staircase, with under-lit treads. Amongst the *Canberra*'s many memorable interior spaces, a teenagers' room, called the 'Pop-Inn', stood out on account of its 'grafitti'-style wall murals by a youthful David Hockney. Alas, these delightfully witty decorations were quickly panelled over, perhaps because the ship's rather conservative owners feared that their design might inspire youthful passengers to draw their own versions elsewhere on board.

Both the *Oriana* and the *Canberra* set a very high standard for British shipboard design and the two vessels proved extremely popular, firstly in liner service and later as cruise ships. Indeed, both survived well into the 1990s, the *Oriana* latterly in a static role in the Far East.

By the mid-1960s, the shipping industry was in a state of flux due, in part, to major social and economic changes on *terra firma* and to the advent of jet aircraft and mass car ownership. New ship types – car ferries, cruise ships, container ships and bulk carriers – rendered traditional passenger and general cargo liners obsolete. In this process, even famous established shipping lines came under intense financial duress. Cunard, not surprisingly, was amongst the worst hit. The trans-Atlantic flagships *Queen Mary* and *Queen Elizabeth* had been a winning formula for the company, but the Boeing 707 rendered both hopelessly *démodé* almost overnight. As with many successful businesses which experience a sudden change in trading conditions, at first Cunard seemed unable to decide what best to do. Some of their existing liners were converted to cruise ships, but with limited success. Clearly, the only solution would be to build anew.

With the notable exceptions of the *Canberra* and the *Oriana* – and a few cargo liners and ferries – recent British passenger ships were tepid in comparison with their foreign competitors. It appeared that British liner companies and shipyards were complacently sticking with tried and tested design formulas which had worked in the past and had little understanding of, or affinity with, the exciting technological, aesthetic and social advances associated with the Modern Movement. One of the worst offenders in this regard was the Union-Castle Line, the interiors of whose 1960 *Windsor Castle* and 1962 *Transvaal Castle* exemplified what the poet and architecture writer John Betjeman sarcastically termed 'ghastly good taste.'[16] The former had been drawn up, in part, by the society interior designer Michael Inchbald (1920-), working with Jean Monro, her assistant Evelyn Pinching and Bernard Cayzer, the Deputy Chairman of Union-Castle. Monro was the daughter of Geraldine Monro, a well known London decorator, and both mother and daughter had a penchant for floral patterns.[17] Consequently, the *Windsor Castle* was as fusty as a four-star hotel in Eastbourne. Ornate fireplaces, chintz armchairs, flock wallpaper and Edwardian-style electroliers may have found favour with conservative Afrikaners – but certainly not with the leading members of Britain's increasingly powerful design lobby. The British, it appeared, were simply failing to reflect that the times were, indeed, a-changing.

Of the many outstanding new foreign-flagged liners entering service from the latter 1950s onwards, two stood out, in particular, on account of their radical design. One was an American nuclear-powered passenger-cargo liner, the *Savannah*, and the other was an Israeli passenger liner called the *Shalom*.

Completed in 1961 to a design by the celebrated naval architect George C. Sharp, the *Savannah* was a remarkable vessel. In profile, she was inevitably 'futuristic' – a streamlined, white 'shape of things to come', with the superstructure located aft and 'atomic' graphic designs on the topsides. The *Savannah*'s real wonder, however, was below decks, viewed in the public rooms by closed-circuit television: a Babcock & Wilcox nuclear reactor, but her glories, from a design and style perspective, were the interiors.

Designed by Jack Heaney & Associates, the *Savannah*'s accommodation required to serve more complex functions than those normally associated with passenger-cargo vessels, as she was also a floating showcase for American art, industry and science. The Dining Room was striking, focused around an all-white sculptured mural entitled *Fission*, located behind the Captain's table. All of the cutlery, china, glassware and napery was specially commissioned and decking reflected the most intriguing range of materials and motifs – from the unique use of non-skid ceramic tile in the enclosed promenade deck to a carpet, wrought in two different heights of pile in concentric ovals, in the lounge, which was also fitted with a brass-framed white translucent vinyl dance floor.

The French-built *Shalom* of 1964 was a conventional steam turbine liner – but with an equally avant-garde interior, largely the work of the Israeli architects Al Mansfeld and Ben Kaplan. As the name suggested, the vessel was themed around ideals of peace and international goodwill, aims entirely in keeping with the spirit of the Modern Movement. Indeed, the ship was intensely co-ordinated in a manner with which no existing British liner could compare – and the result was as captivating as it was glamorous. Floating stair-treads with spindly balustrades ascended against backgrounds of op-art wall paintings; Arne Jacobsen chairs on pedestals were grouped in front of full-length curtains and plate glass partitions; collages and photo-murals in stark black-and-white contrasted with dazzling upholstery and abstract works by leading Israeli artists.

In January 1965 *Shipping World and Shipbuilder* interviewed Cunard's Chairman, Sir John Brocklebank (1915-1974), who was asked whether '…the forthcoming commissioning of the new Italian liners and… the *Shalom* presents Cunard with a stiff challenge to build a vessel which, in the travelling public's opinion, is at least the equal of these ships, if not actually surpassing them?' Brocklebank replied: 'Certainly it does… When we are ready to reveal her passenger layout, it will be seen that ingenuity, imaginative planning and attention to detail have produced a winner… The Atlantic trade always has been a challenging one… heightened by the tendency of foreign governments… justifying state support of their national lines… a policy that has determined the highest class in ship design and performance…'[18]

Although neither the *Savannah*, nor the *Shalom* was commercially successful, due respectively to the complications associated with nuclear propulsion and to serving exclusively kosher food, their designs set a high benchmark for shipboard modernity and, in the flux of 1960s modernisation, the increasingly powerful British design lobby leaned heavily upon Government and Cunard's directorate to follow suit. Of Britain's most prominent liners, the *Canberra* and the *Oriana* were the exceptions proving the rule that typical British ships were drawn up by engineers and then furnished in chintz and potted palms by friends of the Directors' wives. Thus, the average British liner may have been solidly constructed and as seaworthy as the lagging technology of British shipyards would allow but, all too often, they lacked the sense of overall design co-ordination and modernity that had long typified Scandinavian and Italian vessels – and which now was found on American and Israeli ships as well.

Brocklebank, whose main expertise was cargo shipping and who had only reluctantly taken on the Cunard Chairmanship in 1959 when Colonel Denis Bates died suddenly, went on to argue that the new Cunarder should be a three-class ship. This, he felt, would be more profitable and have greater passenger appeal. While he acknowledged that two classes could be successful in medium-sized liners, such as Cunard's own *Carmania* and *Franconia*, he continued to believe

Above left: The Dining Saloon on the American nuclear ship **Savannah**. *(Peter C. Kohler collection)*

Left: The Lounge on the **Savannah**, *featuring table tops made from sections of petrified log. (Peter C. Kohler collection)*

Above: The main staircase on the Zim liner **Shalom**. *The op art mural panels were painted by Ron Agam on a corrugated surface, so that much like a hologram, a different image could be seen from either side. (Bruce Peter collection)*

Below: The **Shalom**'s *Circle Lounge featured full-length curtains and groups of Arne Jacobsen 'Egg' and 'Swan' chairs, arranged under pools of diffuse light. (Bruce Peter collection)*

that passengers preferred three classes in larger vessels – citing Italy's *Michelangelo* and *Raffaello* as exemplars, on which 'three classes are more attractive on all counts.'[19] Indeed, with the consent of the Italian Line, Cunard's technical staff closely studied the layout and arrangements for the subdivision of classes onboard these liners with a view to emulating significant aspects of their design in the Q4.[20] As history proved, however, these ships, with their heavily subdivided accommodation, had limited potential for cruise operation and, in fact, lasted in service for only a decade. Fortunately a more progressive approach came to prevail as the planning of the new Cunard flagship developed.

Forging a New Britain

On *terra firma*, meanwhile, Britain was changing rapidly. The final end to wartime rationing in 1955 had unleashed a property boom as, in the immediate post-war years, entrepreneurial speculators had bought up pieces of land with an eye to erecting high-rise offices. Simultaneously, local authorities had been given sweeping development powers by Attlee's Government to build new housing and civic facilities on an unprecedented scale. Harold Macmillan's subsequent Conservative Administration became enthralled with increasing car ownership which, itself, was seen as a sign of growing prosperity and so, through an unholy alliance between private property speculators, central government and regional councils, Britain's cities experienced an orgy of rebuilding with new urban motorways smashing through the existing cityscape and high-rise flats and offices sprouting up everywhere.

The architecture and design journals were filled with articles and images of these grand schemes which appeared to reflect an unstoppable momentum for modernisation. Indeed, anybody arguing in favour of clinging to the past came to be viewed as deeply eccentric and out of step with the times. Britain always has been a nation with a soft spot for entrepreneurship and, in a sense, the 1960s construction boom reflected the *laissez-faire* spirit of the first Industrial Revolution a century before. (Even if much of this reconstruction was modernist in appearance, the pattern of development often was in stark contrast to the

structured and controlled approach to planning required by 'true' modernism and, besides, much of what was built appeared to the layman to be of inferior quality to what had been replaced).

In 1964 Harold Wilson led Labour back into government, albeit with a majority of only four. Opening the science debate at the Party's conference in Scarborough the previous year, Wilson famously argued that Labour's aim would be to 're-state our Socialism in terms of the scientific revolution… The Britain that is going to be forged in the white heat of this revolution will be no place for restricted practices or for outdated methods on either side of industry.' The idea of a rational, scientific approach to structured change was entirely in line with the modernist rhetoric, then informing architecture and design debates. This also reflected the veneer of confidence generated by urban redevelopment and through Britain's burgeoning pop culture. Even so, while London and the affluent Home Counties were 'swinging', Britain's industrial heartlands – from which Labour drew its support – were stagnating. Ironically, that situation would be thrown into sharp focus during the design and construction of Cunard's new flagship liner.

Tony Benn, initially Wilson's Postmaster General, became the Minister of Technology in 1966, with special responsibility for industrial modernisation. Benn, like Wilson, believed that, for British manufacturing to compete with Europe and America, a structured approach would be required to support clusters of inter-dependent industries – for example, steel, shipbuilding and the ship supply businesses. This was in line with policy in France and Italy, to name two countries which have managed to retain their shipbuilding industries. Yet, according to Benn, this aim ran contrary to received wisdom amongst Government officials – particularly in the all-powerful Treasury. Wilson's Government hence found itself in an unequal struggle against Britain's *laissez-faire* traditions and the increasingly entrenched and fractious disputes between management and the unions. As Benn ruefully recalls: 'I felt it was absolutely crucial to keep skilled men and women in manufacturing jobs to benefit our economy, but shipyard owners appeared to be an old boys' club, who casually won contracts over drinks with shipowners in their gentlemen's clubs. By the 1960s, that, surely, was no way to do business.'[21] This notwithstanding, the Labour Government considered shipbuilding to be a vital national industry and so the construction of a new flagship for Cunard was viewed favourably, especially as, by then, shipyards were beginning to close in increasing numbers, unable to win orders in the face of foreign competition.

It was hoped that the prestigious Cunard project would, in itself, become an advertisement for the quality and technical brilliance of Britain's shipbuilding industry – in the same way that Concorde was intended to position Britain as a world leader in civil aviation and the tilting Advanced Passenger Train (authorised in 1967) was to promote Britain's advancement in railway technology. Alas, in all three cases unforeseen events negated these worthy aims.

Since the Second World War, overall employment rates had remained remarkably high as Britain was required to export goods to America to earn dollars in order to repay its war debt. This situation masked an underlying lack of investment in traditional heavy industries – including shipbuilding – in contrast to the former Axis powers which had rebuilt their industries using Marshall Plan aid. Another consequence of the export drive was that prosperous Americans were more likely to have an affinity with the best of British design and consumer goods than many Britons, the majority of whom had far less spending power.

In contextualising the American response to the forthcoming Cunard flagship, the liner historian Peter C. Kohler asks rhetorically:

'What did Americans of the sort who'd cruise or cross – then a pretty tiny slice of the population – want from QE2 back in 1969? Why, precisely what Brits told us we wanted. Hard as it is to believe, back when America put man on the moon, what really rocked the world was Britain. Music, cars, aeroplanes, architecture, design… it was all British and all cool. Twiggy, Carnaby St, 007, VC-10s, Triumph Stags, The Who, The Beatles etc etc. I remember rich friends at school whose parents really dressed like the models in the brochure and had square Lucite vases with yellow daffodils in them. And they had a Jag in the driveway or at least a Rover 2000. And we all had bronze green Raleigh Sports three-speed bikes of course. Only the maid's children had yucky American Schwinns. How uncool is that?'[22]

Yet, as Kohler observes of the existing Cunard fleet: 'Oddly, I think we Americans rather liked the toffee-nosed aspects of the old Cunard at least as far as paying for First Class and expecting nothing less.'[23] So great had the decline in trans-Atlantic travel become by the mid-1960s, however, that the danger to Cunard of losing their existing traditionally-minded clientele was thought to be considerably less than the danger of the company's passenger business becoming an irrelevant anachronism altogether.

It seems that Britain's expanding middle class, in particular, perceived Cunard to be a shipping line run by the aristocracy principally for the benefit of the aristocracy, whereas P&O, with their splendid new *Canberra*, appeared brilliantly to capture the more egalitarian spirit of the post-war nation. David Trevor-Jones, who cruised regularly on P&O liners with his parents during the 1960s, observes:

'When Cunard first announced the intention to build a new flagship, it was less than two decades since the war had ended. Back then, most people felt that the sacrifices required should be fairly rewarded and that everyone should enjoy the fruits of victory. Equally, those who were perceived to have had an easier war – meaning the upper classes – were less respected than before, while entrepreneurs and self-made people were admired. Although my parents and I visited the great Cunard liners in Southampton, they would never have wanted to sail with Cunard, even although they could have afforded to do so. They simply felt that Cunard's ships were floating versions of Pall Mall clubs and not for middle class people like us.'[24]

In an article titled 'A Week at Sea or a Week at Butlins', published in *Shipping World and Shipbuilder* in January 1965, John Rose, the Public Relations Officer of Ocean Travel Development, stated that his brief was 'to destroy the upper class image of sea travel and replace it with one attuned to the democratic standards of the Affluent Society… to sell the attractions of sea travel to the new executive class, and to the increasingly well-to-do members of the middle class.'[25] In designing the new flagship, Cunard would therefore have to work hard to give themselves a new, more egalitarian image in keeping with the meritocratic spirit of the era.

CHAPTER 3

Q3 - THE THIRD QUEEN

THE normal life expectancy of an ocean liner is between 25 and 35 years, measured as much by how long the machinery can be expected to last and metal structures remain intact against the strains of motion and ravages of sea water as by the changing trends in lifestyle ashore against which her accommodation and services must remain up-to-date. As early as 1951, Cunard's then Chief Naval Architect, Robert K. Wood, started making preliminary sketches and drawings for a new generation of Cunard *Queens*, in anticipation of the *Queen Mary*'s replacement around 1965 and the *Queen Elizabeth* five years later. At John Brown's shipyard at Clydebank, meanwhile, speculative drawings of the machinery arrangement, based on the existing *Queens*, were prepared at Wood's request. These drawings would form the basis for the propulsive arrangements for the new ship.[26] Detailed planning, involving Cunard's Technical Department, was started in 1955 for what was eventually to become a 75,000-ton North Atlantic express liner with nominal provision for off-season cruising, codenamed Q3.[27]

For shipping lines, fleet renewal is a major expense to be anticipated in much the same way that the average household must foresee periodic replacement of the family car. Normally this is financed by setting aside funds out of a new ship's revenues during her initial years of service while she is most popular and profitable, and by borrowing to cover any shortfall as the time for building new tonnage approaches. In the scale of the largest shipbuilding projects, where construction costs and taxation levels were highest, Cunard received government-backed loans for the *Lusitania* and the *Mauretania* of £2.6 million and, later, for the *Queen Mary* and the *Queen Elizabeth* at £4.5 and £5 million respectively.[28] With these loans duly repaid, and the ships having proved themselves to be commercially successful, Cunard felt that they were in a solid position to borrow once again from the public purse to build a successor to the by-then famed and venerable *Queens*.

By the Macmillan era of the latter 1950s, however, Government help would be less of a certainty. With non-stop trans-Atlantic jet air travel, introduced by BOAC's de Havilland Comet jetliner flights between London-Heathrow and New York-Idlewild in 1958, followed by Pan American's inaugural Boeing 707 service between New York-Idlewild and Paris-Orly,

trans-Atlantic flying times were reduced to under eight hours and, for the first time, offered the convenience and comfort of a truly viable alternative to sea travel. In 1958 a crossover point was reached when more people crossed the North Atlantic by air than by sea, with 937,000 sailing against 1.193 million flying.[29] The figures continued to grow in favour of the airlines as sea travel diminished, with two million passengers crossing by air and only 800,000 by sea in 1962. While the numbers travelling by air had doubled, sea crossing had only diminished by twenty per cent, showing that, in fact, there was an exponential growth in overseas travel and indicating, it would also seem, that travel was becoming more diversified in meeting the expectations of both those wanting swift passages from one place to another and others preferring to take advantage of the shipboard experience itself, by opting to sail rather than fly.

Harold Macmillan's Conservative Government convened the Chandos Committee under Viscount Chandos (Oliver Lyttelton, 1893-1972) to advise the Minister of Transport, Ernest Marples, on possible future prospects for British express passenger shipping on the North Atlantic. In late 1960, the Committee recommended that the Treasury lend Cunard £18 million, repayable at 4.5 per cent interest over 25 years, towards construction of a single 75,000-ton liner, designed and built specifically for three-class express trans-Atlantic service year-round, with an added stipulation that the ship's use for cruising was expressly forbidden.[30] The idea was that this would operate in tandem with the French Line's soon-to-be-completed liner *France*, whereby the sailing schedules of the two liners would coincide to retain weekly sailings in both directions, alternating between the *France* and the new Cunard ship.[31] The Government's interest in this, however, appeared to be motivated more by the short-term objective of providing immediate employment in a politically sensitive part of the country to build the ship without any regard for its ultimate commercial fortunes once in service.[32] That would be Cunard's business, and there would be no question of there being any operating subsidy.

In an act of desperation to sell the idea of a new trans-Atlantic flagship to government, to the general public and to a sceptical news media, Cunard's directorate contacted the noted industrial designer

James Gardner (1907-1995). According to his autobiography, The ARTful Designer:

'The national press were attacking the Government with sarcastic headlines. Apparently, these guys had gone mad, proposing to throw millions in public money at a useless 'white elephant'... The press realised, of course, that no one in the Government gave a damn for the ship; their interest was to provide employment in a politically sensitive area.

James Fitton, an artist friend of mine – velvet jacket and flowing bow tie – who happened to have an IN with the Cunard Directors, suggested that if, in place of words, they offered the press an exciting visualisation of the ship, it might turn the heat off.'[33]

Britain's pavilion for Expo '67 in Montreal and the Museum of Tolerance in Los Angeles, designed in 1993 shortly before the end of his life.

Gardner met Sir John Brocklebank in the *Aquitania*-era elegance of the Arthur Davis-designed executive suite of the Cunard Building at Liverpool's Pier Head during the latter stages of the Q3 project to discuss creating a visualisation of the proposed new liner for the press. The idea would be to present a public convinced that the whole project was a colossal waste of money with an outward impression, at least, that this ship would have something in common with the emerging jet age and the world of the de Havilland Comet, Boeing 707 and Douglas DC-8.

An early model prepared by Cunard for the proposed Q3. The design lacks coherence and appears to be an engineer's solution.
(Design Archives, University of Brighton)

'Red Funnel Syndrome': James Gardner's cartoon makes fun of the Cunard Directors' obsession with traditional smoke-stacks.
(Design Archives, University of Brighton)

Cunard's initial Q3 proposal, viewed from the stern quarter. There is a certain similarity to the **Carmania** *and* **Franconia**'s *deck arrangement – and also to the* **France**. *(Bruce Peter collection)*

Gardner was widely regarded as one of Britain's most imaginative designers, whose work included just about everything from illustrations, theatre sets and airliner interiors to household products. Born in 1907, his precocious talent and drawing ability earned him a scholarship to attend Chiswick College of Art in 1924. By the latter 1930s, Gardner had established himself as a designer, early clients being Imperial Airways and Shell. During the Second World War, he produced designs for camouflage, dummy tanks and landing craft to confuse the enemy – work which brought him to prominence in government circles. A man of wit and remarkable perception, he was perhaps best known for his exhibition work, including 'Britain Can Make It' in 1946 and his subsequent collaboration with Misha Black and Hugh Casson as principal co-ordinating architects for the 1951 Festival of Britain. Later, he worked with Basil Spence on

Gardner mused to himself that he had never before designed a 'white elephant' as he was shown plans and a model of what had become a veritable ocean-going block of flats, drawn up by Cunard's Technical Department. Worse still, this lacklustre proposal actually looked as though a committee of engineers had designed it. Perhaps inevitably, the superstructure was topped by a single enormous ovoid red-and-black Cunard funnel.

According to Gardner's autobiography, Brocklebank's main concern seemed to be 'Whatever you do with the rest of her, the ship must have traditional Cunard funnels. It's the insignia of the line, you know, Cunard red.'[34] Gardner's somewhat romantic renderings of a sleek modern space-age liner with two tall, gently-tapered white stacks – one as a funnel almost two-thirds aft and the other a combined mast and exhaust above the bridge housing, forward –

were a visual knockout. The Cunard insignia appeared rather as an escutcheon on the superstructure sides, below and slightly ahead of the forward stack – 'Cunard red, you know' – and Brocklebank apparently bought it.

While Cunard and John Brown had been exclusively involved in the preliminary design phase from April to September 1959, Cunard were obliged to place the ship out to competitive tender in the UK. In March 1961, invitations were issued to five large British shipyards: a consortium of Vickers-Armstrongs/Swan, Hunter & Wigham Richardson, Cammell Laird, Harland & Wolff, Fairfield and John Brown.

Throughout the ensuing period, John Brown used their excellent relations with Cunard to the full, principally through Cunard's Chief Naval Architect, Robert K. Wood, much to the annoyance of the other shipbuilders.[35] Over the decades, the close relationship between John Brown and Cunard resulted in many Clydebank-trained naval architects working for Cunard and both Wood and his successor, Dan Wallace, were ex-Clydebank men. Despite his familiarity and affection for Clydebank, Wood, nevertheless, conducted himself in a thoroughly professional and even-handed manner.[36]

In July 1961, after months of work by the competing shipbuilders in preparing detailed costings, the tenders for Q3 were submitted. In the following month, however, Lord Aberconway, Chairman of John Brown & Company, commenting in the Annual Report for 1961, said that 'the new Queen is vital to Clydebank if continuity of employment is to be maintained and to hold together Clydebank's skilled labour force. If the contract is lost, the yard will be severely underemployed.'[37] The implication was clear: John Brown must win this order; if not, a low volume of orders through the yard would make it uncompetitive.

In keeping with tradition, the principals of the tendering shipyards were invited to the opening of tenders at Cunard's Liverpool offices. When the tenders were opened by Sir John Brocklebank, Cunard's Chairman, both Lord Aberconway and Mr John Brown, Clydebank's Managing Director, were shaken to find that the Vickers-Armstrongs/Swan Hunter consortium had submitted the most attractive tender.[38] Moreover, they had prepared two designs –

one, the all-steel four-shaft ship that Cunard had requested in the specification, and the other, a smaller, lighter, two-shaft alloy and steel design.

The disturbing news for John Brown was that the Vickers-Armstrongs consortium's four-shaft, all-steel design was preferred on cost and delivery grounds to their own. Clydebank's price was £1.8 million higher, principally because the John Brown hull was a heavier and stiffer structure than the consortium's and required more power and, therefore, more expense to propel it.[39] However, it was the consortium's smaller two-shaft design which caused Cunard to pause. Many of the features it embraced were based on the Oriana, a ship which incorporated not only an aluminium superstructure but also some novel steelworking features.[40] The Clydebank tender was based almost entirely on steel, in compliance with Cunard's specification. At this time, John Brown had little practical experience of aluminium construction. As Roy Turner, Vickers' Naval Architect, put it: 'We had just built the Oriana; John Brown's hadn't.'[41] From Cunard's point of view, despite its predilection towards Clydebank, the fact remained that the designs advocated by the Vickers-Armstrongs/Swan Hunter consortium were cheaper, more interesting and, in the smaller ship proposal, placed an entirely different perspective on Q3.

The trick was that, with only half as much machinery needed to drive two, rather than four, propellers, other services and working areas could be relegated to hull compartments below the waterline, freeing more space above the Plimsoll mark for passenger accommodation and public spaces. By also building an aluminium alloy superstructure and adopting other lightweight metalworking techniques, the ship could be built higher above the waterline without compromise to her stability, achieving the greater exposure to natural light and the outside world for the cabins and public areas Cunard had already sought in Q3.

The smaller overall size was more in line with other high-performance new liners such as the France, at a measure of 66,350 tons, and the new 45,900-ton Italian Line Michelangelo and Raffaello that would provide a 26.5-knot service speed between New York and the Mediterranean when delivered in the mid-1960s. These adopted an unusual three-quarters-aft

The final design model for the stillborn Q3: James Gardner produced a very distinctive ship with two dramatic smoke-stacks, the forward of which vented the galley and also served as a signal mast. (Bruce Peter collection)

asymmetrical machinery layout, with mirrored arrangements of boilers and turbines on opposite sides of the centreline in two separate engine rooms, one forward of the other. This provided the same level of operational security as the quadruple-screw *United States* and the *France* by having two fully-isolated sets of machinery that could be run independently of one another. Other relevant Italian examples included Costa Armatori's 30,567-ton *Eugenio C.*, built for express service between Genoa and Buenos Aires, and the *Oceanic*, at 27,644 tons, originally designed for Home Lines' North Atlantic service and completed for full-time cruising. Apart from their generally *Canberra*-like layout, with machinery aft, the Costa and Home Lines ships each featured remarkably compact propulsion plants, using only three high-performance boilers and twin turbines.

The idea of a smaller ship was, in fact, nothing new for Cunard, as the Chandos Committee had questioned the Line's requirement for Q3 being so large, and an earlier Government committee, reviewing Cunard's application for a loan to build *Queen Elizabeth*, had suggested in 1936 that, perhaps, a smaller ship of around 50,000 tons would be more economical to build and more practical in operation.[42]

For the Clydebank men, the experience of apparently failing to win the Q3 contract came as a tremendous shock. Lord Aberconway was distinctly unhappy at the prospect of letting the new Cunarder slip through his fingers. As the meeting progressed, however, Mr. John Brown successfully argued that the alternative Vickers-Armstrongs/Swan Hunter proposal for a twin-screw design was very different from that requested by Cunard and suggested that John Brown & Co should be given the opportunity to re-tender on a similar basis. Cunard agreed to consider this proposal and the meeting ended without any decision.

At the point of signing a building contract for Q3, however, Cunard finally decided that this was the wrong type of ship for the times and so the project was scrapped on the drawing boards. As passenger traffic figures on the North Atlantic continued to decline, Sir John Brocklebank announced on 19 October 1961 that the contract for the Q3 was to be postponed while Cunard reappraised the type of ship they required. Postponement, followed by cancellation, came as a blow to John Brown's. Great disappointment was also expressed on Tyneside where Q3 would probably have been built, had a contract actually been awarded.[43]

CHAPTER 4

THE DEVELOPMENT OF Q4

QUOTED in 1961 as suggesting a Georgian-style interior for Q3,[44] Sir John Brocklebank announced in October 1963 that the revised Q4 ship, later to be launched as the *Queen Elizabeth 2*, would be rather closer to the spirit of Jacqueline Kennedy than to Queen Victoria.[45] As flattering as it was to the American First Lady and the great sense of contemporary elegance, grace and style she brought to the White House, this came little more than three weeks before the world was horrified by the tragic assassination of President John F. Kennedy on 23 November 1963. Nonetheless, it had been an entirely apropos reference for a much anticipated change in design direction at Cunard. There was no apparent attempt to capitalise on Sir John's remarks, no doubt largely out of respect for the widowed former First Lady and for the American people at a time of great sadness. This notwithstanding, the point had been made in terms that would appeal to Cunard's largely American clientele, but details of the ship's architectural and interior design were still negotiable and far from being finalised.

Everyone realised that the whole concept of Q3 was still inclined more towards Cunard's past than it was in the direction of Jackie Kennedy or, for that matter, the emerging jet age. Yet, in British architectural and design circles, the professionals still wanted something more mainstream modernist to reflect the nation's best architectural and industrial design aboard the Merchant Marine's new flagship. Additionally, the nation's popular culture was then riding on the crest of a high wave. The whole world rocked to the music of The Beatles, the Rolling Stones and the Dave Clark Five. In the elegantly informal fashion scene of mid-1960s *Swinging London*, the *mod* mode was set by the mini-dress, Biba styles and other bright, simple and relatively affordable apparel from young trend-setting designers such as Mary Quant and Barbara Hulanicki, whose work seemingly appealed to people of all ages and in every walk of life. The new Cunard flagship would also have to be *mod*, or as close to it as the Cunard Line could possibly be dragged.

Meanwhile, as no order had been placed for Q3, Cunard gave more serious consideration to developing the alternative, smaller, twin-screw concept which it code-named Q4. As this would be a radically different ship, the Chandos Committee's terms for a Government loan no longer applied.

Cunard's renewed application for direct Treasury assistance was turned down by the Ministry of Transport, although a loan of £17.6 million was obtained under the Government's Shipbuilding Credit Scheme, set up to help shipowners willing to book building contracts with British yards. Cunard had to mortgage their fleet immediately to raise £4 million to make the initial payments to secure the building contract and qualify for Shipbuilding Credit Scheme assistance. Since this would only be paid upon the ship's delivery, interim financing for the difference between the initial payment and the loan amount was secured from a consortium of British banks at 0.5 per cent above the Bank Rate, as further instalments had to be made at various stages of building. The remaining £3.8 million, making up the final contract price of £25.4 million, was raised by Cunard through investment allowances and out of their own financial resources.[46]

Cunard's design team was headed by Chief Naval Architect Dan Wallace (1916-1979) and Technical Director Tom Kameen (1916-). The former was responsible for the overall design and construction of the Q4 and the latter for the mechanical operations – including everything from the engine room to the galley, the plumbing and the air conditioning. Working with Cunard's directorate, their initial job was to establish the optimum size, capacity and speed of the new liner. Wallace had begun his career as an apprentice draughtsman at John Brown's shipyard in 1931 and the first ship on which he worked there was the *Queen Mary*. In 1951 he joined Cunard as their Assistant Naval Architect, later succeeding Robert K. Wood as Chief Naval Architect in 1964.[47] Kameen had started his apprenticeship at Cammell Laird's yard in Birkenhead in 1932, joining Cunard four years later as an engineer officer. In this role he served on board the *Aquitania*, the *Berengaria* and the *Queen Mary*, to which he was posted during the Second World War. During the latter stages of the war, however, he was stationed in New York, serving the Ministry of War Transport there before returning to Cunard in 1945 as the Line's Assistant Superintendent Engineer in Southampton. He became the Technical Director in 1963.[48]

Wallace and Kameen were both highly-experienced

and affable gentlemen, whose accumulated knowledge and unflappable determination steered the Q4 project through to a successful conclusion.

The 1960s, now under way, would prove to be a tumultuous period for shipbuilding in Britain and for John Brown at Clydebank. A series of high-wire events unfolded that shook the shipyard to its core while, at the same time, it prepared to tender for the ship that would become the QE2.

While Cunard deliberated upon the type of vessel the new Q4 should be, the prediction that Lord Aberconway made about John Brown's Clydebank shipyard not being able to hold its skilled workforce together if it did not win the Cunard contract began to assume reality. Its traditional ability to tender for prestigious contracts, such as well-appointed passenger ships, resulted from a balance of know-how through experience, competitiveness and having the appropriate skills to hand. Indeed, the shortage of skilled labour was an issue that dogged shipbuilding throughout the 1960s. Management knew that labour was difficult to re-employ if, because of a gap in production, it had been necessary to let skilled trades go. With the completion of Union-Castle's *Transvaal Castle* in December 1961, the unfortunate process of releasing men from the fitting-out trades began.

With one eye firmly fixed on the possibility of building the Q4, retaining a large complement of finishing trades became of vital importance. Consequently, during 1962 the company tendered for the Norwegian America Line's *Sagafjord*, a 24,000grt cruise ship, and a contract that would have maintained John Brown's traditional business and kept key trades together. However, the order went instead to the Société des Forges de la Méditerranée (La Seyne sur Mer). John Brown's price was £160,000 higher than the best British price, which was that of Swan Hunter at £5,630,000.

The next tendering opportunity lay with the Swedish American Line, which was considering the construction of a new intermediate liner to replace the existing *Kungsholm* of 1953. Almost certainly, concerns over John Brown's growing uncompetitiveness conditioned the Board's attitude towards this contract. The process started on 17 December 1962 when Clydebank's Managing Director wrote to the Swedish American Line, asking that they be permitted to

tender for the new ship, initially code-named the *Salholm*. The Swedish American Line was known throughout the shipbuilding industry for commercial astuteness. Following intensive negotiations in Gothenburg between John Brown and the Swedish American Line, it was agreed that John Brown would tender for this ship by the deadline of 4 June 1963.

John Brown's tender was successful at £6,780,000, carrying with it a stipulated delivery date of October 1965.[49] To ensure every chance of winning the contract, a price had been quoted based on charges only, with no profit and with no escalator clauses to protect against inflationary rises in labour and material costs. In other words, provided nothing went wrong, the yard would break even. The ship, later named the *Kungsholm,* was laid down on 1 January 1964. By the end of that year, it was clear, for a number of reasons, that the delivery date could not be met, forcing the yard to re-negotiate a delivery date of 19 December 1965. The new contract specified that delivery beyond then would incur penalties of £3,000 per day.

As the *Kungsholm* began to take shape on the building berth at Clydebank, Cunard were well into the process of determining the specifications for their new Q4.

Vickers-Armstrongs' imaginative Q3 design, meanwhile, had earned them a development contract from Cunard, signed in May 1963, to work out a concept proposal to build Q4 at Barrow. Although Cunard maintained a dialogue with John Brown's throughout the development period of the new ship, technically important work had been lost to Vickers-Armstrongs. There, the design developed into a ship of 57,000 tons with two shafts. Unlike Q3, Q4 was to be capable of negotiating the Panama Canal and, therefore, able to cruise from ports on either coast of the United States.

On 19 August 1964 invitations to tender were issued to Fairfield, Cammell Laird, Harland & Wolff, Vickers-Armstrongs/Swan Hunter and John Brown. In October, Cammell Laird dropped out of the competition, to be followed by Fairfield in November. The main John Brown Board met at The Sanctuary, John Brown's London office, to discuss and approve the terms of the quotation for Q4. In consideration of the great prestige of the contract, it was agreed to cover full costs and full charges but include no profit, although this was kept secret at the time. The Board felt that 'extras', by way of changes to the contract during construction, would ensure no loss. It was their view that the contract for this ship simply must be won.[50]

On 30 November the tenders from the remaining three shipbuilders were opened. With a tender price of £25,427,000, John Brown's price was the lowest and the delivery date of May 1968 the earliest. However, Sir John Brocklebank and his staff were shocked to

The troublesome **Kungsholm** finally nears her delivery to Swedish American Line, leaving behind serious debts for John Brown & Co's Clydebank shipyard. Nowadays, she is the German-operated **Mona Lisa**. (J.E.K. Smith)

note that all three tenders were in excess of the £22 million set aside for the ship. John Brown's were advised that their tender was the lowest but that the price would have to be cut down further before a contract could be signed. Cunard asked the yard to reduce the cost of the ship by approximately £1.5 million. To qualify in time for the loan under the Government's Shipbuilding Credit Scheme, it was essential that the final figure be reached quickly. A team of Cunard personnel, led by Dan Wallace and Tom Kameen, came to Clydebank to meet with John Starks, John Brown's Technical Director, and George Strachan, the Director of the Engine Department. Over the course of three weeks, with beer and sandwiches at weekends, the cuts were made.

The contract for Q4 was finally signed on 30

December 1964. There was much jubilation in the yard and on the Clyde as work for a large number of people on the world's most prestigious shipbuilding contract had been secured for three years. Cunard, too, were delighted that the old partnership was in business once again. Tom Kameen recalls that John Brown's were held in very high regard by Cunard, based, partly, on the technical excellence of the two original *Queens* and, partly, on the 'terrific support and assistance given to Cunard in running their fleet.'[51] In a report written in 1965, Lord Aberconway noted that:

'The winning of the order for the large new Cunarder at the end of December last was a great triumph, and a fitting reward for the hard work put into the project and tender by our management and staff. We are particularly proud that our offer was accepted and the contract signed only thirty days after we submitted the tender. We have long experience of the fine co-operation that we know we shall continue to receive from Cunard and with this we are confident that the ship will be a worthy product of British design and workmanship.'

In December 1964, no one could have foreseen the troubles that would lie ahead. During the course of 1965, other substantial contracts were booked, or in progress, at Clydebank. These included the 12,000-ton cargo liner *Glenfinlas* for the Glen Line, the 18,000-ton bulk carrier *Cape St Vincent* for charter to Lyle Shipping Co, and the partial conversion of the *Queen Elizabeth* for cruising, to be carried out during 1966. The latter contract enabled continuity of employment to be maintained for finishing trades after the departure of the *Kungsholm*. Additionally, three jack-up drilling rigs for the North Sea were ordered by International Drilling Co Ltd, the first North Sea orders to be placed with any shipbuilder in the UK. Work in hand included the *Kungsholm*, the lumber carrier the *Vennachar*, the assault ship HMS *Intrepid*, the partial conversion of the intermediate liner *Sylvania* and a second 70,000-ton tanker for BP, the *British Confidence*.

The *Kungsholm* was launched on 15 April 1965 and taken the short distance to the basin for fitting-out to begin. The late arrival of drawings for the *Intrepid* delayed her completion which meant that both vessels were now in contention for the limited number of men of the finishing trades, a position which management had sought to avoid in their original production schedules.[52] Much to the irritation of the Royal Navy overseer at Clydebank, more men were assigned to the *Kungsholm* than the assault ship. Given the penalties for late delivery on the liner, there was a simple and compelling logic behind this. The Navy could wait. At the same time, the yard was hit by a rash of disputes and the completion of the *Kungsholm* was subjected to no fewer than eight stoppages by finishing trades, principally plumbers and electricians[53]. In a letter to the Swedish American Line dated 31 January 1966, Company Secretary Robin Williamson sought to explain the position:

'As evidence of the difficult labour conditions prevailing in this period, it is interesting to note that increases in wage rates in the shipyard of approximately 20% in nine months were awarded. The excessive demands made by labour, in an economy where the demand for skilled and unskilled labour developed to far exceed the supply, were met in an attempt to keep delay to a minimum, albeit at a cost not predicted at the time when extension of delivery was agreed and totally unforeseen at the negotiation of the contract.'[54]

Williamson continued that, in conceding to high wage demands, senior management had:

'...not only to deal with difficulties as soon as they arose, but also foresee many of them and avoid disruption of work before they materialised. Despite these efforts, from time to time the underlying discontent and uneasiness of the workpeople erupted in overt actions... It cannot be too strongly emphasised that these incidents are only the culmination of day-to-day continuous difficulties the like of which our shipyard has never before experienced.'

The effect of this was to delay the *Kungsholm*'s delivery until 11 March 1966, resulting in significant penalty payments. More importantly, the actual cost of building the ship had risen out of all proportion to the original tender of only a few years earlier. By 7 January 1966 the loss on the *Kungsholm*, excluding penalties, was a staggering £2,474,000.[55] John Brown had no option but to swallow this bitter pill. At the end of the contract, losses had accelerated beyond £3 million.[56] Ironically, in the *Kungsholm* Clydebank had produced a magnificent ship, equal to the finest

traditions of the shipyard. A comment in the yard report for February 1966 offers some explanation and confirms the view that the Swedes were exacting in their demands: 'Inspectors have been most severe ensuring a quite exceptionally high standard of material and workmanship which is most costly.'[57] The Swedish American Line were delighted with the ship they received. They had every reason to be. If John Brown's failure to win the Norwegian America Line contract for the *Sagafjord* late in 1962 had contributed, in some degree, to the *Kungsholm* debacle through a cut-throat price, management at Clydebank must have been chastened to note that the *Sagafjord* contract had driven her French builder out of business.

In 1965 a number of events occurred that would have repercussions up and down Clydeside and beyond. At the beginning of that year, Government concerns over the future of shipbuilding in Britain prompted Roy Mason, Minister of State for Shipping, to lead a fact-finding delegation to Japan, now the world's largest and most successful shipbuilder. He visited eight yards and had discussions with the Japanese Shipbuilders Association. The short report published as a result of this visit listed points that suggested why the Japanese industry was so successful:

A permanent labour force organised in one shipyard union, paid at marginally lower rates than in the UK.

A management structure which contained large numbers of men at middle management level with control of individual shops.

Middle management staff were invariably technically qualified graduates with practical experience in the work for which they were responsible.

The widespread use of planning and production control techniques and of computers in these fields as well as in ship design. In every case where facilities were being extended, construction docks were favoured in preference to slipways.[58]

It was against this background of concern for the industry that the President of the Board of Trade, Douglas Jay, set up the Shipbuilding Inquiry Committee in February 1965, under the Chairmanship of Reay Geddes. This committee, known as the Geddes Committee, was given one year in which to report on the changes necessary to restore the British shipbuilding and marine engineering industries to prosperity. While the Committee gathered to its task, John Brown & Company, similarly motivated to cure their ills, conceived an extraordinary construction project to build an entirely new super-yard at Clydebank. At the heart of this scheme lay the proposal to straighten the River Clyde by eliminating a bend in the river adjacent to the existing yard. This involved diverting the river and using the redundant section of river-bed to build three enormous building docks. The project, biblical in scale, was taken seriously and supported by leading political and industrial figures in Scotland. At an estimated £25 million, however, it would require considerable Government support and a financial commitment that John Brown could not provide alone, given their parlous financial position. Nevertheless, the Shipbuilding Inquiry Committee agreed to examine the proposal as part of its remit.

Attention now focused on Q4, Clydebank's Ship No 736, the keel for which had been laid on 5 July 1965 on the same berth that her famous Cunard predecessors had been constructed. Just four months later, however, one of Britain's foremost shipbuilders, the Fairfield Shipbuilding & Engineering Co Ltd, collapsed despite a £34 million order book. The Fairfield yard had been Clydebank's great rival during the late nineteenth century, while both yards were considered to be the most important on the upper reaches of the river. The failure of this leading yard added momentum to Government efforts to find a remedy for the increasing problems bedevilling British shipbuilding.

The Q4 Design Team

As early as March 1962 Cunard's Chairman, Sir John Brocklebank, gave some indication of how the new flagship would appear and, with an emphasis on design, how this would be achieved:

'The decision to build 'Q4' is a major turning point in Cunard history, and the design concept of the ship is a complete break with tradition. The Company has no intention of abandoning its hard-won position as the leading North Atlantic shipping line. Cunard policy is changing as the trade is changing, and the Company is beginning 1962 with positive evidence that it is applying its know-how and resources to producing a ship which will be the pacemaker on the North Atlantic, and will be equally successful as a cruise ship.'[59]

Regarding the liner's external appearance, he announced that James Gardner had been re-appointed to style the Q4's superstructure and to design the livery. Thus, Brocklebank was confident 'that the exterior profile of 'Q4' will be both attractive and forward-looking and, when the time comes to tackle the interior decoration, the same progressive policy will be pursued and a team of the very best designers will be engaged'.[60]

This was, of course, merely a continuation of the bad old British tradition of only employing interior architects to work on passenger ships once the planning of the structural steelwork was well advanced, meaning that the interiors would have to be inserted around existing columns and bulkheads. Modernism, in contrast, required that edifices of all kinds should be conceived from the inside out, the location of structural elements following the functional requirements of their programme. As events unfolded, however, a modernist approach to the layout and planning of Q4 came to prevail – although nobody could have predicted that when the project was initially announced.

At first, the Chairman's wife, Lady Brocklebank, almost inevitably assumed responsibility for the Q4's interior design. To begin with, she selected Jean Monro, Evelyn Pinching and Michael Inchbald to decorate the onboard spaces, based upon their existing work for Cunard and Union-Castle Line.

Monro, Pinching and Inchbald had recently redesigned the public interiors and cabins aboard Cunard's intermediate-class liners *Saxonia* and *Ivernia*, when these were adapted for a greater cruising role in 1962-63 and renamed the *Carmania* and the *Franconia*.[61] While the original intent of the refit was only to add air conditioning and fit *en suite* toilet facilities to a greater number of cabins, the opportunity was taken to add a swimming pool and lido decks and to remodel the interiors. A curved staircase was added to the original mezzanine-plan main lounge and a new cocktail bar introduced, while the cabins and public spaces were redecorated in a bright and fresh contemporary style that made few historical references. This, in itself, was a significant change from the eclectic original design of these ships, although they were still by no means of the Modern Movement, either in terms of aesthetics or intentions.[62]

While Inchbald's style was more overtly contemporary, Monro's input in selecting soft furnishings arguably purveyed an element of gentler, feminine charm. Moreover, Cunard's North Atlantic rival, the United States Line, believed that ships needed a woman's touch as the choice of trans-Atlantic sailing, they believed, was most likely to be made by the lady of the household. Thus, interior design of the *America* and the *United States* was carried out by Anne

proposed Q4 was potentially a vast project and, irrespective of style, it was doubtful whether Monro, Pinching and Inchbald would be capable of handling the work alone. Following Casson's advice, Lady Brocklebank formed an in-house design committee with Cunard's Vice-Chairman, Anthony Hume, and their Chief Naval Architect, Dan Wallace, and began to assemble a diverse team of architects and designers to handle various parts of the ship. Casson suggested that, for a start, his friend Dennis Lennon (1918-1991) would be a good choice. Moreover, Lennon's office had previously designed the Royal Box at the Royal

James Gardner, who co-ordinated the external design of the Q4. (Design Archives, University of Brighton)

The interior designer Michael Inchbald was an early appointee to the design team. (Gallagher collection)

The architect Dennis Lennon ended up co-ordinating the Q4's interior design. (Design Archives, University of Brighton)

Urquhart and Dorothy Markwald of the New York firm Smyth, Urquhart & Markwald,[63] with the *United States*, in particular, reflecting a style similar to that of Monro, Inchbald and Pinching's work for Union-Castle and Cunard.[64]

Although conservative by instinct, Lady Brocklebank was, nonetheless, well travelled and an informed observer of the lifestyle trends and expectations of the travelling public, with a practical point of view and the ability to understand and work with technical drawings and other material from Cunard's design department and the shipbuilders. Slightly later in the process, she met Sir Hugh Casson, who was well known for his work on HMY *Britannia* and for Casson-Conder's highly-acclaimed *Canberra* project. Using his famous charm, Casson reputedly attempted to persuade Lady Brocklebank that, at least, some more progressive British architects and designers ought also to be involved. After all, the

Opera House in Covent Garden and had also been invited to make proposals to renovate spaces in Windsor Castle, and so he was a known and respected name in 'establishment circles.'

Lennon had trained at the Bartlett School of Architecture under the traditionalist Professor Sir Albert Richardson, who strongly disliked the Modern Movement *per se*. Lennon apparently rebelled and became very interested in modernist art and design aesthetics, if not in the radical leftist politics which typified much modernist discourse, particularly at the Architectural Association School from the latter 1930s onwards. As with Sir Hugh Casson, Misha Black and James Gardner, he was regarded as a moderate progressive, rather than a radical iconoclast.

The war, however, intervened in his architectural career and Lennon joined the Royal Engineers. He had a distinguished war record, serving first in France, where he was taken prisoner in 1940. He escaped, however, winning the Military Cross for his bravery, and later served in North Africa and Italy. As with so many young British architects of progressive persuasion, Dennis Lennon had begun his career in exhibition design, working initially in the office of the high-profile modernists E. Maxwell Fry and Jane Drew.

Upon founding his own practice in 1950, Lennon had a peripheral role in the Festival of Britain, producing mainly furniture designs – but this brought him into contact with Casson, Gardner and Misha Black, who later designed the QE2's synagogue.[65]

Having been appointed by Lady Brocklebank, Lennon, in turn, suggested that Jon Bannenberg (1929-2002) would be another suitable designer. An émigré from Australia, Bannenberg initially had wanted to be a concert pianist, and so he studied at the Sydney Conservatoire of Music. He left for England in 1952 to pursue both his musical passion and a new interest in theatre set design (including for

the Australian to be 'a likeable, rumbustuous and personable young man.'[67]

Other members of Lady Brocklebank's eclectic seven-strong interior design team were the society interior decorator David Hicks and the Austrian émigré designer Gaby Schreiber. It was hoped that this diverse group of architects and designers would give the liner's public rooms and cabins the necessary variety of atmospheres to stimulate and delight passengers – and to attract a broad clientele of various ages, social and cultural backgrounds.

David Hicks (1929-98) was born in Coggeshall, Essex and schooled at Charterhouse. Thereafter, he studied painting at the Central School of Art and Design in London, after which he launched his interior design career with the decoration of his own house in London in 1954. Early clients mixed the aristocracy, media and fashion worlds (Vidal Sassoon, Helena Rubinstein, the Duchess of Rutland and Mrs Condé Nast). Hicks married Lady Pamela

Jon Bannenberg drew up some of the Q4's most striking interiors.
(Design Archives, University of Brighton)

The interior designer David Hicks, who decorated the Q4 Room. (Gallagher collection)

Gaby Schreiber poses with a model of the Q4's complex theatre auditorium.
(Design Archives, University of Brighton)

London's Old Vic). In 1954 he and his wife Beaupre opened an interior design business and, when a client showed him plans for a new yacht, Bannenberg responded that 'it was terrible. "So", he said, "If you're so bloody smart, do it better." So I did. Fortunately, his original design was so bad, it wasn't hard to improve on it!'[66] The yacht became the centre of attention at the 1963 London Boat Show and Bannenberg's involvement in luxury ship design had begun. Quickly, Dennis Lennon and Jon Bannenberg became friends and mutual advocates. Lennon found

Mountbatten in 1960 and thereafter decorated apartments for HRH Prince Charles and Princess Anne at Buckingham Palace. As with Michael Inchbald, his output was richly varied and he was particularly admired for his colourful modern fabric and furniture designs – indeed, he and Inchbald were two of the pioneers of interior design as a professional discipline in post-war London's high society.[68]

Gaby Schreiber (c.1912-1991), in contrast, was trained in Vienna and Berlin and, being very well-connected, she escaped to Britain in 1938 with her husband, the liberal Jewish publicist Leopold Schreiber, who was twenty years her senior. Thereafter, she formed an interior design business in Chelsea, Sykes & Schreiber, with Daniel Sykes, a young socialite whose sister was married to the Earl of Antrim. During the Second World War, Schreiber's career took a radical change in direction when she became a consultant designer to Runcolite, a plastics manufacturer (later, in 1951, she married its director, William Fischbein).

Gaby Schreiber Associates was formed in 1943 and their work comprised mainly design for plastic moulding – such as meal trays, bathroom and kitchen units. In 1946 Schreiber designed the Women's Dress Hall at the 'Britain Can Make It' exhibition in the V&A, a commission which brought her into contact with James Gardner. Later, in 1948, she was commissioned to design cafeterias for re-modelled Marks & Spencer stores in Holloway (London), Leicester and Brighton. In the same year, she toured the United States where she visited the offices of the furniture designers Marcel Breuer, Herman Miller and George Nelson and the industrial designer Walter Dorwin Teague. Schreiber appears to have been greatly influenced by these men – and, more generally, by the optimism and glamorous design imagery of post-war America. Consequently, Schreiber firmly aligned her practice with modernism's growing corporate wing, rather than its social ideologues.

Later still Schreiber, like Gardner, became an important designer for BOAC, drawing up first the cabin for the 1958 Comet IV, then the 1960 VC-10 (a project carried out with Charles Butler) and, later still, BOAC Boeing 707 and DC-7S cabins. Since the 1940s, BOAC, like the United States Line, had a policy of employing women designers to bring a desired 'feminine' touch to their 'plane interiors, crockery and stewardess uniforms. The fact that Schreiber additionally had modernist sympathies must also have helped her career as the technologically-charged aesthetics of the jet age developed during the 1950s. A remarkable (and, unfortunately, unsung) designer, Schreiber brought to Cunard a great deal of expertise and contemporary thinking about corporate image and identity.[69]

Before the new Cunarder actually came to be outfitted, however, the entire concept for the liner would be subjected to a great many radical changes – and not all of Lady Brocklebank's chosen designers survived this period of transition.

Given that the liner was going to be built with the benefit of a generous Government loan, the Council of Industrial Design, led from 1959 by Paul Reilly, lobbied hard for progressive architects and designers to be more centrally involved – indeed, Reilly and his COID colleagues privately held the view that certain of the designers and decorators already selected by Lady Brocklebank were 'a pretty useless bunch of people.'[70] Moreover, Reilly was particularly keen to promote technology and engineering design – both themes echoed by Harold Wilson's Government. Initially, Cunard were reluctant to engage constructively with the Council of Industrial Design, despite Reilly's best efforts.

Behind the scenes, meanwhile, the society photographer Lord Snowdon (Antony Armstrong-Jones, 1930-), who was married to HRH Princess Margaret and, as a member of the Council of Industrial Design since 1961, was an enthusiastic promoter of contemporary British design, argued that the new liner should be a 'national ship' and a showcase for progressive art, design and architecture. Being married to Royalty and sympathetic to the modernist-orientated design lobby, Snowdon was well positioned to help encourage Cunard to enter meaningful negotiations with the Council of Industrial Design. He recalls:

'We were deeply concerned that the new liner would be rather fragmented in terms of onboard style due to the very different approaches of the group of designers which had been assembled by Lady Brocklebank. We certainly did not want the ship to be a floating piece of chintz, representing the worst of British bad taste… Jean Monro, for example, was not even a professional designer but, instead, ran an interior decoration shop in Sloane Street, inherited from her mother.'[71]

In March 1965, the Council of Industrial Design invited Cunard's directorate to a meeting at their Haymarket offices, where they were shown portfolios of work by twelve architects and designers, all of whom the Council believed would give the ship its favoured modernist aesthetic.[72] Amongst those presented were Neville Ward of Ward & Austin – well known for his interiors for British Railways ships and a contributing architect to the Tourist Class spaces on the *Oriana* – and a young interior design graduate from Glasgow named John McNeece. During his diploma year at the Glasgow School of Art, McNeece had devised interiors for three David MacBrayne car ferries – the *Clansman*, the *Columba* and the *Hebrides* – which had been positively reviewed in *Design* magazine. His subsequent interiors for Scottish civic centres – most notably the council chamber and committee rooms of the Lanark

highest possible standard. With this object in view, the President of the Board of Trade will continue to keep in the closest touch with the company and the Council of Industrial Design.'[73]

With so much external pressure being brought to bear, Cunard's Directors evidently had no alternative but to engage as best they could with the pro-modernist architecture and design lobby. In May 1965 another meeting was therefore convened, this time at Cunard's Liverpool headquarters. There, Paul Reilly

A cabin decorated by Jean Monro on the **Transvaal Castle** *(above)*

and James Gardner's cartoon of Lady Brocklebank and her friends. (Ann Haynes and Design Archives, University of Brighton)

County Council headquarters in Hamilton – were equally praised by the Council of Industrial Design. However, neither Neville Ward nor John McNeece was considered to be sufficiently 'glamorous' or 'establishment' to be worthy of employment by Cunard, yet McNeece subsequently launched himself as a leading specialist cruise ship interior designer and, as we shall see, much later in his career, he helped to master-mind the QE2's 1994 refit.

Although Cunard, apparently, remained unconvinced by the merits of any of the Council of Industrial Design's suggested designers, with a Government loan involved, the Council had political leverage. Shortly thereafter, on 29 April, Roy Mason, the Minister of State for Shipping in Harold Wilson's Government, told the House of Commons:

'Discussions between Cunard and the Council of Industrial Design are ongoing. The company is well aware of the Government's concern that arrangements for supervising the interior design of the new ship should ensure that the result achieved will be of the

met Lady Brocklebank and Dan Wallace to discuss the selection of designers and the co-ordination of their work in more detail and, as a result, Reilly left with the invitation to prepare a second showing of work by suitable Council of Industrial Design-approved candidates.[74]

Some months later in November 1965, after suffering illness, Sir John Brocklebank took early retirement, aged only fifty, and, with him, Lady Brocklebank withdrew her involvement in the design of Cunard's new flagship.

A Fresh Design Approach

The new Cunard Chairman, Sir Basil Smallpeice (1906-1992), was an airline man. Although trained as a chartered accountant, he had become a Director of the nationalised British Transport Commission in 1948, before joining BOAC two years later. His long association with the airline ended in 1963 when he resigned in support of the Chairman, Sir Matthew

Slattery, after a policy disagreement with the Conservative Minister of Aviation, Julian Amery, about reducing the airline's debt burden.[75]

Cunard's involvement with BOAC had begun in 1960 when the Conservative Government had passed the Civil Aviation (Licensing) Act to allow private businesses to compete with nationalised corporations on the major international jet trunk routes. That year, Cunard had purchased Eagle Airways and announced the intention of buying three Boeing 707 jets to

gentlemen's club in London's Pall Mall which Gardner described as being 'a marble mausoleum watering hole where Establishment dinosaurs gather to sip port and fart gently after lunch.'[76] Smallpeice wanted to find out about progress on Q4's above-the-waterline external styling and to discuss how the interiors might best be co-ordinated. Gardner, however, was frustrated by the interference and obstruction of Cunard's traditionalist Vice-Chairman, Anthony Hume, and so he told Smallpeice of his irritation in no uncertain

Theo Crosby was a late entrant to the Q4 design team. (Design Archives, University of Brighton)

Stefan Buzas who, with his partner Alan Irvine, designed much of Boat Deck. (Gallagher collection)

The Royal College of Art students Elizabeth Beloe and Tony Heaton. (Design Archives, University of Brighton)

compete with BOAC on the main trans-Atlantic services. BOAC, however, quickly appealed to the Minister of Aviation, effectively forcing Cunard to merge their airline activities. Consequently, the two joined forces to form a new company, BOAC-Cunard, with the latter subscribing 30 per cent of the £30 million capital, together with two aircraft. The idea was to offer air-sea trans-Atlantic packages, an innovative idea which enabled passengers to fly in one direction and sail in the other.

This brought Sir Basil Smallpeice onto Cunard's Board – but he was unimpressed by the shipping line's rather quaint managerial style. Headquartered in Liverpool, but operating mainly from Southampton, the Line had no Managing Director and a very hierarchical corporate structure. Smallpeice brought to Cunard both a modern jet age approach to management and an appreciation of the importance of modern corporate design.

Shortly thereafter, Smallpeice invited James Gardner for afternoon tea at The Athenaeum, a grand

terms. Consequently, Hume was forcibly retired. As Smallpeice reassured Gardner at another meeting of the two in The Athenaeum: 'Don't concern yourself. When an executive reads of his retirement in *The Times*, it's a *fait accompli*.'[77]

Smallpeice, however, evidently felt that, as the Council of Industrial Design had sought both overtly and covertly to influence Cunard towards a modernist design agenda for the Q4, it would be politic to attempt to reach some sort of face-saving compromise on the final choice of interior architects and designers.[78] Strong central control would be required to co-ordinate the ship's internal spaces so as to ensure a harmonious outcome. Thus, it was decided that Dennis Lennon, hitherto a subordinate member of the Brocklebank-appointed design team, should be appointed to direct and synchronise the work of all the other interior designers. Paul Reilly and James Gardner both agreed with Smallpeice that Lennon would be the ideal candidate for this onerous task.

Lennon was not only well-connected in British

progressive architectural and design circles but was also very friendly with such contemporary artists as Henry Moore and John Piper who regularly visited his Fitzhardinge Street office. Another frequent visitor there was Sir Hugh Casson, whom Lennon knew from Festival of Britain days and who acted as an advocate and adviser when he was appointed to co-ordinate the interior design work on Q4. Indeed, in bringing together architects, artists, designers, fabric and furniture makers, Lennon's revised team arguably would be working in the tradition of the Arts & Crafts Movement and, for that matter, the early Bauhaus.

Meanwhile, the traditionalist interior decorators chosen by Lady Brocklebank – most notably Jean Monro and Evelyn Pinching – were sidelined, to be replaced by more progressive and 'mainstream' disciples of the Modern Movement. Originally, Monro had been commissioned by Brocklebank to design a veranda bar, lounge and library for Cabin Class in what was to have been a three-class ship, while Pinching was to have drawn up the observation lounge and indoor pool. As the Q4 project evolved, however, the Cabin Class lounge and veranda bar were merged with another lounge space on Boat Deck, above, to form the Double Room. Moreover, the initial drawings supplied by Monro and Pinching evidently did not meet with Dennis Lennon's approval and so their remaining public rooms were re-allocated and they were relegated to designing only cabins and crew accommodation. Doubtless only too aware of what was happening, both left the project in 1966. The 'old school' decorators had lost out – and the modernist designers had won.

Jo Pattrick, the wife of Michael Pattrick, Head of Central Saint Martin's College of Art and a very close personal friend of Sir Hugh Casson, replaced Monro and Pinching in April 1967.[79] Pattrick was commissioned to design the officers' and crew accommodation, as well as the ship's hospital facilities. At around the same time, Cunard's first female Director, Lady Tweedsmuir (1915-98), former Under-Secretary of State at the Scottish Office, was brought into the project to lend the sort of practical outlook from the passenger's viewpoint that had been Lady Brocklebank's speciality.

However, with Dennis Lennon effectively calling the shots, even those who survived the initial restructuring of the design team were placed under stricter control. For example, Lennon's office collaborated with the eclectic Michael Inchbald on the Queen's Room and Quarter Deck Library to ensure that his work remained largely in the modernist idiom, while David Hicks was allocated the Q4 Room – a combined lido café and night club – and teamed with the trendy architectural practice of Garnett, Cloughley, Blakemore & Associates to make certain that his work also conformed. This latter firm, headed by Patrick Garnett, had recently completed eye-popping interiors for the restaurant and bar, run by Butlin's at the top of the Post Office Tower, then one of London's most fashionable hang-outs. Yet Gaby Schreiber – who was admired by Sir Basil Smallpeice and James Gardner for her earlier BOAC design work – was given a freer reign than her fellow surviving designers from the Lady Brocklebank era.[80] Besides, Schreiber is remembered for her effective mixture of charm and steely determination, which enabled her to succeed in what was, otherwise, a male-dominated and rather nepotistic field. She drew up the Theatre auditorium, amidships, as well as a conference room and a block of luxury cabins on Two Deck. Jon Bannenberg, meanwhile, handled the immense and complex Double Room, Tourist counterpart to the Queen's Room, as well as the card room and indoor swimming pools.

Other new appointees to the interior design team – Theo Crosby (1925-1994) and Stefan Buzas (1915-) – were, not surprisingly, both well known in Council of Industrial Design circles and personal acquaintances of Lennon.

When Lennon had been employed by E. Maxwell Fry and Jane Drew in the latter 1940s, he sat at a drawing board next to Theo Crosby. Born in South Africa, Crosby had studied architecture at the University of the Witwatersrand in Johannesburg, before moving to England where he had a distinguished career as an architect, designer, sculptor, journalist and academic. His multi-disciplinary practice, Crosby/Fletcher/Forbes, run jointly with the graphic designers Alan Fletcher and Colin Forbes, handled architectural projects, interiors, graphic design and advertising. Crosby designed the Look Out lounge, forward on Upper Deck, but Crosby/Fletcher/Forbes were also commissioned to create a complete graphic identity for the ship. In a move to assert the sort of corporate design aesthetic that was already being used by other national commercial institutions, such as British Rail and BOAC, this was to include all printed items – from brochures, sailing schedules and deck plans to ticket folders, menu cards, cabin 'Do Not Disturb' notices and to the four-language signage throughout the ship's accommodation.[81]

Later, in the 1970s, Crosby/Fletcher/Forbes expanded and the firm was renamed Pentagram, becoming arguably Britain's foremost design agency of the era.

The Hungarian émigré Stefan Buzas – whose previous commissions included the 'The Land' exhibit in the Dome of Discovery at the Festival of Britain, the South African Airways travel bureau in London's Piccadilly and the glamorous interiors of Manchester Airport – was admired by Lennon for his 'wonderful interiors and for being delightful to work with.'[82] Having arrived in England, via Vienna, in 1938, he became a student at the Architectural Association. With a group of contemporaries, he became one of the founders of the practice of James Cubitt & Partners in 1948. Buzas' partner Alan Irvine (1926-) served in the RAF during the Second World War before joining Basil Spence for nine months to work on the remarkable Sea and Ships Pavilion for the Festival of Britain. Thereafter, he studied design as a post-graduate student at the Royal College of Art before leaving for Milan, then a ferment of post-war Italian style. Having subsequently taken part in a Council of Industrial Design exhibition in Stockholm, also involving Buzas, the two went into partnership in 1965.[83] Buzas and Irvine drew up the 736 Club, art gallery and Boat Deck shopping arcade.

Perhaps inevitably, Dennis Lennon & Partners designed the largest share of the interiors, including the two main dining rooms and Grill Room, the Midships and Theatre Bars, the Upper Deck Library and many of the passenger cabins, along with the circular Midships Lobby where passengers boarded the ship.[84] Additionally, Lennon's assistants designed all other deck lobbies, vestibules, stairways and other linking elements that were critical to bringing a sense of unity to the work of so many different designers.

Intriguingly, Lennon, Crosby, Buzas and the Pattricks were all acquaintances of Hans and Elspeth Juda, who edited an up-market arts and design quarterly called *Ambassador Magazine*. Lord Snowdon was also a member of the 'Ambassador Set' and photographed them together at various parties thrown by the Judas. Other members of this grouping of influential people and mutual advocates included the grocer and art collector John (later Lord) Sainsbury, George Christie (of Glyndebourne Opera House fame), the fashion designer Mary Quant and Eric Sharp of ICI Fibres, which later supplied synthetic textiles to the completed QE2.[85]

A number of special commissions included an invitation to Sir Hugh Casson, then Professor of Interior Design at the Royal College of Art, for the children's and teenagers' facilities to be designed by his students. A competition was held among eight or nine of the interior design students, from which Sir Hugh and Lady Casson selected a joint submission by Tony Heaton and Elizabeth Beloe as the winner.[86] The two students were then given the opportunity to work in Dennis Lennon's office during the summer of 1967 to work up their design to the required level of resolution.[87] Heaton recalls:

'I think that Sir Hugh and Lady Casson probably chose our scheme because they saw we could work together, whereas the other students were real individualists. Besides, Elizabeth was a textile designer, whereas I had studied interior design as an undergraduate in Manchester, so we complemented each other very well... We spent six weeks working in Lennon's office, which was a whirlwind of activity. All the time we were there, a steady stream of important people – ranging from the other designers to Cunard Directors and even HM The Queen – appeared in the office to look at the large models and renderings of the various interiors for the ship.'[88]

When Dennis Lennon started up his practice, his first employee was a youthful architectural graduate from the North London Polytechnic, Brian Beardsmore, later joined by Lennon's brother-in-law, Bernard Wehaan, who was South African and who concentrated mainly on business and administrative matters rather than design.

Typically, in the mid-1960s, Lennon's firm numbered between eight and ten people, but it grew significantly to handle the Q4 project.[89] To assist with

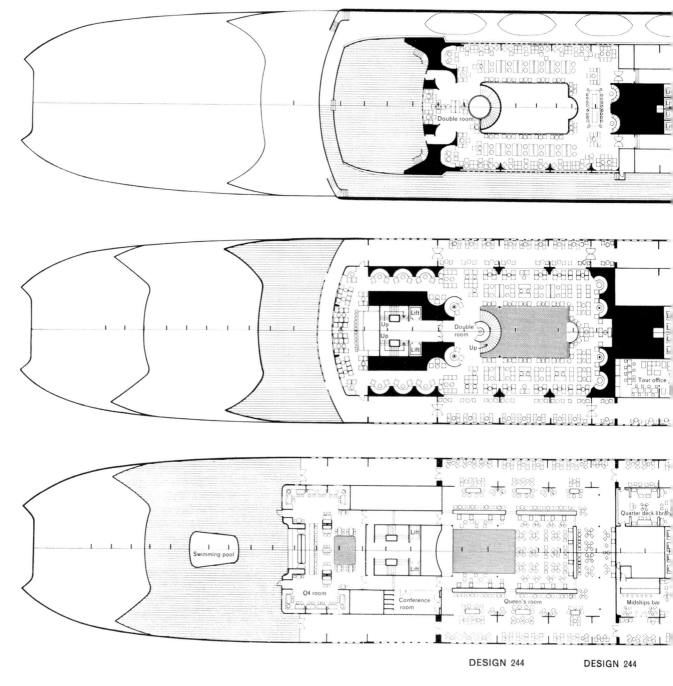

Double room

DESIGN 244   DESIGN 244

*The three main public room decks of the **Queen Elizabeth 2**'s original deck plan. (Bruce Peter collection)*

co-ordination, Lennon employed George Gibbon as his senior architect. As with Bernard Wehaan, Gibbon was South African and is remembered for being very competent in orchestrating Lennon's design team and also acting as a 'go between' to James Gardner to co-ordinate the internal and external look of the ship. For example, the arrangement of window openings in the superstructure had consequences for both the

interior atmosphere and exterior appearance of the liner. Although an effective and diligent designer and project manager, Gibbon's religious background (he was Plymouth Brethren) made it difficult for him to fit into the otherwise liberal and bohemian atmosphere of Lennon's office and, subsequently, he returned to South Africa.

Later, the architect Simon Monk and the furniture

Boat Deck

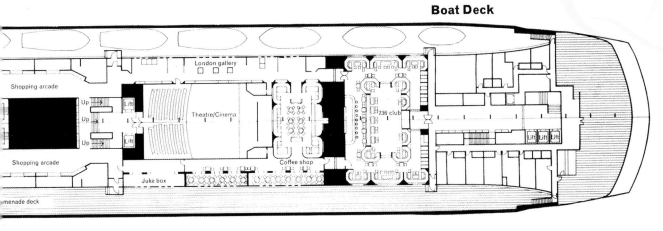

Upper Deck

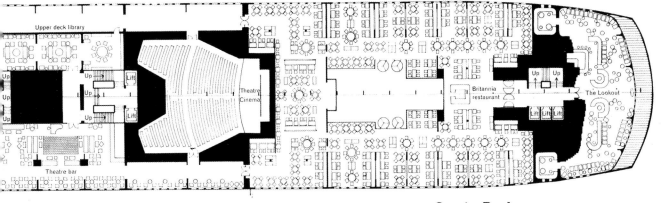

Quarter Deck

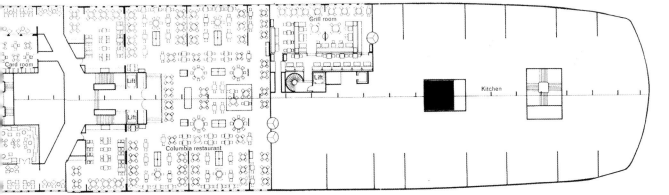

and interior design graduate James Herbert joined the firm – and these two men were the most centrally involved in drawing up interiors for Q4. They were assisted by the interior designers John Salmon and Jim Gordon and by a Norwegian couple, Nils and Margaretta Borch-Johnsen. An Australian interior designer, Ann Tilley, became Lennon's personal assistant and 'organiser' to help him deal with the many bodies and individuals who were to be involved in seeing the project through to completion.[90] To

assist Lennon's team with detailed design issues and with the specification of suitable components, the architectural practice of Tabb & Hazlehurst, which had recently assisted Swedish American Line's architects with the *Kungsholm* project, was appointed in a subordinate role to lend expertise and to take some pressure off the main Q4 designers.

Brian Beardsmore recalls that Lennon's office was run rather like an atelier with numerous young architects and designers passing through, enjoying

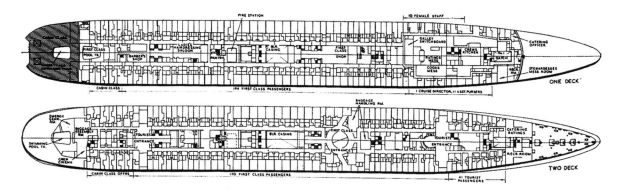

The decks containing cabins and machinery in the hull and lower superstructure. (Bruce Peter collection)

brief stints in what was a stimulating atmosphere with a broad diversity of retail, hospitality and public housing projects being tackled. Recent commissions then included London's Cumberland Hotel, 32 restaurants for J Lyons & Co, large housing estates for the Camden Borough Council and advisory work on a major revitalisation of the Rome Opera House. Beardsmore himself was responsible for much of the hotel design work carried out by Lennon's office and, although he was not personally involved in designing the Q4 interiors, it seems reasonable to argue that the reputation of the Lennon office for this type of work must have been a factor in helping to secure the Q4 commission. Indeed, James Gardner, in his autobiography, rather mischievously commented that Lennon would neither veer in the direction of Danish modern nor high-tech German Bauhaus and – if he did slip at all – it would, at least, be in the safer direction of the very best International Hilton.[91]

Upon being appointed to master-mind Q4's interiors, Lennon faced two immediate challenges. Firstly, he instinctively believed that Q4 should be a two-class ship – and this went against the view of Cunard's directorate which was still determined that there should be three classes. Secondly, Lennon had to persuade Dan Wallace that he should be taken seriously, as he correctly feared that the all-powerful Chief Naval Architect would resent what might have been viewed as his 'interference' with the overall planning of the ship. Beardsmore recalls that 'Dennis was as charming as he was forceful and, after lengthy and sometimes quite heated discussions, he won over both Cunard and Dan Wallace. Indeed, towards the

end of his three-year involvement, he and Wallace became good friends and mutual admirers. In fact, the QE2 turned out to be such a fine ship as a result of their excellent working relationship.'[92] Furthermore, Wallace's background as a John Brown man enabled him to bridge a potentially awkward gulf between Cunard's industrial and interior design teams, led by Gardner and Lennon, and the shipyard's technical staff, who were very suspicious of any designers, other than 'proper' naval architects and engineers, being involved at all in the Q4 project.

Tom Kameen recalls that 'behind closed doors, the naval architects and engineers often referred to the interior designers as 'the Teasy-Weasies' because they knew how they wanted the QE2 to look, but some appeared to have only the most superficial idea of the technical consequences of their decisions until we told them what could and couldn't be achieved on a ship. Out of the many designers involved, only Lennon was really trusted and respected by the technical people, who felt that he was a man of true substance.'[93] Kameen's commentary reflects a wider issue of professional demarcation in British industry as a whole, in which experts with potentially overlapping skills often were unnecessarily dismissive of each other's contributions. This situation was, in fact, endemic from the boardroom to the shop floor and shipbuilding was, arguably, more acutely affected than most, meaning that few British vessels achieved the same level of aesthetic and technical integration as the best of their foreign rivals. The Q4 project, however, proved to be a brilliant exception to this rule and, in fact, the ship that emerged was as complete a work of

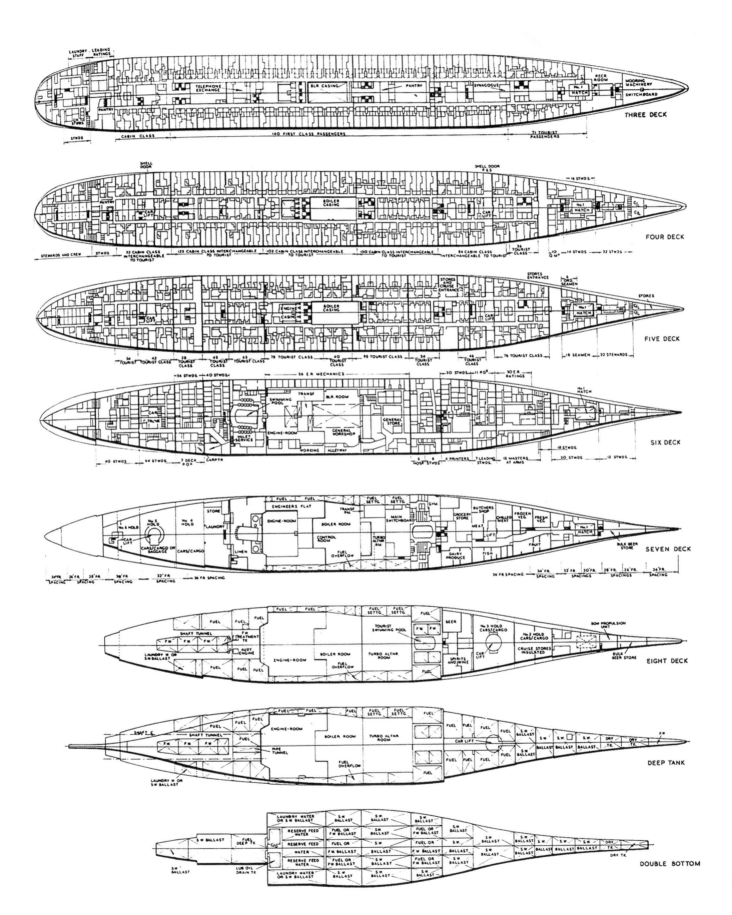

THREE DECK

FOUR DECK

FIVE DECK

SIX DECK

SEVEN DECK

EIGHT DECK

DEEP TANK

DOUBLE BOTTOM

art as has ever gone to sea.

Before actually beginning work on Q4, Lennon made an expenses-paid trans-Atlantic crossing from Southampton, via Cherbourg, to New York on the *France* to get a better idea of the scale of the task and the type of detailing which would be required. Monk was permitted to join him only for the overnight Southampton-Cherbourg leg, before taking the ferry home. Lennon also took the design team on study tours to various places of significant modern design in London that he thought were appropriate references. In addition, he set up an ongoing exhibition in the basement of his own studio, where other team members were encouraged to drop in and discuss the project. Without wishing to exercise too great an influence over their own individual creativity, he encouraged the designers to develop their own interpretations of the approach collectively, while still allowing the opportunity 'for individuals to put across their ideas.'[94]

As the project progressed, Lennon made frequent trips to Clydebank with Herbert and, occasionally, Monk to check on progress, to discuss issues to be resolved with Dan Wallace and to brief John Brown's naval architects and draughtsmen on the detailed design of the interiors. As Beardsmore recalls: 'Dennis was a stickler for detail and insisted on the best possible materials being used.'[95]

Designing from the inside out

With Dennis Lennon now taking a leading design role, alongside James Gardner and Dan Wallace, the planning of Q4's passenger accommodation and facilities was given primary consideration, with the all-important propelling machinery, auxiliary engines and generators, air conditioning plants and myriad other supporting services arranged with as little compromise as possible to the liner's hotel domain.

From the days of Q3, Cunard had already decided to abandon the conventional arrangement of public rooms on the promenade deck – dining rooms as low down as possible to minimise the effects of motion at sea, and cabins located on the decks in between – favouring an absolute linear split between the ship's cabin and communal areas. The new Q4 layout was also to take up this approach, with all passenger cabins located exclusively on the uppermost five hull decks and the public spaces, including the dining rooms and galleys, arranged throughout the three principal superstructure decks, above.

This allowed a uniform height to be maintained throughout the full length of each deck, with those housing the public spaces given the additional headroom needed for their larger open areas and vertical height on the cabin strata maintained at a comfortable minimum. The overall reduction in top-weight achieved by building the superstructure of aluminium allowed one more deck than would have been possible in a steel structure. A 150 to 230 mm (6 to 9 in) height reduction was achieved throughout the cabin decks by routeing cabling and piping through aircraft-style profile openings in the deck girders, thereby avoiding loss of finished ceiling height in the rooms. Electrical and plumbing distribution lines were run above the passages where a reduction in height was acceptable. [96] Thanks also to detailed engineering planning allowing a 900 mm height (3ft) reduction of the machinery spaces, there was also room enough for one more stratum of cabins in the hull than would otherwise have been possible in a ship of this size.[97]

Overall, the design concept sought to push the passenger spaces outwards and upwards, so that daylight could flood into the ship, making her bright and airy. In line with modernist practice in architectural design, the ship would have a single central service core, filling the middle sections of the lower decks, with parallel cabin corridors to either side and, consequently, the liner would be able to boast more outside rooms than any other in her size and class. Indeed, nearly all cruise ships built since have emulated this formula, which offered a significant advance over existing practice.

To maximise the amount of clear and unencumbered passenger area at the ship's sides and throughout the upper decks, all machinery and other working installations were concentrated as low as possible in the hull, or innermost along the centre axis of the lower passenger decks. The most powerful twin-screw steam turbine machinery ever to go into a passenger ship was shoehorned into only three of the hull's fifteen watertight compartments, slightly aft of amidships. This occupied less than a third of the ship's length, compared with installations aboard the old *Queens* at half and two-thirds the length of the *Queen Elizabeth* and the *Queen Mary* respectively. It allowed more space below the waterline to be made available for ship's stores and other working spaces, in turn freeing valuable internal volumes on the decks above for passenger accommodation. The boiler and engine room uptakes, along with principal ventilation shafts, were consolidated into a single cluster of casings, running up through eight passenger decks.

All vertical services and accesses, such as stairways and lift-shafts, were arranged along the ship's centreline, with the deck openings for these confined to the 8.8-metre (29ft) width of the boiler room uptake so as to retain the maximum structural strength of each deck – and the ship as a whole. Air conditioning and ventilation machinery, conveniently housed on the uppermost decks since mechanical shipboard ventilation was first introduced, was relocated to a series of plant rooms, located along the centreline on Three Deck. This, in effect, formed a functional, though non-structural, service core along the ship's centreline, bounded by the funnel uptake's breadth and flanked to either side by the fore-and-aft cabin corridors. The essence of this was continued through the two cabin strata above, where centreline spaces among the stairways and lifts, the uptakes and various other vertical cores were occupied by ship's offices, cabin service pantries, hairdressing salons, some of the shops, the synagogue and even an exclusive aperitif bar for the Grill Room on the deck above. The corresponding spaces on the two decks below were occupied by double rows of inside cabins, arranged back-to-back along the centreline.

The Inverted Hotel

While the notion of the ocean liner as a sea-going hotel traces its origins to the time of Cunard's *Umbria* and *Etruria* of the 1880s and to the lavish 'grand hotels' of the era on *terra firma*, Q4 was significantly to update the whole concept in line with the modern urban and resort hotels ashore, developed since the Second World War. This involved organisational change as well as a more contemporary approach to both the sleeping accommodation and public areas. Catering, housekeeping, entertainment and the traditional purser's functions were all organised into a

single hotel department under a Hotel Manager with direct responsibility to the ship's Captain. The objective of this was to bring all aspects of the ship's operation affecting the passengers under a single management hierarchy, based on modern hotel organisation ashore. This approach had already been successfully tried in 1968 aboard the *Carmania* and the *Franconia* before being implemented aboard Q4. This, along with the consolidation of all catering services for passengers and crew around a single centralised food service complex, reduced the hotel staff complement to around 650 persons, about 100 fewer than were needed aboard the old *Queens*.[98]

The complete separation of Q4's sleeping accommodation and public areas into two distinct zones, one above the other, already contributed significantly to creating a more hotel-like feeling, as found in modern high-rise examples ashore. Sir Hugh Casson described the ship as 'a hotel on its head: three decks of public rooms of great variety of size and character, above five decks of bedrooms.'[99]

With the dining rooms, various lounges, cocktail bars, night club, discotheque, auditorium and even a business centre, all arranged together as a single vast suite of public spaces, this created a far stronger impression of modern hotel living than had been possible with previous generations of ships' plans, where passengers had to descend through several accommodation decks to reach the dining rooms, after having taken their aperitifs in one of the promenade-deck lounges.[100] Banished too were the old-style U- and H-shaped lounges, worked into the available spaces surrounding multiple funnel uptakes, along with the enclosed promenade decks through whose often damp and chilly metal and teak wood milieu was filtered any view beyond the ships' sides. While, all too often, there was little more than fog and rain to be seen on winter North Atlantic crossings, cruise passengers were already getting used to full-beam public rooms with large floor-to-ceiling windows in the newer Scandinavian hybrid liner-cum-cruise ships, for example Swedish American Line's *Gripsholm* (1957) and Norwegian America's *Sagafjord* (1965).

Sensitive, perhaps, to the preferences of British passengers to continue enjoying at least some vestige of the traditional shipboard experience, Q4's designers chose to retain the essence of the promenades, adapting them as the principal circulating arteries among the public rooms on Quarter and Upper Decks, with these brought fully into the architectural and climate-controlled milieu of the ship's interior. Following the example of the *Gripsholm*, in particular, this saved considerable space by, in effect, bringing the promenade's function inboard and doing away with the additional galleries and other circulating spaces that would otherwise have been needed. Extending aft from the main restaurants on these decks, Q4's interior promenade allowed smaller spaces – such as the libraries, cocktail bars, writing and card rooms – to be arranged directly either side of the central boiler and engine casings, with these being accessed from the promenade at their outer sides or being integrated directly as part of the circulating space, as in the Theatre Bar on Upper Deck.

This was the antithesis of the *Canberra*'s layout where her machinery-aft plan was exploited to arrange the First Class public rooms around a central axis, with an outward perspective of infinite spaciousness through the Meridian Room main lounge with its outer corners also opening into connected spaces beyond. The periphery circulation pattern by way of Q4's promenades, inevitably, brought a less dramatic entry into the large public spaces, which were entered from their corners, losing the sense of infinity achieved in the *Canberra*. Functionally, though, this simplified the planning of those spaces to be used for dancing or entertainment, with the dance floors, bandstands or stages being given their rightful places as central focal points.

The promenades were integrated into the peripheral areas along either side of the Queen's Room on Quarter Deck and the Double Room's main level on Upper Deck, extending the latter fully to the ship's sides, as in the *France*'s vast Tourist Class Grand Salon. The promenades, however, retained their own distinct architectural identity, largely by being routed through the large round-cornered openings in the ship's transverse structural web-frames. These formed a repeat pattern of flattened arches when viewed from either end.

Where Quarter Deck had additional height to accommodate the main galley and its need for overhead ventilation and exhaust piping, the greater headroom allowed the floor level in the public spaces amidships and aft to be raised slightly, by about 300 mm (1 foot), so as to optimise viewing of dancing and entertainment features in the Queen's Room and also to provide a slightly raised entry to the Columbia Restaurant. This took advantage of variations in deck level along the centreline, so that the two centre-most stair-landings coincided with the raised floor level, minimising the need for steps or slopes in the circulating areas. On Upper Deck, the peripheral areas of the Double Room's main level were also slightly raised in a similar manner.

Other modern hotel features of the public spaces included a 24-hour coffee shop, the art gallery and a business centre with a conference room, along with facilities for photocopying, and ship-to-shore telephone (in those days before satellite communications). The conference room was reached from an inner passage running alongside the aft main stairways and also accessing the Q4 Club, aft, or the Queen's Room, forward, which could be closed off from the main promenade circulating spaces. This, in effect, formed a separate inner loop within the peripheral promenade circuit, with the sophistication of a discreet means of circulation among these rooms when used for private functions.

Apart from the diversity of pubic rooms aboard Q4 and their consolidation into a single contiguous suite of connected spaces, the absence of enclosed promenade decks surrounding the public decks also added to the sense of a building. On first experiencing this when the ship was new, one passenger was overheard asking the rhetorical question: 'When does this place get to the other side?'[101]

Cruising first

As a liner of unprecedented originality and sophistication, and with a progressive design team, the new Cunarder seemed destined to become one of the most exciting things to emerge on the world scene from Swinging Britain of the 1960s. Yet, the one remaining hangover from Q3 was that, as late as the summer of 1966, she was still to have had three passenger classes, at a time when the *Rotterdam* and the *France* had more flexible two-class arrangements. Delivered in the mid-1960s, at about the time Q3 was to have made her debut, Italian Line's *Michelangelo* and *Raffaello* stood alone as the last three-class liners. Fortunately, with Dennis Lennon's persuasion, Cunard had the opportunity to rethink this aspect of Q4's design when, during construction, her delivery was postponed from May 1968 until the end of that year.

Essentially, the lower two classes were to be amalgamated and their public rooms on Upper and Boat Decks consolidated, and the remaining division between the Tourist and First Classes de-formalised. Cabin and Tourist Classes were already to have shared the same dining room, forward on Upper Deck, with this becoming the Britannia Restaurant on the revised plan. The major structural change was that the Cabin and Tourist main lounges, aft on these two decks, were amalgamated into a vast single mezzanine plan multi-function room (the Double Room), while the spaces for smaller lounges and other rooms were rearranged.

In essence, Q4 was to be completed following cruise-ship design trends, in general, with various particulars of plan and outfitting specially arranged to meet Cunard's need for a fairly flexible two-class service on trans-Atlantic crossings.[102] Other large modern ships, such as the *Rotterdam* and the *France*, followed the traditional approach of each class having its own main lounge-cum-ballroom and some sort of café bar as a conjugal contemporary replacement for the once strictly male preserve of the smoking room. These were laid out one deck above the other, with separate stairways for each class arranged to bypass the deck belonging to the other in line service, and with various doors that could be opened to join both suites of spaces when cruising. This was never entirely satisfactory as it left cruise directors with duplication, rather than diversity, in the function of the combined spaces in which to keep their passengers amused and happy.

Q4, in contrast, was one of the first large ships designed with a single integral suite of public spaces, primarily oriented towards cruising rather than multi-class line service. Apart from their designated trans-Atlantic roles as main lounges for First and Tourist Class, the Queen's Room and Tourist Double Room were, otherwise, spaces of entirely different character that complemented, rather than replicated, one another's function. While the Double Room was created

to have a sense of infinite spaciousness for various groups of people all to be doing different things at the same time, the Queen's Room followed more the function of a traditional ballroom and, as needed, could be closed off from its peripheral areas, creating a more intimate smaller space of quite different character for private parties or other special events.

The dark and intimate promenade Midships Bar cocktail lounge and the Theatre Bar, in First and Tourist Classes respectively, also retained marked differences of function and ambience when the ship was in cruise or trans-Atlantic service. Likewise, the two night-spots had differing alternative daytime roles, with the Q4 Room becoming the lido lounge and bar for the Quarter Deck swimming pool and the 736 Club spending its daytime hours as a café, with the discotheque installation darkened behind its smoked Plexiglas front. In no sense, however, were rooms designated for either class of differing quality in terms of planning, materials, fit and finish.

Along with Cunard's decision to locate all dining rooms on the upper decks came an extensive rationalisation of the entire approach to serving these, again as was originally planned for Q3. Where provision in the old *Queens* was distributed among a central galley conglomerate, serving the First and Cabin Class dining rooms, and separate kitchens elsewhere for the Grill Room, Tourist Class and various officers' and crew's wardrooms and messes, all catering on the new ship would be handled by a single, entirely centralised, hotel-style complex, fully forward on Quarter Deck. This was arranged around a single open-plan central cooking area, including the bakery, with multiple ranges, ovens and other equipment laid out so that each *chef de partie* could work independently, but adjacent to the service counter sections, where their particular specialities would be picked up by the dining stewards.[103] The complex was staffed at various levels, according to demand around the clock, maintaining a level of service for on-duty crew and ad hoc cabin service outside regular passenger dining hours.

Service difficulties encountered in the QE2's early years were probably more a matter of the galley's scale rather than its concept. This probably had more to do with the fundamental difference of adapting sound hotel practice to the peculiarity of shipboard service peak loads, seldom experienced ashore, with all patrons dining in two-sitting relays at set times of the day.

The Columbia Restaurant and Grill Room were directly aft of this catering complex, and the Britannia Restaurant, above, was served by escalators, as already found aboard the highly-successful Dutch ships *Willem Ruys* and *Rotterdam*. The 24-hour Coffee Shop, 736 Club and officers' wardroom on Boat Deck were supplied by lift from the same complex, along with the various crew mess rooms down on One Deck where these, in effect, formed a widened part of the ship's core spaces, flanked by passenger accommodation to either side. Pantries in the core areas of the five accommodation decks were arranged for hotel-style room service to cabins around the clock, with direct lift access to the main galley.

Store rooms, larders, cold lockers, wine cellars and the handling areas for these were arranged with lift access directly below in the forward hold areas of Seven Deck. The forward baggage and automobile holds, needed for Atlantic service, were also provided with horizontal access so that these could be used for additional ship's stores when needed for world cruises or, indeed, an entire cruise season. Shell doors in the hull, providing for cars to be driven on board, could also be used for stores to be handled by fork-lift trucks, with sufficient space available for these to manoeuvre within the working areas on board. Only the forward-most Number 1 hold had a conventional trunkway and hatch, worked by cranes on the bow deck, although this also had internal horizontal access, allowing it too to be worked laterally from the pier, by way of the working passages on Six and Seven Decks and a stores lift descending to its lowest level on the double bottom's inner shell.

Structure and Strength

The elegant hull and superstructure that contained all of this was a masterpiece of naval architecture and marine construction, capable of moving at a top speed of 32.46 knots as demonstrated when the completed

Above: Another hull prototype is tested in a simulation of more 'stormy' weather in the test tank. The display model of the completed QE2 in Glasgow's Museum of Transport was built using one of these models as its basis. (Gallagher collection)

Right: One of the several timber hull models of the Q4 undergoes wave-tank testing to ascertain the optimum form in a variety of sea conditions. In service, the QE2 has proven to be an outstandingly robust 'sea ship' in even the worst Atlantic weather. (Ian Johnston collection)

liner ran her sea trials in November 1968.[104] At the waterline, the bow lines were very fine and slightly concave in form as these widened out to the midbody's straight and parallel lines, creating a minimum amount of wake and surface drag along the ship's sides and around the likewise slender, though slightly convex (rather than concave) afterbody form. Below the waterline, the shape was more yacht-like, with the rectilinear midbody lines dissolving into a continuous, gently curvilinear form around the bilge keels, with the bow's narrow waterline profile opening up into a substantial bulbous forefoot. While the bow's narrow waterline entry cut through the surface with minimum flank turbulence, its blunt underwater 'nose' was devised, in effect, to 'de-tune' and reduce the amplitude of wave created by the forward part of the hull, achieving a propulsion economy of 7,460 kilowatts (10,000 shaft horsepower).[105]

Above the waterline, the hull and superstructure were suffused as a single, though bi-metallic, structural entity. The superstructures of conventionally-built liners – such as the old *Queens* – were, essentially, deckhouses, supported pretty much as free-standing structures atop the hull. Their mass was supported by a steel strength deck, forming a 'breastplate' for the hull's structural rib-cage, with the keel as its backbone.

In Q4, by contrast, the entire superstructure formed a strengthening element, countering the keel, with all levels of the hull upwards from One Deck and the four superstructure strata above these being longitudinally, as well as laterally, framed.[106] From Quarter Deck up, the superstructure, along with the funnel and mast, were constructed entirely of aluminium, though the funnel casing itself was steel. Alloy was also used for internal structures down as far as Two Deck. The external riveted bi-metallic lap joint between the steel hull and aluminium superstructure encircles the ship at a point just beneath the large Quarter Deck windows.[107] To prevent electrolytic corrosion of the alloy, caused by sea water and airborne salt spray where the two metals are joined, the butt edges of the join were covered with a neutral cold-setting Araldite fillet, isolating the steel and alloy from direct exposed external contact.

The alloy superstructure was stressed so as to take up the relatively large bending and twisting forces passed up from the hull's movement, as well as the weight of the lifeboats, their davits and launching gear and the substantial external forces of wind and rain while under way at full speed. The inherently greater elasticity of the alloy was better able to take up the greater movement and larger structural stresses so high up in a sizeable ship than could be absorbed by a comparable steel structure.[108] Yet, this also called for the precaution of widely-rounded corners and gently-bowed upper and lower edges for the large Quarter and Upper Deck windows to minimise the possibility of eventual fracturing or tearing of the alloy under stress at the corners of large openings, such as these.[109]

Without the structural stiffening elements of a conventional strength deck and the lapped plating of a traditionally riveted hull, special attention had to be given to the added rigidity that could be gained from internal web-frames, extending several metres in from the ship's sides. The intervals of these varied according to the differing lengths of various watertight compartments, as their dimensions were determined by the need to house assorted machinery and other working installations on the lower decks. Added strength was gained in the superstructure sides by maintaining a solid area of shell plating, a full hull-frame width of 900 mm (3 ft) to either side of each web, resulting in the irregular appearance of the ship's Quarter and Upper Deck window groupings.[110] The topsides' structural weight economies had to be counterbalanced with an extra 750 tons of steel added to the double bottom to maintain an acceptably low centre of gravity in the interest of overall stability at sea. This was accomplished mainly with double-thickness plating of the bottom and by closing up various intervals in the inner plating of the double bottom, as well as with added stiffening in places susceptible to damage from corrosion and vibration.[111] As a result, the liner had an exceptionally robust hull bottom, a factor which helped to ensure such a long operational career.

There was no overhang of the superstructure beyond the ship's sides, as there was in the old *Queens*, the more modern examples of the *Rotterdam*, the *France* or, for that matter, the *Oriana* which was otherwise a prototype for much of Q4's lightweight structural innovativeness. Instead, the ship's sides were absolutely flush all the way from the turn of the bilge keels, below the waterline, to the outer edge of the boat deck. Internally, exactly the same arrangement of structural and web-frames and the lines of internal supporting columns was maintained throughout, with the one exception that the centre line of columns was discontinued from Quarter Deck upwards to provide greater openness along the centre axis in the public rooms. On the public room decks, Dennis Lennon made a virtue of the web-frames by expressing their form, with its distinctive curved corners, as a repeated element along each side of the restaurants and promenade arcades. Indeed, the idea for these actually originated in Lennon's office and began as a series of speculative drawings which were passed on to Dan Wallace, who examined the structural implications and engineered a solution. This aspect of the work took nearly a year to achieve – but it enabled the free-flowing open-plan ambience which made the liner feel so distinctive and so much more modern and spacious than any other large passenger ship hitherto. Indeed, throughout the duration of the project, Lennon's office worked closely with Wallace and Gardner to achieve as harmonious an effect as possible. This also included thinking carefully about the shapes of the windows in the shell plating and so, long before the liner was actually fitted out, the bare bones of the distinctive and spacious onboard style were already inherent in the structural aluminium and steelwork.

Although falling short of being the type of monocoque construction proposed for streamlined high-speed liners during the 1930s by the visionary American designer Norman Bel Geddes, Q4's advanced bi-metallic construction probably came closer to achieving an aviation-style structural integrity than any other large ocean going passenger ship ever built.

Power and Propulsion

At the time she was built with her original steam machinery, the QE2 had the largest boilers then ever built for shipboard use and the most efficient high-powered steam turbines ever to go into a merchant ship, making her the most powerful twin-screw ship of her time.[112] Significantly lighter and more compact than the machinery of the old *Queens*, the QE2's power plant consumed only about half as much fuel to yield a similar performance at 28.5 knots for trans-Atlantic service, along with the additional latitude to be run efficiently at lower speeds for cruising. Of the three watertight machinery compartments, the boiler room was centre-most, with the propulsion turbines aft and the 16.5 megawatt electrical turbo-generator plant forward. Logically, this placed the steam-raising plant amidst its two main consumers with the advantage of feed lines to these being as short and direct as possible.

A steam plant was required to produce the necessary power output to drive the hull at Cunard's specified 28-knot service speed. At that time, interestingly, the most powerful diesel plant yet fitted to a passenger ship was the two Götaverken V6-9V engines fitted to the *Kungsholm*, built by John Brown's immediately before the QE2 was constructed, yet the service speed was only 21 knots and it would be some years before a diesel plant capable of maintaining speeds similar to a steam turbine ship could be designed.

The three main boilers were a larger version of the Foster Wheeler External Superheater D-type (ESD) units fitted aboard the *Canberra*. These superheated the steam to 950 degrees Fahrenheit by convection from the boiler's exhaust gas flow, with the operating advantage of reducing the working temperatures of the steam tubing. This minimised the risk of clogging inherent in radiant superheating.[113] Triple-boiler installations of this type were also successfully used in the likewise compact machinery arrangements of the mid-sized fast Italian liners *Eugenio C.* and *Oceanic*, with the larger *Michelangelo* and *Raffaello* each having four ESD boilers, paired up in their two engine rooms. The Q4 was originally to have had four boilers, following the example of Holland America's *Rotterdam*, which could maintain full service speed with only three of these in use, allowing one to be shut down for maintenance without serious loss of headway. Q4's fourth boiler was one of the items sacrificed to cut the original building price. With hindsight, this proved to be a false economy. Indeed, a lack of spare boiler capacity subsequently would compromise the liner's reliable operation as a steam ship.[114]

The main turbine sets were designed by Pametrada

(PArsons Marine Experimental Turbine Research and Development Association), founded in 1944 to consolidate and rationalise marine turbine research and development for both defence and merchant shipping in Britain. Each of the two double-reduction geared turbine sets, with single steam flow from the first high-pressure stage feeding to double-flow low-pressure stages and then to an under-slung condenser, was designed to yield maximum efficiency at the ship's design service speed of 28.5 knots. An added reserve margin was available by increasing the steam temperature to 1,000 degrees.[115] Electrical power was generated by three main 5,500kW AEI turbo-alternators, backed up by twin diesel-powered emergency generator sets. This was distributed at 3,300 volts, 60-Herz three-phase AC for consumption by large items, such as the steering gear, bow thrusters and stabiliser motors, and stepped down by transformers to 415 and 240 volts for other services such as lighting and domestic use in the accommodation.

The 5,207 rpm speed of the propulsion turbines was stepped down through double-reduction gearing to the 174 rpm turn of the twin six-bladed propellers of 5.79 metres (19 feet) diameter. Following extensive model testing of four- and six-bladed alternatives, a six-bladed design was finally chosen as it exhibited the best combination of high propulsion efficiency and low vibration-causing cavitation.[116]

Other equipment included twin 746 kiloWatt (1,000 hp) bow thrusters, with a combined thrust of 22 tons. As in the *Oriana*, one of the first ships to use these, their hull tunnels were fitted with steel covers, closing flush into the underwater shell plating to maintain smooth lines of flow past these when steaming at full speed.[117] The QE2 was also fitted with two sets of retractable power-operated fin stabilisers. Rather than carrying large quantities of fresh water, pumped aboard from ashore as with the old *Queens*, flash evaporators installed in the QE2's main engine room were able to produce 400 tons of potable water daily of sufficiently high quality that it could be used for both domestic purposes and as boiler feed water without additional treatment. Sea water was taken in through two raked 900 mm (3 ft) diameter intake pipes, passing through the ship's double bottom, beneath the engine room.[118]

The machinery spaces were supervised from an air-conditioned engine control room. This was spacious, ergonomically designed and laid out with a series of consoles, giving 'push button control of all the major machinery.'[119] Cunard were particularly proud that a Ferranti 'Argus' computer was installed to process all data in relation to machinery control and the management of the ship's onboard services. Whether the officers and crew dared trust this (fairly primitive) computer is a moot point – but it did signify that the QE2 was as bang up-to-date as the technology of the era would allow.

The new Cunard flagship, nonetheless, represented a final chapter in the illustrious history of merchant seafaring under steam. She, along with the Deutsche Atlantik Line's *Hamburg* also delivered in 1969, were to close out the era of passenger steamship building, against the formidable competition of diesel engineering virtually monopolising the passenger ferry and cruise ship markets.

Architecture and Style

As advanced as the ship was structurally and in her engineering and other technical systems it was ultimately the work done by her architects, industrial and interior designers that would give an image and persona in the public's perception and experience of her. Given that several architects and interior designers were to collaborate, an essential unifying element among their individual creative signatures was to be derived from what Sir Hugh Casson described as the 'ruthless standardisation of such linking elements as staircases, corridors, door furniture and sign-posting.'[120]

From his original concept for Q3, James Gardner, in fact, visualised Q4's realisation as a great yacht with a graceful flourish of line and form, rather than yet another grand ocean liner.[121] The work already done by Dan Wallace and the naval architectural teams both at Cunard and John Brown & Co helped Gardner along in this direction by giving him a very elegant and fine-lined waterline profile and bow form with which to work.

The superstructure front was stepped back, wedding-cake style, in a similar fashion to the *Canberra*, though in parabolic, rather than semi-

Top: The uncluttered expanses and dynamic forms of the QE2's original Bridge and Signal Decks. The sweeping forms around the base of the funnel and sheltering the sports deck are similar to those in some modern concrete architecture on terra firma of the same period. (Bruce Peter collection)

Left: The QE2's wheelhouse was – and remains – a masterpiece of modern ship design. James Gardner devised the shape to give the impression that it was pulling the ship's dead mass forward. (David Trevor-Jones)

Above centre: This impression of forward motion was further enhanced by the swept-back forms of the bridge wings. Here, we see the view aft beneath the port-side bridge wing. (David Trevor-Jones)

Above right: The QE2's remarkable forward-leaning mast. (Bruce Peter collection)

circular, lines of form. This reflected the curvature of the navigating bridge front, its lines spreading out in a series of widening concentric arcs down through three levels to the open bow deck. Remarkably, compound curves of the type rendered in metals of one-tenth the thickness for aircraft manufacturing were achieved successfully in the ship's altogether heavier construction. Believing that it was necessary to engender an impression of great speed, Gardner chose to raise and rake the bridge front forward, rather than back, to create the illusion of it pulling the ship's mass along behind it.[122] Towards the stern, the aft ends of Upper, Quarter and One Decks were cascaded down between gently-tapered glazed windscreens, each turned in gradually from the ship's sides, providing protection for the open deck areas from the wind and concealing the deck stairways and other cluttering items from view. Between these screens, large expanses of teak-planked sun deck were arranged as a series of tiers, enabling passengers to lounge in relative shelter around two outdoor swimming pools. Whereas Cunard's pre-war liners

had only moderately-sized sun decks – reflecting a belief that only the working classes who laboured outdoors had suntans – the new flagship would be designed to enable all of the passengers to find outdoor space to bronze themselves to their hearts' content. After all, in the jet age, coming home from holiday with a tan was now *de rigeur* as a status symbol for the wealthy and upwardly-mobile. To maximise the deck area aft, the Q4's stern profile was spoon-shaped, giving a much more full-bodied form than on Cunarders of recent decades which, since the *Queen Mary*, had had cruiser sterns. The *France*, too, had a slender stern profile, but recent Scandinavian and Italian liners also provided more outdoor space aft. The recent conversion of the *Carmania* and *Franconia* provided a precedent for the tiered deck arrangement and for the glazed shelter screening on either side.

Gardner's greatest triumph, however, was the ship's funnel, an inspired combination of old and new ideas, resulting in a form that was sophisticated, highly effective – and also iconic. Apart from venting exhaust emissions from the ship's machinery, the funnel also

Having executed a sharp turn to starboard, the QE2 surges towards the camera in this striking aerial view. (Bruce Peter collection)

The mighty bow towers over the shipyard. The slender entry at the waterline and the bulbous bow are notable aspects of the design. (Gallagher collection)

QE2's tapering stern lines are emphasised by the subtle curves of the windscreens on each side of the extensive sun decks. (Bruce Peter collection)

had to keep these away from the large open lido decks used by passengers. After looking at the great ovoid funnel favoured by the naval architects, with a flat fin at the top – ostensibly devised to keep the smoke above its under-draught – and thinking again of his own tall white alternative from Q3 days, Gardner quietly asked himself: 'Hell, who's supposed to be designing this ship anyway?'[123] His original idea, in fact, was borrowed from the old Victorian notion of a tall black stovepipe funnel that would carry smoke and smuts high up above the ship though, at the time, he probably never thought of it that way. Extensive wind tunnel tests were carried out at the National Physical Laboratory at Teddington, which showed that this functioned more effectively than Dan Wallace's proposal but, in certain winds, the soot and gases could still fall to the decks due to a vacuum in the stack's lee. With help from both the shipyard's technical people and from the National Physical Laboratory's scientists, seventeen different models were tested to perfect the design.[124] Eventually a solution was found by wrapping a white cowl around the sides and back of Gardner's tall stack to about three-quarters of its height and venting return air from the accommodation through this to push the exhaust gases up and away from the decks. By adding a wide wind scoop at the funnel's base to pick up air currents from above the deck and concentrating these up-draughts behind the cowl, a second low-pressure spot was eradicated when winds blew across the ship's quarter. Gardner was now armed with scientific evidence that a version of his tall stack would be much more effective in keeping the lido decks clear of soot than a traditional Cunard funnel, as fitted to the company's existing post-war liners.

This notwithstanding, some of Cunard's Directors still had doubts about ditching the old notion of a big red funnel – 'the insignia of the line, you know, Cunard red.' Having given Gardner's design work unqualified support up to this point, Sir Basil Smallpeice decided that, on this controversial issue, diplomacy was required and so he decided to pass the buck. In an unexpected bout of conservatism, he elected to ask for The Queen's opinion when showing

Left: Scientists at the National Physical Laboratory discuss a range of models of funnels to be tested in a wind tunnel for the Q4 project. (Gallagher collection)

Above: The process by which the final design solution evolved, with inspiration apparently drawn both from the 'romantic days of sail' and from someone's old boot. (Bruce Peter collection)

a model of the Q4 to her at Buckingham Palace at a special private audience, arranged in relation to Her Majesty's invitation to launch the ship in September 1967. As an alternative to his own favoured modernist design, Gardner was asked to bring along a conventional Cunard funnel that could also be shown on the model. Understandably, he feared that Her Majesty might opt for tradition in the absence of a suitable explanation being given for the rationale informing his provocative black-and-white smoke stack. As the model was gingerly being wheeled into the Palace, Smallpeice discreetly buttonholed Gardner for the funnel in Cunard house colours. 'Awfully sorry... it fell off this morning – and someone trod on it.'[125] If looks could have killed... Anyway, The Queen was spared having to make the choice, and it would be Gardner's funnel after all.

As building work progressed, Dan Wallace started worrying that perhaps the liner's upper decks, mast and funnel were reaching too high up to the sky. He explained that a ship at sea is like an inverted pendulum, and the higher she goes, the wider she swings. To make his point, Wallace took Gardner up on a shipyard hoist. 'Two more decks to come, then the fan house and that eighty-foot funnel of yours,' said Wallace, motioning skywards with his umbrella. 'And the dog kennels,' added Gardner, though the wind blew that one away from the naval architect's ears. Point taken though, as a wiser Gardner later pencilled a sketch in his notepad of the ship's unfinished decks rising ever higher into the sky above Clydebank, before whittling away at a piece of cheddar from the fridge as he modelled a refined and slightly lower profile for the bridge housing. However, his elegant tall and slender funnel would stay.[126]

Gardner's mast was equally remarkable. His original Q3 styling model had a combined foremast and forward funnel in a tapering white stack. Although Q4's engine room was located two-thirds aft, the galley was forward, meaning that an exhaust was required to vent heat and cooking odours. Gardner therefore reworked the Q3 proposal into a remarkably bold and sculptural mast which leaned slightly forward to reinforce the dynamic form of the

Above: The Q4's evolving funnel is subjected to wind tunnel testing at the National Physical Laboratory in Teddington.
(Ian Johnston collection)

Right: The sophisticated workings of the final design solution, showing how air was forced upwards immediately behind the smoke stack to prevent exhaust from being sucked down. (Gallagher collection)

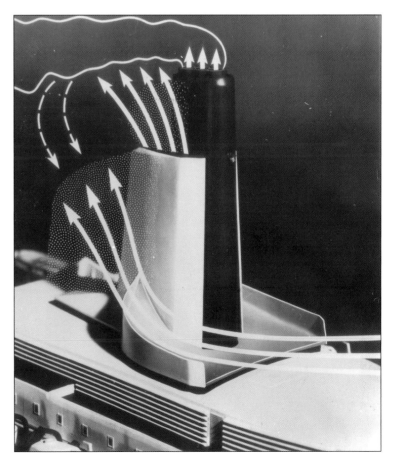

wheelhouse, immediately below. Otherwise, the main challenge was to fit the various navigation lights, arms and pieces of radar equipment in a systematic and aesthetically pleasing manner. As with the funnel, the outcome was a masterpiece of imaginative and elegant modern design.

Between mast and funnel, Q4 had yet another large sheltered deck area – this time dedicated to sports and fitness. In order to protect passengers from strong headwinds as they exercised, Gardner surrounded this with a large aluminium shelter

freeboard height as a ship inevitably pitches fore-and-aft while in motion at sea. As an added safety consideration for her North Atlantic role, the forward decks were, instead, sloped upwards in a straight line from a point just ahead of the mainmast to the bow, and those aft towards the stern, from about where the Quarter Deck lido ended. Gardner's solution was to superimpose a beautifully-curved sheer line where the contrasting hull and superstructure colours meet on the ship's sides, bringing it up across the Two Deck porthole line and around the curved top of the bow.

*The new lido decks of the **Franconia**, seen here during conversion at John Brown & Co, evidently influenced those of the Q4. (Bruce Peter collection)*

Part of the elegantly tapered windscreening, sheltering the QE2's extensive lido and recreational deck areas towards the stern. (Gallagher collection)

James Gardner's model of the final solution to the problem of designing the aft lido areas shows the subtle curves of his design. (Gallagher collection)

screen, the top edge of which was cut in a gentle curve rising towards the signal deck. This not only directly echoed the shape of the scoop at the base of the funnel but also indirectly referenced recent modernist architecture on *terra firma* – for example, edifices by Oscar Niemeyer, such as the Government buildings in Brasilia and his role in the United Nations Secretariat Building in New York, or Eero Saarinen's sculptural TWA Terminal at John F. Kennedy International Airport, also in New York. Smaller additions to Q4's topmost decks were disguised with similar upward-curving accents, making for a bold and harmonious composition.

Whatever else might have been outside Gardner's design influence would instead be skilfully camouflaged with paint. One of the key economies in Q4's construction was that the decks were built flat and without the conventional long parabolic lines of sheer that turn the decks up slightly towards the bow and stern as a means of maintaining a constant

The lesser slope, aft, was compensated by the tapered glazed windscreening above.

The ship's livery was also altered to give a less severe appearance, befitting her alternative cruising life. The hull was painted a very dark charcoal grey colour, called anthracite, as it was thought that a black hull would have produced too overwhelming an effect without the balancing force of a couple of big red funnels above. The lifeboats also needed special consideration so that the dissimilar line of boats, excursion launches and fast rescue craft would not spoil the otherwise smooth and uncluttered appearance of the ship. These were arranged with the larger covered launches amidships, following the top contour of the superstructure and the funnel's base structure. To obscure the clutter of davits and other boat-handling equipment from view, the walls of the superstructure along Boat Deck, and the handling equipment itself, were painted khaki instead of the usual white. The effect of this was quite remarkable when the ship was viewed at a distance, since the boats appeared to be free-standing. On deck, it also served to reduce dazzle effects from the sun, a welcome touch, no doubt, on tropical cruises. The deckhouse below the bridge was also painted the same colour, giving the bridge itself a distinctive cantilevered appearance. Forward on Quarter Deck, directly beneath the bridge wings, the word CUNARD was painted in bold, red capital letters – much like the branding on a modern jet aircraft fuselage.

Shapes, Forms, Materials, Finishes

The ship's crisp and elegant modernism was, as much as anything else, an expression of the materials and finishes used throughout her interiors, both public and private. In place of the traditional brass, teak hardwoods and all those exotic Empire veneers that drummed and creaked as the old *Queens* plied back and forth between the Old and New Worlds, the QE2 made extensive use of modern durable materials that were as hard-wearing and easily cared for as they were elegant and functional. Rather than having to be constantly groomed and polished, they only needed to be wiped clean. The more technical approach to detailing brought its own sophistication with, for instance, the GRP window surrounds on Quarter and Upper Decks being fitted absolutely flush around the window frames themselves, without the usual area of white-painted metal around such openings where conventional finishing techniques are used.

Some 186,000 square metres (two million square feet) of Formica laminate went into the QE2.[127] These included silky-smooth finishes and various textures with a warmer look and feel, including a weave with the nap of taut denim, used extensively for walls in the accommodation passages, and a parchment-like Hessian finish for cabin ceilings, with its lustre created by fine ridging only visible when illuminated horizontally.[128]

Facings for the inverted trumpet-shaped columns, ceiling lattices and various other elements of the Queen's Room interior, along with the inside surrounds for the large Quarter and Upper Deck windows and deck light fixtures for one of the outdoor swimming pool lidos, were produced in glass fibre reinforced plastics (GRP) made for the QE2 by

Glasdon Manufacturing Limited in Blackpool. Don Sibebottom, Glasdon's enthusiastic then 22-year-old Managing Director, had approached Cunard in the early planning stages of Q4 with ideas for using lightweight glass fibre plastics aboard ships. The company's ability to produce items in the required forms and shapes realised considerable economies over alternative fabrication in metal.[129] While concerns were expressed at the time of the QE2's building about how long these materials would last, the Queen's Room has ultimately proven to be one of the

Extensive use of GRP mouldings was made throughout the QE2, but nowhere more so than in Michael Inchbald's striking Queen's Room. (Bruce Peter collection)

ship's most enduring interiors. Although non-load-bearing, the window surrounds have in fact fared better than the aluminium plating that has since cracked in some places around the outside corners of these openings.

Glasdon – who in their early days made GRP tubs for the Wonder Bath, to be fitted in older houses built without indoor plumbing – have since grown and diversified into the international Glasdon Group, manufacturing just about everything from complete modular buildings and industrial products to street furniture and rubbish bins.[130] In passenger ship interior design, since QE2 was introduced, the usage of GRP mouldings for window surrounds and other shipboard details has become common orthodoxy.

(J.F.K. Smith)

CHAPTER 5

CONSTRUCTION, LAUNCHING AND DELIVERY

THE construction of Q4 at Clydebank took place against a background of industrial decline, economic and social turmoil. As work progressed, the financial position of the John Brown shipyard continued to deteriorate. The ship had been laid down before the true scale of losses on the *Kungsholm* had been learned. By 1966, the picture was clear, prompting Lord Aberconway in his report for that year to include the following chilling statement about Q4:

'The outcome of this contract, decisive perhaps for the continuance of Clydebank as a shipyard and for the future livelihood of those who work there, depends greatly on how well our team of management, staff and workpeople work. I cannot emphasise to each of them too strongly how much it is in his own interest that he should strain every nerve to make this contract come out on the right side, and not let it come out on the wrong side.'[131]

In the wake of the *Kungsholm* disaster, in June 1966 Lord Aberconway wrote to John Rannie, now Clydebank's Managing Director, under the heading 'Clydebank Liquidity', to ask for a projection of cash and trading forecasts for the next three years. The letter pointed out what John Rannie knew already: the previous three years had accumulated losses of over £4 million. While these losses had been made good by transfers from the parent company, Rannie was to assume henceforth that there would be no further subventions, out of shipbuilding reserves built up in better days, from the parent. Thus, the John Brown Report and Accounts for 1966 optimistically stated:

'No further moral debt from John Brown to Clydebank remains... (and any) remaining indebtedness of Clydebank to John Brown will be in the ordinary course of business. For the purposes of this exercise (forecasting to 1969) that indebtedness should be regarded as having to be repaid at an early date, and the weight of financing deemed thereafter to be placed upon the bank.'[132]

In years gone by, profits from the Clydebank shipyard had supported other areas of the John Brown Company whereas now, as a habitual loss-maker, Lord Aberconway was signalling that the shipyard was on its own. After much consideration and several re-forecasts, Robin Williamson, Clydebank's Financial Director, responded to Lord Aberconway's request and sent the forecast to the firm's Sheffield headquarters on

Saturday 17 September 1966. The projections from 30 September 1966 to 31 March 1968 kept below the assumed bank overdraft limit of £850,000, but the indebtedness to the parent company would rise from £3,560,000 to £5,860,000. The forecast losses were:

Year to 31 March 1967   £269,000
Year to 31 March 1968   £391,000
Year to 31 March 1969   £1,230,000 with Q4 making no profit and the yard empty.[133]

The actual loss for 1967 alone was £932,175. It seemed certain that, under the terms of Lord Aberconway's letter, the Clydebank shipyard would close after the Q4 had left.

In October 1966, in preparation for future eventualities, the shipyard and engine works were split into two separate businesses. This was in recognition that the shipyard would probably fail or be merged with other Clyde yards, in line with the recommendations of the Shipbuilding Inquiry Committee's Report. The engine works, which a few years earlier had seemed to be in terminal decline through the contraction of marine work, was showing all the signs of making a dramatic recovery, courtesy of General Electric and industrial gas turbines. Renamed John Brown Engineering (Clydebank) Limited, the works, unlike the shipyard, would remain firmly under the wing of the John Brown parent.

In March 1966 the Geddes Committee published its report, recommending the creation of large shipbuilding groups on Britain's main shipbuilding rivers and their districts. Rationalisation was implicit. The theory was that, through merger, shipbuilding firms would reduce costs by directing resources such as marketing, design, purchasing, personnel, training and management services via one organisation. The report did not subscribe to the view that large building docks were necessarily the way forward, commenting that improvements in industrial relations might, on their own, be more useful. Thus, John Brown's scheme for a super-yard would not be supported. With Government finance to back the report's recommendations, merger discussions began on the basis that a large shipbuilding group would be formed on the upper reaches of the Clyde. In one scheme under discussion, employment in the group would be reduced from 13,000 to 7,500.

Above left: The Q4's keel-block, the first section of the new Cunard flagship, stands on wooden supports, while the **Kungsholm** *is fitted out in the background. (Philip Dawson collection)*

Left and above: The Q4's hull begins to take shape on the launchway. (J.E.K. Smith)

Below left: The bulbous bow is craned into position. (J.E.K. Smith)

Below right: One of the Q4's low-pressure turbines is assembled in August 1967. (J.E.K. Smith)

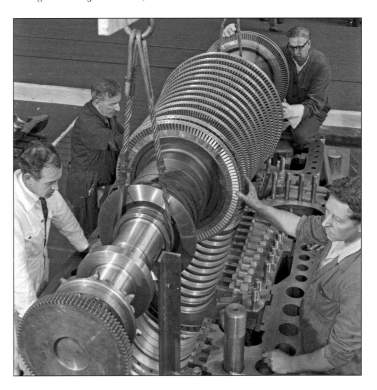

Top: A large section of stairway, forming part of Quarter Deck near the entrance to the Columbia Restaurant, is moved into position. At this point, where the steel One Deck joined the aluminium Quarter Deck, a special riveted bi-metallic joint was made with sleeves around the rivets to keep the two metals from touching. (J.E.K. Smith)

Left: In what was to become the galley on Quarter Deck, a welder fits supports to the floor which will subsequently hold kitchen equipment in place. (J.E.K. Smith)

Above: In August 1967, the balcony of the Theatre Auditorium is fabricated from aluminium alloy, later to be moved on rollers. (J.E.K. Smith)

Understandably, the trade unions and the workforce generally viewed these events with considerable concern.

In the midst of these discussions, the hull and superstructure of Q4 took shape. During his frequent visits to Clydebank, James Gardner wryly observed the severe conditions of shipyard life there, which had not changed significantly since the early twentieth century:

'Through the spiked shipyard gates – another world. Teams of tough Glaswegians… treat the game of 'workers-v-bosses' as they would knock-out football and… a man who becomes worn out is replaced by his son. Visitors who are not 'shipmen' are considered twerps and discouraged – and that goes for pale-faced intruders from down south…[134]

Gardner was, however, impressed by the skill and organisation of the yard:

'While the smooth-sided hull was slowly growing on the slipway, it was startling to see a chunk of superstructure, larger than a house, swing from a giant crane, to be welded neatly into place. Delicate lines drawn with a 2H pencil became muscular men fighting the stiff resistance of steel. At one point, where the observation deck swept in forward of the bridge, there was, what John Brown's Chief Draughtsman termed, a 'discrepancy.' A tapered section of steel plate sailed two feet outboard when it should have met another plate in an uninterrupted curve. "What the hell are you going to do about *that*?" I asked. Then I forgot about it. Why? The tough gang had sprung that heavy plate inboard and then welded it for good. Not a kink, yet sufficient tension there to knock a bus over.'[135]

The Q4 was brought to launch on time on 20 September 1967. The many uncertainties surrounding the shipyard's future were temporarily forgotten as thousands of people flocked to the yard and the opposite bank of the river in time-honoured fashion. As with the previous *Queens*, the name of the new liner had been kept a secret. Yet, not surprisingly, speculation over what she would be called resulted in extensive press coverage, to the extent that the former *Goon Show* star Spike Milligan called his 1969 BBC TV comedy sketch show Q5. Various names of British establishment figures – from Winston Churchill to Princess Anne – were bandied about as possible choices but, given that the project name all along had been Q4, it was most likely that the flagship liner would receive a 'Queen' name.

At 14.28, HM Queen Elizabeth christened the ship *Queen Elizabeth the Second* and pressed the button.

Then nothing happened. For just over a minute, it appeared that the hull did not move. Workers lining the decks high above shouted 'Give us a shove!' and, for fun, the Shipyard Director George Parker leaned on the bow and pushed. By coincidence, the liner began to move at that very moment and Parker waved his bowler hat triumphantly. The new flagship then slid gracefully into the Clyde, leaving a cloud of dust and debris behind her. At the same time, aircraft from 736 Squadron flew overhead in an anchor formation. It was a magnificent spectacle and the Royal Party was visibly moved.[136] Most importantly, the QE2 was on schedule.

Although the launching received great positive publicity, one sour note was caused by Cunard's refusal

James Gardner's cartoon of the Q4 soaring above Clydebank. (Design Archives, University of Brighton)

to invite any of the architects and designers to attend, apart from James Gardner and Dennis Lennon. Sir Hugh Casson had attempted to intervene on behalf of his friends some weeks before, but Cunard declined to budge, leading Casson to write in disgust to *The Times*.[137] His letter alerted the *Daily Express* to the fact that at least one designer, Jon Bannenberg, had decided to show up on launch day anyway. In a typically flamboyant gesture, Bannenberg – who apparently had been unimpressed from the outset by what he saw as the high-handed and hierarchical attitude of Cunard's management – flew his entire office team to Clydebank and camped out with a champagne picnic in a field opposite the shipyard so that all of his staff could, at least, watch the launching spectacle from a distance. After all, as he pointed out, the interior designers had devoted three years of their lives to the Q4 project. Of course, the *Daily Express* sent a photographer to capture Bannenberg and his colleagues with the ship looming in the background, across the river. Under the headline 'The Uninvited – or how Mr Bannenberg missed the party', he was quoted as saying that 'I felt that ship was as much mine as anyone's. I've designed damned nearly a third of its interior. And no one on earth was going to stop me seeing it hit the water, invitation or no invitation.'[138] Back in the latter 1960s, however, even the most distinguished architects and interior designers apparently were considered to be mere functionaries, rather than the high-profile celebrities they are today. A Cunard spokesman brazenly told the *Daily Express* that 'There was not sufficient space to invite them all. We only had 700 special invitations' – which only made matters worse.[139]

After the launching, the QE2 was moved to the fitting-out basin, where she was to be completed. Meanwhile, in the engine shops, now known as John Brown Engineering (JBE), the ship's turbine machinery and boilers were well advanced. Pametrada, the Newcastle-based designers of the liner's machinery, had ceased to exist in 1967 and so John Brown Engineering recruited the nucleus of Pametrada's design team specifically to work on the liner's machinery contract.

Meanwhile, to prepare for merger with other Clyde shipyards, the Clydebank yard was first de-coupled from John Brown & Co (Clydebank) Ltd, to become John Brown & Co (Shipbuilders) Ltd on 25 January 1968. However, the new company was only a stepping stone to the wider merger and had an existence of just two weeks. On 5 February 1968, John Brown & Co (Shipbuilders) was sold to Upper Clyde Shipbuilders (UCS) in exchange for 1,199,999 £1 shares in the new company.[140] Lord Aberconway had been relieved of a loss-making subsidiary but had gained a major shareholding in the Government-supported UCS. John Rannie, formerly the Managing Director of the Clydebank yard, was made Special Director in charge of the QE2 outfitting project.

Upper Clyde Shipbuilders Ltd

The shipbuilding map of the Clyde had been redrawn and the former John Brown shipyard was now known as the Clydebank Division of Upper Clyde Shipbuilders Limited, with other shipyards at Linthouse, Scotstoun and Govan. The new company set about the introduction of methods to raise productivity, but labour relations only deteriorated as a result.

George Parker, Clydebank's Divisional Director, reported an 'irresponsible and unrealistic' wage demand from sheet ironworkers. On 6 May, the sheet ironworkers went on strike. They returned on the 27th, having won an additional 4d per hour.[141] John Rannie reported that finishing trades were working well on the QE2, although a strike of sub-contract pipe coverers, insulators and plumbers was threatening progress. He was, nevertheless, able to assure his Board that Cunard had agreed to an increase in the ship's price, caused by the higher wage costs.

In August 1968 UCS received an invitation to tender for the conversion of the *Carinthia* and the *Sylvania* into cruise liners, following Cunard's disposal of the ships to Fairwind Shipping Corporation (Sitmar Line) of Monrovia. The work on each ship, valued at between £3 and £4 million, had to be turned down because of insufficient labour. The QE2 was consuming every man that UCS had to spare. With a boom in shipbuilding under way, UCS were receiving a large number of enquiries but lacked the technical capacity to deal with the volume. Similarly, shortages in design and estimating capacity had the effect of reducing steel throughput.[142] By September, the workload at Clydebank was building up, with six ships under construction, including the QE2. Sadly, labour shortages and technical difficulties continued to plague production. One-hundred-and-fifty boilermakers were urgently required while, in protest at a letter which had been sent out to the men urging greater productivity, the engineers held a one-day strike and cranemen a ten-minute token stoppage. The painters, meanwhile, were considering a complete stoppage.

Traditionally, a ship nearing completion gave the workforce the upper hand, although this was often tempered by lay-offs once the ship left the yard. The level of disruption now being experienced was unprecedented in the history of the Clydebank yard which, hitherto, had enjoyed better relations than many other British shipbuilders.

Unfortunately, by the latter 1960s the Clyde shipyards were no longer in a position to recruit the

Above: On a still night in August 1967, the Q4's hull and growing superstructure cast an almost perfect reflection. (J.E.K. Smith)

Left: Fitting the starboard stabiliser fin in July 1967. (J.E.K. Smith)

Below: Shrouded in scaffolding, the Q4 slowly takes shape in this sunny July 1967 view. Working outdoors in the unpredictable West of Scotland climate often was hard going, however, especially during the winter. (J.E.K. Smith)

The Q4 nears her launch day on the slipway. The superb hull form is already apparent – as is the extensive use of aluminium for the superstructure. (The Quarter and Upper Decks are painted in yellow ochre undercoat). (J.E.K. Smith)

Top: Opposite the John Brown shipyard, there were open fields which became popular vantage points for spectators on launch days. Here, the Q4 is viewed from a distance in the early summer of 1967. (Ann Glen)

Above left: The launch platform, crowded with invited guests, as viewed from the press gallery. (J.E.K. Smith)

Above: Seen from a ground-level vantage point, the QE2 begins her descent into the Clyde, with cheering workers waving from the forepeak. (Smith collection)

Left: Mr John Rannie hands HM The Queen the card bearing the name of the new Cunard flagship, as Lord Aberconway looks on. (J.E.K. Smith)

most talented and motivated of workers. Shipyard jobs often were dangerous, dirty and physically exhausting. Much work took place out of doors in the cold and wet West of Scotland climate and, moreover, there was little security of tenure. The more able of the younger generation suddenly had new and more attractive career possibilities – like going to study at university or technical college, thanks to the post-war expansion of higher education, or seeking employment in the cleaner, safer, more comfortable light industries. In addition, the building of new towns at East Kilbride and Cumbernauld denuded the Glasgow conurbation of population as a whole – meaning that the old shipyards often were left with no option but to supplement time-served 'old hands' with less enthusiastic employees whose commitment to their trade was less strong than that of previous generations. Productivity suffered as a result and, sadly, theft and vandalism also increased markedly, causing further delays to building contracts – not least the completion of the QE2. (Incidentally, British Railways simultaneously faced a similar recruitment problem for much the same reason, a factor which hastened the demise of steam traction in 1968).

Throughout the summer of 1968, a series of quality inspections, some by Cunard personnel, were carried out on the ship which had been subdivided into a series of work blocks. These inspections were intended to uncover work that still remained to be done. Thus, for example, an inspection dated 17 June 1968 concerning Block 29 Starboard on 3 Deck noted that for Cabin 83:

Entrance door to cabin needed adjusting

Gap at shipside dresser needed to be closed

The mitre under the shelf support in the hanging space needed to be closed

Plastic strips to complete the corners in the hanging space needed to be fitted

A collar needed to be fitted to the light in the hanging space.

While this was routine and applied to many cabins, a report dated 25 October, less than three weeks from the ship's departure, noted that the target date of 1 November for completion of joinery work would not be achieved and that it was unlikely that the new target date of 19 November would be met either.

John Rannie searched urgently to find the additional 200 joiners he needed to complete the ship.

Delays in the completion programme had been caused when the decorating sub-contractors arrived late, causing ventilation contractors to leave for other work. Nevertheless, Rannie confirmed that the ship would leave Clydebank on 19 November, as originally planned. However, labour difficulties among the work-force and sub-contractors meant that the ship would leave Clydebank in an incomplete state, albeit with relatively minor tasks yet to be finished. At a Board meeting held in September 1968, Rannie diplomatically placed on record that there had been no requests for last-minute alterations or additions to the ship and that Cunard were 'helping us all they can' to get the project finished on schedule. Significantly, he also reported that he had informed Cunard that three areas within the ship would, in fact, be incomplete on departure from Clydebank.[143] In October, 150 joiners were lent from Lithgow's Port Glasgow shipyard to work on the QE2. However, the continuing shortage of boilermakers pushed back delivery times on the other contracts by between four and eight weeks. The best that could be achieved within UCS was the transfer of 68 men from their Linthouse yard. While these transfers speeded up work on the QE2 to an extent, they also posed problems for shipyard security, especially with so many valuable fixtures and fittings lying around awaiting installation. Not surprisingly, in the dying weeks of the outfitting process, pilfering became a very serious problem – and this only served to add further delays and oncosts.

In September, the Board of Upper Clyde Shipbuilders noted that John Rannie would reach retirement age at the end of the year and his service with the company would come to an end. However, as finalising the details of the QE2's contract was likely to take additional time, he accepted the offer of a further six months' service for a retainer of £2,500.[144]

At a Cunard Board meeting on 22 October, Sir Basil Smallpeice described the condition of the ship as follows:

'...Excluding three blocks of accommodation, in the absence of any major difficulty the ship would be reasonably ready by 10 December, but with a large number of minor fittings to be fitted before 24 December. The main engine had been tested, ship stability was satisfactory and certain trouble with the rudder was under investigation. As had been expected the final stages of completing the ship were attracting

Top left: After a brief pause, the **Queen Elizabeth 2** glides majestically down the slipway and into the River Clyde, while jubilant shipyard workers and their families wave and cheer. (*J.E.K. Smith*)

Left: Viewed from a crane, the **Queen Elizabeth 2** slips down the launchway, surrounded by admiring crowds. (*Smith collection*)

Above: Viewed from the far side of the River Clyde, the **Queen Elizabeth 2**'s stern touches the water for the first time. (*Smith collection*)

Below: Four Steel & Bennie tugs (nearest the camera, the **Strongbow** and the **Thunderer**) manoeuvre the newly-launched **Queen Elizabeth 2** towards the fitting-out basin. (*J.E.K. Smith*)

a certain amount of labour difficulties. One sub-contractor had already offered his labourers a substantial bonus for remaining to complete their work by 19 November and other labour forces, including UCS' own men, were looking for similar payments.'

Although such payments were outside the Price Variation Agreement, such was their desperation to get the ship delivered that Cunard agreed to make a contribution towards them. [145]

On 19 November 1968 the QE2 left Clydebank, on time, for the Firth of Clyde Dry Dock at Greenock, under the command of Captain William Warwick. Sir Basil Smallpeice, Cunard's Chairman, and a distinctly chilled-looking young Prince Charles were also on the bridge. About 100 cabins remained incomplete and several hundred men were on board, working continuously to finish them. At Greenock, John Rannie addressed his men, exhorting them to do their utmost to carry the work on to completion. On 27 November the Cunard Board met and Sir Basil Smallpeice confirmed that, because of the incomplete state of parts of the ship, difficulty was anticipated at the press visit on 10 December. Smallpeice thought this would be addressed by a briefing, explaining that John Brown men would be working throughout the trials period.[146]

The QE2's first technical trials were carried out between 26 and 30 November but had to be abandoned when oil fuel contaminated the feed water system because of a faulty non-return valve. At a stroke, delivery was delayed by one week while the trouble was located and rectified. This required a lengthy period of cleaning out in dry-dock and forced Cunard to cancel a charity cruise, scheduled for Christmas. Cunard took these events in their stride and agreed that final acceptance trials would be conducted on a 10-day trip to the west coast of Africa, where the air conditioning plant would also be tested.

Trials resumed on 17 December. John Rannie, John Starks and Graham Strachan were on the bridge as the liner worked up speed over the measured mile off Arran. Contract conditions for speed and power were 32 knots and 110,000 shaft horsepower. The QE2 lived up to expectations, recording a speed of 32.5 knots at 117,000 shp. It seemed that all was well. The ship returned to the Tail of the Bank, from where she sailed to Southampton and then to the Canary Islands. On Christmas Eve, as she steamed southwards, vibrations

were felt from the starboard turbine. Within hours, the world knew that the QE2 had major technical problems. What should have ended well for Cunard and Upper Clyde Shipbuilders rapidly became a disaster. The spectacular failure of the turbines also highlighted the incomplete state of the liner. While Cunard had been fully aware of this, in the full glare of the media they had little alternative but to reject the ship outright, which Sir Basil Smallpeice did very publicly.

In the last hours of his employment, John Rannie and UCS Chairman Anthony Hepper argued over the condition of the ship, resulting in Rannie's six months' consultancy being withdrawn. When the QE2 docked at Southampton on 2 January 1969, Rannie slipped quietly away and into retirement. UCS Technical Director John Starks took over the completion of the ship, for which there was now plenty of time. Nevertheless, this work took until 14 February. The turbines were a different matter, however. They had been designed by Pametrada, which no longer existed, and constructed at Clydebank by John Brown Engineering, therefore, Upper Clyde Shipbuilders could do little until the extent of the damage was determined and a timetable decided for repairs.

When the QE2 berthed at Southampton on 2 January, senior men from John Brown Engineering were at the quayside. Three days later, after the machinery had cooled, inspection of the turbines was carried out. The metal debris visible as the turbine casings were lifted off indicated that the damage was considerable. On inspection, it was clear that the rotors would have to be returned to Clydebank for repair. It was equally clear that repair was going to take much longer than a week.[147] The rotors were air-freighted to Glasgow the following day. Graham Strachan, Managing Director of JBE, placed Jim Turner, the Director of the Marine and General Engineering Division, in charge of co-ordinating the turbine repair. John Brown engineers quickly realised that the cause of the failure was steam excitation. This can develop when the frequency of vibrations set up inside the turbine results in premature metal fatigue of the blades, causing them to snap at the root. The most convenient solution was to redesign and manufacture blades with thicker roots. Sourcing the molybdenum steel, from which the blades were made, began quickly, and

*On a still November day in 1968, the **Queen Elizabeth 2** nears completion in Upper Clyde Shipbuilders' fitting-out basin. The Clyde-class bulk carrier **Volnay** is under construction at the adjacent berth. (John Peter)*

manufacturing the redesigned blades was set in hand.

The Clydebank diagnosis was met with scepticism by Cunard's consultants, the Technical Investigation Department at Lloyds. When Cunard discussed the failure with Associated Electrical Industries (AEI), with whom turbine orders for Cunard container ships had recently been placed, both JBE and UCS threatened legal action. After all, AEI was a competitor. On 5 February, JBE held a press conference to announce an interim report on their findings. This confirmed their initial diagnosis of steam excitation causing blade failure, which they attributed to a design error by the now defunct Pametrada[148]. Sir Basil Smallpeice's reaction was publicly to demand an independent assessor. Newspapers ran headlines quoting the Cunard Chairman saying: 'What Reliance Can We Place on John Brown Engineering?'[149]

The national importance of the QE2 and the bitter disagreement between JBE and Cunard required the involvement of the Minister of Technology, Tony Benn. On 10 February, Benn convened a meeting to appoint an independent assessor, with Sir Basil Smallpeice, Anthony Hepper and Sir George Gardner, JBE's Managing Director, in attendance. Gardner had previously suggested to Benn that Sir Arnold Lindley, President of the Institution of Mechanical Engineers and a former Managing Director of GEC, should be considered. Lindley was eminently suitable and Benn had little difficulty in obtaining approval.

On 11 February, Tony Benn arrived at Clydebank to see the damaged turbines for himself, commenting later at a press conference: 'I have come here today to take the steam out of the situation and put it back into the turbines', a comment which was greatly appreciated at Clydebank.[150] Meetings between UCS, JBE and Cunard remained difficult, in stark contrast to the friendliness that had existed between John Brown and Cunard in the past. With the exception of formal meetings, communication between the parties was discouraged and only took place after thorough vetting by lawyers.[151]

Sir Arnold Lindley's report was made public on 28 February and vindicated the Clydebank engineers. At a press conference, Sir Arnold stated:

'Steam excitation is a phenomenon well known to steam turbine engineers not only in Britain but also in Europe and America. In the case of marine turbines which operate under variable speed conditions, this excitation is particularly difficult to avoid. It should be made clear that there is no reflection whatsoever on the quality of workmanship or of the material used in any part of the construction of the turbines. The remedial measures proposed [by JBE] were adequate, and when complete, trials could be resumed with every confidence.'[152]

By 21 March the rotors had been returned to the QE2 and the turbines closed up. Successful basin trials were conducted two days later and, on the following day, the ship embarked on an eight-day cruise to the west coast of Africa. Cunard made the welcome gesture of inviting all those who had worked on the ship on the trial trip. The QE2 was formally accepted by Cunard from her builders at noon on 18 April 1969. The terms provided for an extension of the guarantee period in respect of any turbine defects, should the first annual overhaul not take place by 18 April 1970. Her first scheduled voyage, a preview cruise for travel agents, was planned for 22 April and her maiden voyage to New York for 2 May. In April, Cunard prepared to press a claim of £2 million against UCS for losses and delays in the QE2 contract. Anthony Hepper told Sir Basil Smallpeice that, if he persisted, it would force UCS into liquidation. The threat of a counter-claim from UCS for alterations and delays to the contract during earlier construction phases brought the issue to a close.

The final cost of the QE2, as calculated by UCS in an internal memo of 27 March 1970, was £28,062,467.[153] UCS survived the construction of the QE2 only to lurch from one crisis to another, finally succumbing to insolvency in July 1971. The last vessel to be built at Clydebank left in 1972. The yard never built another ship but continued as an offshore yard until the end of the 1990s when it finally closed, along with the former engine works, latterly known as Kværner Power. From 2002 onwards, the works was dismantled and the site redeveloped. Today, a solitary crane stands on the location where the QE2 – and some of the most famous ships in modern British history – were built. In the end, the difficulties of her construction, set against the background of an industry in terminal decline and a country about to experience de-industrialisation, gave way to the realisation that, in the QE2, Britain and the Clyde had produced a masterpiece.

Top left: Upper Clyde Shipbuilders employees celebrate in the Double Room during the QE2's delivery voyage from the Clyde to Southampton. In the background, it is apparent, however, that the ceiling and bulkhead finishes are incomplete and that there was considerable finishing work yet to be done. (J.E.K. Smith)

Above: Crowds of spectators admire the QE2 as she rests in the dry-dock at Greenock during her problematic initial sea trials in December 1968. (John Peter)

Left: Anthony Hepper and a distinctly strained-looking Sir Basil Smallpeice face the press in the Q4 Room prior to her delivery voyage. (J.E.K. Smith)

Below: The completed **Queen Elizabeth 2** at sea. (Bruce Peter collection)

CHAPTER 6

A 'PLEASURE ISLAND'

WITH the trials and tribulations of the QE2's construction and delivery behind her, Cunard, the design profession and the public at large could finally assess whether the building of Britain's new national flagship had been worthwhile. To ensure that the ship was given a high-profile entry into service, both Cunard and Upper Clyde Shipbuilders produced an avalanche of publicity material. The press packs, distributed to all of the popular magazines and newspapers, were substantial, detailing each novel aspect of the QE2's design and every innovation and luxury to be enjoyed on board. From telephones and *en suite* bathrooms in the cabins, to an onboard computer and the latest radar installations, the liner was presented in all of her wondrous complexity and statistical superlatives.

A Striking First Impression

While the standard of architectural design was remarkably high throughout the ship as delivered, a number of individual rooms were especially outstanding. The circular Midships Lobby on Two Deck, the point where First Class travellers would

embark on trans-Atlantic service and where all cruise passengers would normally board, was designed largely by Lennon's assistant, James Herbert, to make an immediate first impression and set the tone for what Cunard were avidly promoting as being a sci-fi experience, similar to climbing into a spacecraft.[154] The initial surprise was that the space was circular, rather than rectangular as most shipboard entrances are, and that it was entered diagonally, via short passages from the gangway hatches in the hull's sides. This, in fact, served to make the transition from existing gangway placements at the trans-Atlantic terminal ports to the lobby's location, adjacent to the midships stairways and lifts.

The lobby space itself was wrapped around a single fibreglass-clad white centre column, in the same up-turned trumpet shape to be found in the Queen's Room, rising out of a sunken, circular seating area. Above, a concentrically-serrated fibreglass ceiling was dramatically illuminated from spotlights, concealed in the backs of the seating banquettes around the room's sunken centre feature. Dennis Lennon had intended this to give the impression that 'you have dropped a pebble in the sea, the rings getting bigger as they

Above: The spectacular circular Midships Lobby, showing the remarkable ribbed GRP ceiling, which was supposed to resemble ripples caused by a pebble dropping in still water. (Cunard Archives, University of Liverpool)

Top left: The Double Room, viewed from its balcony level on Boat Deck with the small bandstand at the base of a smoke-tinted curving glass panel at the far end of the dance floor. (Bruce Peter collection)

Above: The Theatre Bar, amidships on Upper Deck, was brightly furnished in shades of orange. (Design Archives, University of Brighton)

Left: A busy, late-night gathering place at the heart of the ship, it proved to be enduringly popular. (Design Archives, University of Brighton)

Below: The Look Out Lounge, designed by Theo Crosby, offered a splendid panoramic view over the QE2's bow. (Bruce Peter collection)

Top left: The entrance to the 736 Club on Boat Deck. As with all of the QE2's public rooms, there were tinted plate glass doors with brushed aluminium handrails and leather details. (Alan Irvine collection)

Top Right: The London Gallery. (Alan Irvine collection)

Middle and bottom left: The 736 Club empty and in full swing. (Alan Irvine collection and Bruce Peter collection)

Above: Heaton and Beloe's Coffee Shop, featuring murals by their Royal College of Art colleague, Tim Sarson. (Bruce Peter collection)

circulate.'[155] While the effect was most successfully created in models, it turned out to be impossible to apply the reflective foil to the ceiling at full scale, and the painted surface ended up looking more like the grooves in a gramophone record. Contrasting hues of the emerald green settees and of the dark blue carpeting and leather wall-coverings further heightened this area's sense of drama.

Lounges, Bars and Entertainments

When the QE2 was first delivered, great emphasis was placed on the informal, leisure-orientated atmosphere on board the ship. There was, supposedly, something for every taste and occasion.

Claimed to be the largest interior in any passenger ship afloat at the time, the Double Room, occupying the aft ends of Upper and Boat Decks, was an

lighting and matrix of spot down-lighters above the dance floor, served to counter the visual impression of its great fore-and-aft length. The use of stainless steel and glass in the surround of the opening through Boat Deck, and the sepia-tinted glass balustrades and aluminium handrails, surrounded the key focal point of this vast space – a remarkable curved staircase, connecting the two levels. This was reflected at the forward end of the double-height central void by a circular bandstand, set within a frameless glass half-cylinder, extending up through the room's full double-deck height.[156]

Jon Bannenberg himself felt that the QE2, as a whole, needed to be 'a fantastically exciting ship,'[157] and that his Double Room – with its warm hues of red, plum and orange, enlivened with elements of metal and smoky tinted glass – needed something more spectacular that would go beyond the design

A view looking along the length of the London Gallery. This relatively narrow space was squeezed in between the Theatre Auditorium and the port-side Boat Deck promenade. (Alan Irvine collection)

Part of the QE2's Boat Deck shopping arcade, designed by Stefan Buzas and Alan Irvine to sell a broad range of modern British consumer goods and fashion clothing. (Alan Irvine collection)

enormous all-purpose space of no particular set function but rather provided for many people all to be doing different things at the same time, without disturbing one another or getting in each other's way. It was actually a rather old-fashioned mezzanine-plan space, similar to those revitalised by Michael Inchbald and Jean Monro on the *Carmania* and *Franconia* earlier in the decade, though given a couple of new twists in its inception aboard the new Cunarder. The room's slatted aluminium ceiling, with its inset fluorescent

cosmetics of colour, brightness and texture to breathe real life into the space, where people could feel good, relax and enjoy themselves. Thus, he envisaged his spectacular curved stairway, its arc sweeping into the double-height central space rather than recoiling back away from it. As a key focal point of the room, this was to be an epic descent, 'where ladies could sweep down feeling elegant and regal,'[158] and where young people, in particular, would feel welcome to perch themselves on the steps to take in the show, or merely enjoy the life-beat of the space itself.

The large, quadrangular Double-Up Bar, forward of the glass bandstand cylinder and extending some two-thirds of the Boat Deck opening's full width, was intended to give a greater social focus to the room's mezzanine level than it might otherwise have offered. At its opposite end, the room looped around the aft-most main stairway on Upper Deck, where the Double-Down Bar overlooked an open lido deck, aft. Yet despite its superlatives of size and capacity, the arrangement of numerous intimate seating groups with high-backed upholstered seats, fitted into semi-circular alcoves in the walls around the room on both levels, allowed for conversation and other pursuits to continue, undisturbed by entertainment, dancing or other activities going on elsewhere. The Double Room's furniture was designed by William Plunkett and consisted of remarkable low-slung lounge chairs and settees, with chromed metal frames and broad horizontal bars, upholstered in orange and somewhat resembling sausages.

Gaby Schreiber's Theatre auditorium, located amidships on Upper and Boat Decks, was the only other space to occupy two levels. Intended to be used also as a conference room, lecture hall and church, Schreiber concentrated on achieving an effective technical solution in terms of sightlines, lighting and acoustics and so the auditorium was rather understated. Indeed, *The Architectural Review* rather cruelly observed that Schreiber had been given 'an impossible brief which may explain the barren quality of the design.'[159] Seating 530 on chairs designed specially by Schreiber with removable Bernat Klein upholstery in two shades of mauve, and with flat walls painted silvery-grey, in terms of detailing the space had something of the quality of an airliner cabin. Given Schreiber's background, this may not have been surprising. Nonetheless, it functioned well and has survived in a fairly intact condition.

The Theatre Bar, designed by Dennis Lennon and one of his assistants, John Salmon, was between the auditorium and the Double Room on Upper Deck in what was 'one of the more swinging areas of the ship.'[160] Intended to attract 'much of the custom from late-night cinema crowds, this is one of the bars that stays awake when most of the ship is asleep. Its personality is probably best expressed by its grand

piano, which is bright red. So is one wall, which is made of fibreglass and moulded in an egg-crate pattern. The dance floor in the Theatre Bar is always busy.'[161]

Opposite the bustling and lively Theatre Bar, the Upper Deck Library, also designed by Dennis Lennon's office, was a 'cathedral of calm...cool and still, a place of deep leather sofas, with slatted blinds to counter the tropical sun. The book-shelves are lined with blue leather, and a paler blue tweed is used in some of the chairs. No footstep sounds in the thick-ribbed beige carpet, and there are gay, striped Conran fabrics at the windows.'[162]

Forward on Upper Deck, and most obviously accessible by walking through the Britannia Restaurant, the Look Out lounge by Theo Crosby was created as a modern adaptation of the forward-facing rooms aboard the old *Queens*. *The Architectural Review* enjoyed the fact that:

'Here, one is unquestionably on a ship and on a ship in the 1970s... On the back wall, Gillian Wise's reflective screen of stainless steel and bronze-anodised vertical strips, incorporating a stainless steel bar at one end, helps to increase the apparent width of the room... The concealed perimeter lighting successfully emphasises the sweeping curve of the front wall.'[163]

Moving up to Boat Deck, the L-shaped Coffee Shop and teenage Jukebox arcade were designed by the Royal College of Art students Elizabeth Beloe and Tony Heaton. Decked out in shades of red, yellow, orange and blue, these spaces were so radically different from anything that had ever previously gone aboard a Cunard ship as to be quite startling. The white floor covering and dark ceiling were a total reversal of what was normally expected, while the bright wall laminates featured 'pop' murals by a fellow RCA student, Tim Sarson. A horizontal mirrored ribbon strip above the upholstered Coffee Shop booths added to the cheerful sense of modernity.

In keeping with the room's 'Swinging London' character, Coffee Shop patrons were served by stewardesses in white blouses, navy mini-skirts, nightshade stockings and mid-heeled black leather dress pumps. There was also an alternative trouser suit, preferred for evening service in the 736 Club, and – a couple of years later – a cute sailor-style mini-dress in navy and white with a V neck, worn with

Left and below left: The lofty and luxurious Midships Bar on Quarter Deck, designed largely by Dennis Lennon's assistant, Jim Gordon, was finished in dark green and silver and illuminated by onion-shaped brass wall-mounted lights above the rosewood coffee tables. The space is nowadays the Chart Room and is recognisable from Salmon's original design. (Jim Gordon collection)

Above and below right: As befitted First Class, the Midships Bar offered table service from Cunard's most senior and experienced stewards, but passengers could also enjoy over-the-bar service, perched on velvet-upholstered stools. Jim Gordon achieved a very high standard of finish – the ceiling, for example, is completely smooth and without the joints. (Bruce Peter collection)

white Cuban-heeled Mary Jane pumps. Hardy Amies, the well known couturier favoured by HM The Queen, was appointed as Cunard's special adviser to design and select uniforms for the QE2's hotel staff. The teenage 'Jukebox', adjacent, with its distorting mirrors and arcade games, was 'drenched in a continuous torrent of pop music...The young people who gyrate there seem as oblivious of the racket as they are of the older, uncomprehending passengers who pass, wincing, through to the Coffee Shop.'[164]

Heaton and Beloe's Children's Playroom also used modular components in bright colours. This was 'practically indestructible. There are no don'ts.'[165] The floor was a bright yellow and orange 'hopscotch' pattern, with doors covered with blackboard panels, stools and furniture which doubled as building blocks and small enclosures where 'solitary games can still be overlooked by the ship's nannies.'[166]

The Coffee Shop layout was essentially a half-scale rendition of the larger Buzas and Irvine-designed 736 Club next door that served as a night club and discotheque for the 'grown-ups.' This room had a dark, sumptuous feel created by the use of latticed wood screens, dividing its seating alcoves, with a similar Indian laurel wood-grained finish being used on the walls above the high-backed dark taupe leather banquette seating units. There was a shallow white ceiling vault above the dance floor, with recessed coloured spotlights and loudspeakers. The idea was to focus discotheque sound and lighting effects on the dance floor so that others, seated elsewhere in the room and at the bar, could carry on conversation and other activities. An additional lighting effect, created using low-wattage bulbs in standard marine signal lamp housings, bracketed on the latticed screen dividers, was described by *Design* magazine as giving a 'twinkling fairy light effect.'[167]

The London Gallery, also by Buzas and Irvine, was managed by the highly-regarded contemporary art dealer, Marlborough Fine Arts, and had been suggested by Dennis Lennon to display – and sell – works by well known British artists. John Piper, Ben Nicholson, Francis Bacon, R.B. Kitaj and Graham Sutherland were among those represented – and prices ranged from £35 to £20,000. The gallery was the first – and only – example of its kind on a ship and, although it did introduce a vogue for cruise ships

to sell art (of sorts) on board, only the QE2 displayed paintings and sculptures by critically-regarded contemporary artists, whose works would have been equally at home in modern art museums on *terra firma*. Writing in *The Architectural Review*, the art critic Robert Melville observed:

'The first exhibition... was admirable both in quality and variety and the price range, with Kokoschka's 'Istanbul' well into the five-figure bracket and some of the lithographs and silk prints available for only a few pounds, allowed for everyone on board to be a potential buyer...'[168]

Outwith the London Gallery, the QE2 was remarkably devoid of installed artworks, at least in comparison with her foreign contemporaries. Apart from the few pieces described elsewhere in this chapter, the only other major commission was for a series of three tapestries by Helen Banynia, based on newspaper photographs of the ship's launching and displayed as a triptych in the main First Class staircase. Otherwise, the QE2's art consisted mainly of framed lithograph prints and so the gallery really was the focal point for art lovers and collectors.

Further aft still, the shopping arcade (Buzas and Irvine again) sold 'everything from everyday toilet articles to Mary Quant make-up, from beachwear to fine Wedgwood.'[169]

The most sophisticated public rooms, intended for First Class passengers when the QE2 was on trans-Atlantic liner service, were on Quarter Deck. The Midships Bar, by Dennis Lennon and his assistant Jim Gordon, was opulent in character. Indeed, it was:

'...Prodigiously rich whilst remaining restrained to the point of severity. Apart from the gold leaf wall of the bar the décor is in muted shades of green – sofas in rich green leather and mohair velvet, onion-shaped brass lamps shining onto rosewood drinks tables. In here, there is a discreet popping of champagne corks. The staff are veteran stewards who sailed in both the earlier *Queens*.'[170]

Opposite, the Card Room, by Jon Bannenberg, was equally restrained. Again, dark green was chosen as a restful and absorbent backdrop to allow well-heeled passengers to concentrate on their bridge-playing. Inboard, three booths were provided for additional privacy. Next door, in the Quarter Deck Library, by Michael Inchbald, rich woodwork, leather and brass

Left: View down one of the side arcades, outboard of the Queen's Room, showing how the extensive usage of fibreglass engendered a sense of unity between these spaces. (Bruce Peter collection)

Above and below: Passengers pose on Michael Inchbald's chairs in the Queens's Room during the delivery voyage from the Clyde to Southampton. Oscar Nemon's bust of HM The Queen has yet to be installed and so a floral display fills the niche instead. (Bruce Peter collection)

were used 'to create a nautical effect. Writing chairs are in black leather and deep Chesterfields evoke the smoking room atmosphere of ships long gone.'[171] *The Architectural Review* pointedly chose to ignore this one space with overtly 'retro' references – but it did prove popular with passengers and it survived unaltered until the QE2's 1994 refit.

Without doubt, the best-loved and most enduring of the First Class interiors, however, was the Queen's Room, designed by Michael Inchbald and described by Sir Hugh Casson as being 'a split-level confection in white, lemon, orange and dark green.'[172] Although the room impressed him as a 'stunner', he seemed to feel, however, that the imagery was perhaps 'a bit too California.'

The Q4 Room, designed by David Hicks with Garnett, Cloughley, Blakemore & Associates. (Andrew Richardson)

Almost square in shape, the Queen's Room was distinguished by its remarkable latticed fibreglass ceiling which was indirectly illuminated by fluorescent tubes, concealed above the latticework and reflecting diffused light off a flat, white deckhead above. By day, this created the impression of a pergola in a sunny garden. The oblong lattice openings, with their rounded ends, ran fore-and-aft, reflecting the orientation of the ceiling sections themselves and giving the room a more natural impression of its

length being greater than its width. These latticed elements appeared to float freely in light above the surrounding ceiling panels, from where they were also indirectly illuminated by concealed cornice fixtures. The overall effect was an ingenious *coup de théâtre* that overcame the difficulty of designing a large, low-ceiling space. The four supporting columns in the room were formed in white fibreglass as slender inverted trumpets, a shape reflected in the Saarinen-inspired white Lurashell chair-bases and brushed-aluminium table pedestals of the room's original furniture.[173]

Where the raised area of the room's outer reaches descended to deck level at its centre, with its large rectangular parquet dance floor, the two floor heights were separated by low, white-lacquered banquette fixtures, arranged as planter troughs along their length, with cantilevered sectional seating at the room's outer and inner levels to either side. These were interspersed by access points, where there were two steps down to the room's centre. Indirect lighting, concealed beneath the cantilevered seating, gave these an impression of floating free above the close-carpeted floors, while additional up-lighters, encircling the bases of the columns, added to the architectural illumination and general sense of light airiness. The forward and aft end walls were decorated in a bold woodblock treatment on a mirrored background and a niche, holding a bust of HM The Queen sculpted by Oscar Nemon, was centrally located on the forward wall. In an effort to avoid the forlorn look of an empty bandstand during daytime hours, Inchbald arranged a system for continuously changing abstract light images to be projected onto a white, curved stage backdrop, representing firelight, mountains or clouds as dictated by the mood of the hour.[174] The Queen's Room was one of the QE2's most notable – and enduring – design successes and 'it drew an exclamation of delight... when Her Majesty visited the ship on the eve of the maiden voyage to New York.'[175]

The promenade spaces, designed by Dennis Lennon's assistants John Salmon and Jim Gordon as part of the standardised milieu of linking elements, were furnished throughout with British-made Harry Bertoia chairs that were lighter than Inchbald's Saarinen-inspired furnishings for the Queen's Room, though entirely complementary in their style.[176] This

Above: The dignified elegance of the First Class Columbia Restaurant on Quarter Deck was the result of a muted apricot, beige and dark brown colour scheme, accented by brushed aluminium details and soft lighting. (Design Archives, University of Brighton)

Below left: The galley, forward on Quarter Deck, was the largest yet designed for a passenger ship. It was carefully planned and spacious, but stewards had long walks to deliver plates to the restaurant tables, meaning that food was often tepid. (Design Archives, University of Brighton)

Below right: A corner of the Britannia Restaurant, showing Robert Heritage's chairs, designed and manufactured specially for the ship by Race Furniture. (Bruce Peter collection)

was an important consideration, as the promenade spaces formed part of this room when opened up to the ship's full width. Concealed etched-glass sliding wall panels, at the inner edge of the promenade, allowed the Queen's Room to be scaled down to a smaller and more intimate space. This feature proved remarkably practical as a means of providing separate and isolated entry and exit points when the Queen's Room was used for passport inspection and immigration control on arrival at ports where these processes are handled on board the ship.

In its original form, the Queen's Room was an elegant, luxurious and comfortable First Class shipboard space of the highest possible standard, rendered in the same futuristic spirit as the then-anticipated Boeing 747 or Concorde airliner cabins. The curvaceous shapes of the ceiling columns, exposed metal edging strips, ribbed or gaped joins in walls and ceiling facings and rounded edges of the banquette units and other surfaces could also be read as expressing the dynamic of the liner's movement across the oceans.[177] The room's fusion with the promenade circulating spaces, woven through the strengthening element of web-frames, brought an added dimension of unity with the rhythm of the ship's structural design into her interior architectural realm, without appearing to superimpose an overly nautical theme. Indeed, as originally designed, the liner was one of the very few examples of shipboard architecture that conveyed a true sense of the workings beneath its finished and dressed surfaces, in the way that airliner cabins and high-speed train interiors are similarly designed.

Aft of the Queen's Room, the Q4 Room, by David Hicks, working with Garnett, Cloughley, Blakemore & Associates, was a sophisticated night club which doubled as a daytime café and bar for the adjacent lido. Both Hicks and his architectural collaborators had a penchant for bright colours and bold patterns. Thus, the space was lined with dark grey, red and white fabric panels, set in anodised-aluminium frames and with a matching checked carpet. Banquette seating, metal-framed Coulsdon chairs, slatted window blinds and decorative Perspex dividing panels, designed by Rory McEwen and manufactured by ICI, added to the space's night club ambience. However, *The Architecture Review*'s critic, Sherban Cantacuzino,

regretted that the 'demountable ceilings are cheap-looking Marinite panels set in flush metal trim' – which, he felt, spoiled the look of the space, particularly in comparison with Inchbald's striking Queen's Room ceiling next door.

Down on Seven Deck and Six Deck, there were two indoor swimming pools (respectively for Tourist and First Class passengers when in liner service). The one in First Class was designed by Jon Bannenberg and consisted of a fresh, white-tiled space with a rectangular pool basin. The main architectural features were a series of broad, bright red columns which contained the showers. A Turkish Baths was provided in an adjacent space, while there was a sauna next to the Seven Deck pool. In addition, there was a well-equipped gymnasium.

The Restaurants

The main dining rooms, with their large windows overlooking the sea, were an altogether different approach from the cavernous double- and triple-height volumes of space dedicated to First Class gastronomy on the lower decks of the old *Queens*. An overall atmosphere of restrained modern hotelier luxury prevailed in the Columbia Restaurant that would serve First Class passengers in trans-Atlantic service. Designed jointly by Lennon and James Herbert, the room's functionality was extended with the inclusion of a small dance floor at its forward end, revealed by the removal of four tables, and orchestra space gained with two additional tables being taken away. Indeed, to ensure that all of the details were as well resolved as possible, Lennon had a full-scale mock-up of part of the restaurant constructed in the basement of his London office. According to Brian Beardsmore, this enabled him to check that the lighting levels were correct to create the required sophisticated mood and to try out various fabrics and finishes. The space had a copper-coloured ribbed aluminium ceiling (a tint used for metal details throughout the ship, known as Q4 Gold), a mid-grey/brown carpet and matching leather wall panels with apricot curtains. Special attention was paid by Lennon to designing glass table lights, which were powered from sockets in the middle of each table and intended to create an intimate atmosphere, flattering

Above left and middle left: Staff pose in their new uniforms in the bright and airy Britannia Restaurant. The Britannia figurehead, carved by Cornishman Charles Moore, is the only element of this attractive space to survive today, albeit banished to the foyer adjacent to what is nowadays the Mauretania Restaurant. (Bruce Peter collection)

Above: The Grill Room was intended to be seen in the evening, under artificial illumination. Then, the leather panelling glowed and the shiny aluminium accents glinted in the subdued lighting. (Bruce Peter collection)

Below left and right: Janine Janet's sculptures of the four elements in the Grill Room. (Andrew Richardson)

to the diners' clothes and jewellery.

The patriotic red, white and blue Britannia Restaurant, drawn up largely by Lennon's other main Q4 project architect, Simon Monk, was similar, though without the dance floor, and rendered on a larger scale to serve 800 passengers at each of two sittings, rather than 500 at a single sitting as in the Columbia Restaurant. In both rooms, the structural web-frames were used to create a more intimate arrangement of seating alcoves towards the ship's sides. The Britannia Restaurant was, in fact, roughly doughnut-shaped, with its central area being occupied by an enclosed serving area connected to the galley below by two pairs of escalators. Together, these features effectively avoided any impression of this large low-ceilinged

Part of the main First Class staircase, with striking white GRP balustrades contrasting with dark leather bulkheads and carpeting. (Andrew Richardson)

room being a messing hall or cafeteria. The central decorative feature was a ship's figurehead, sculpted by Charles Moore and presented to Cunard as a gift by Lloyd's, the famous London insurance market.

The very popular Grill Cafés from Cunard's old *Queens* were given a somewhat different treatment, with QE2's Grill Room being located port side on Quarter Deck, adjacent to the Columbia Restaurant. The room itself seated only 100 persons and was given a terraced floor so that the innermost tables were

slightly raised to offer an outlook above the heads of those seated nearer the windows. Beneath a ribbed brushed-aluminium ceiling with concealed lighting, the room's rich plum furnishings and wall coverings were highlighted by bright metallic accents of aluminium and chrome. Statues by the French sculptor Janine Janet, made of pearls and sea shells, representing the four elements, were placed near the corners and were the room's singular decorative feature. Diners sat either on plush upholstered banquettes or on elegant Mies van der Rohe Brno chairs in dark red leather. Most remarkable, though, was the entrance arrangement by way of a shimmering spiral stairway, ascending from an intimate aperitif bar located in the core area of One Deck immediately below. The staircase was appropriately similar in scale to its airborne counterpart, leading to the upper-deck lounge on a Boeing 747. The bar and its connecting stairway added a sense of exclusivity to the Grill Room as, in effect, being the sort of place that one needed to 'discover.' The plush spot-lit warmth of the bar's leather-lined interior, according to Sir Hugh Casson, was 'as soft, cosy and dark as the inside of a handbag'.[178]

Stairwells, Cabins, Corridors

All of the cabin corridors, the connecting hallways and staircases were designed and detailed by Lennon's assistant, James Herbert. The stairs were colour-coded with bright fibreglass and enamelled metal claddings covering the balustrades and handrails, the idea being to assist passenger orientation in such a large floating hotel. The cabin corridors were particularly elegant, with hardwood-grained panelling on their inboard walls, evenly washed with diffused light from a continuous recessed strip above. On the outboard side, the cabin doors were grouped in pairs and recessed with a matching lighting strip above each two doors. In between, the walls were clad with removable laminate panels, so that the plumbing for the cabin bathrooms, behind, could easily be accessed without disturbing the cabins themselves. This approach to cabin corridor design has since become more or less standard on passenger ships throughout the world.

Design of the five cabin decks emphasised the hotel

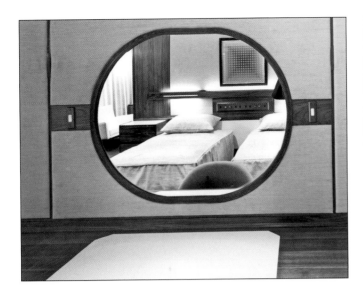

Top left and left: Part of a First Class suite, designed by Stefan Buzas and Alan Irvine. Several of these large cabins could be joined together and space could also be provided in adjacent smaller rooms for passengers' maids or butlers. (Alan Irvine collection)

Above: A First Class cabin, designed by Dennis Lennon's office and offering spacious, hotel-like comfort. (Bruce Peter collection)

Below left: QE2 had en suite facilities in all of her cabins – a first for a liner of this size. Here, a model poses in the bathroom of one of the Tourist Class cabins. (Bruce Peter collection)

Below right: One of the compact, but well-designed, Tourist Class cabins. (Bruce Peter collection)

Top: Within, the wheelhouse was modern and functional with the navigation equipment laid out ergonomically in a series of consoles. In that respect, the design was very different from that of Cunard's earlier passenger liners and Captain Warwick worked closely with Tom Kameen and with James Gardner to achieve this effective arrangement. (Bruce Peter collection)

Above: The QE2's machinery was monitored and operated from the air-conditioned comfort of the engine control room. (Bruce Peter collection)

Right:The crew's accommodation was of a high standard for all ranks. This is a standard cabin, to be occupied by two seamen, designed by Mrs Jo Pattrick. (Bruce Peter Collection)

standard of rectangular, predominantly twin-bedded, rooms, of which the great majority were directly accessed from a pair of parallel passages extending the full length of each deck. Aiming to make these as attractive for longer holiday voyages as for the five-day Atlantic crossing, with natural light and an outside view being one of the most desirable features, 75 per cent of the ship's 2,025 passenger berths were in outer rooms with portholes or windows in the ship's sides.[179] QE2 was the first large British liner to have private *en suite* toilet facilities attached to all passenger cabins and, as delivered, had the lowest number of upper berths, with only 178 fold-away Pullman-style beds fitted in cabins intended for use by families with children or by groups of younger people wanting to travel together at minimum cost. When cruising, however, her passenger capacity was reduced to 1,700.

The cabins were slightly narrower than those aboard the old *Queens* and many extended deeper in from the ship's sides, as there were fewer small inner rooms between these and the main passages. Experience showed that the 2.7 m (9 ft) interval of three hull frames would provide a sufficient uniform width for a standard cabin.[180] This was wide enough that the beds could be arranged fore-and-aft, as aboard the old *Queens*, for greatest comfort while at sea. The dressing table, or writing desk, was relocated as a full-width fitment beneath the outer wall's portholes, rather than against the opposite wall to the foot of the beds as was more conventional. A four-and-a-half frames' dimension was adopted for the de luxe rooms. QE2's cabins averaged an area each of 6.7 m^2 (72 ft^2) compared with the 4.4 m^2 (48 ft^2) mean of rooms on the earlier *Queen Elizabeth*.[181] The furnishing of the larger rooms, in particular, generally followed a more modern plan with sleeping and sitting areas arranged one outboard of the other, as featured prominently in the Swedish American Line *Kungsholm* of 1966, though with the beds oriented beam-wise at the room's outer end rather than fore-and-aft.

QE2's premium-grade suites, by Stefan Buzas and Alan Irvine, were so arranged that de luxe accommodation could be combined, with the furniture being changed in those rooms to be used as living or dining spaces. The larger cabins, located amidships on One and Two Decks, could be joined by way of connecting doors to form suites of two to as many as five rooms. While the reception rooms of grande-luxe suites in the old *Queens* and other liners were often fitted with bathrooms, closet space and other amenities, allowing these to be sold as cabins when they would otherwise be vacant, the QE2 approach was more in line with modern hotel design and considered to be better suited to respond to the diverse needs of line service and cruising. There was considerable additional flexibility for rooms in all fare categories to be joined into suites for use by families or other groups travelling together. This included outer rooms connecting with inner cabins for occupancy by children, or use as dressing rooms in cruise service.[182]

Many of the smaller Tourist Class rooms, aft on Two and Three Decks and amidships on Four Deck, were laid out by Dennis Lennon's assistants using a dovetailed arrangement of the sleeping areas, one inboard of the other for each pair of rooms, and with an extension of each cabin to the ship's side, with portholes at the outer end. Many pairs of these rooms were arranged with connecting doors in their outer alcoves which, in the one room, were furnished with a settee and occasional chair and, in the other, with a combination dressing table and bureau, so that the function of these complemented each other when the connecting doors were opened to join them as suites. The overall layout of these was, in fact, a refinement of the original Bibby-plan idea widely adopted in the all-outside-cabin design of Swedish American Line's 1938-41 *Stockholm* and 1950s-built *Kungsholm* and *Gripsholm*, as well as the five-ship Soviet *Ivan Franko* class of liners.[183] Some of the smaller accommodation on Five Deck was ingeniously arranged in groups with a T-shaped cabin, dovetailed between a pair of mirrored L-plan rooms, at the ship's side and entered from a short secondary passage, also accessing a pair of inner cabins. Entrances to each pair of outer L-shaped cabins, and their adjacent inner rooms, were arranged so that a third door closed to form a small suite, where the inner space could be occupied by children or used as a dressing room.

Gaby Schreiber designed a small block of luxury cabins on Two Deck port side, immediately aft of the

107

angled entrance passages leading to the Midships Lobby. Her styling of these interiors was unique, again reflecting her BOAC cabin design experience, particularly with regard to her airliner-style handling of the porthole surrounds, various other aspects of detailing and finishing, and choice of easy chairs and other furnishings. These consisted of two pairs of double rooms located on either side of a smaller single cabin, so as to be combined in various ways into suites of two or three rooms by way of connecting doors.

Surrounded by cabins at the forward end of Three Deck, the Synagogue, designed by Misha Black, was exquisitely detailed with ash panelling, deep blue carpeting, bronze wall-mounted lighting sconces and buff leather doors to slide across the ark. The space had an aura of meditative quietness and, fortunately, it survived virtually intact until the end of the QE2's sea-going career.

The officers and crew on the QE2 enjoyed an unprecedentedly high standard of accommodation – one reason why the ship enjoyed good industrial relations when others, with less attractive accommodation 'behind the scenes', were troubled by strikes. *The Architectural Review* observed:

'It was a bold decision for Cunard to accept an outside designer in areas which have traditionally been the preserve of their naval architects, and not entirely surprising that second thoughts made them ask Mrs Jo Pattrick not to do any drawings, a request which she understandably ignored. Her judicious selection of finishes and furniture make the crew's quarters…a far cry from the older *Queens* in which the crew were usually given discarded items from passenger areas.'[184]

Indeed, Cunard had to be forced, against their own judgement, towards an enlightened attitude to staff in the lower ranks – a situation which could explain why British shipping lines regularly had union problems whereas Scandinavian lines enjoyed comparatively tranquil labour relations (and Danish, Swedish and Norwegian crews occupied accommodation designed to a high standard). With singular determination, Jo Pattrick prevailed, even although 'Cunard did not always follow the designer's layouts – as, for example, in the Officers' Dining Room on Boat Deck, where the traditional arrangement of long tables was preferred to a free grouping of smaller units, more in sympathy with the irregular shape of the room.'[185] Clearly, it was important for Cunard's traditions that the liner's officers be seated in order of rank, with the Captain at the head of the table.

The crew cabins, by Dennis Lennon's office, tended to sleep two and were spacious and functional, with plenty of storage room – in contrast to their cramped equivalents on the old *Queens*, some of which slept six or more bellboys in one tiny space. The Captain's quarters were designed by Lennon himself as a personal compliment to the Master, William Warwick, whom he greatly admired.

Jo Pattrick also drew up a compact hospital, dental surgery and morgue on Six Deck. This included an intensive care room, an operating theatre, an X-ray room, a dispensary and a physiotherapy room – some of these being remarkable facilities for a liner back in 1969, but commonplace on nearly all subsequent large cruise ships and fully in line with the modernist thinking on health and welfare governing the overall design of the vessel.

Both in the areas to which passengers had access, and behind the scenes, the QE2 was distinguished by the use of modern materials. Wall surfaces in the deck vestibules, stairwells, circulating areas and some of the public spaces were covered in leathers or hides tanned to the colour schemes of individual spaces. Elsewhere, men's gabardine suiting material was used in other spaces, such as the Q4 Room. Stair and passage handrails were made of fibreglass in various colours and, in some places, of bright metals such as chrome or brushed aluminium rather than of traditional hardwood or brass. Indeed, one could almost feel one's way around the ship by the variation of surface texture for just about everything, from differing wall coverings in cabins, washrooms, corridors and public areas to door facings in laminate for private rooms and glass in the public areas, and so on.[186] With all spaces accessible to passengers close-carpeted virtually throughout, this also conveyed a sense of quiet comfort and luxury that was new, and perhaps even strange, to seasoned British passengers, more accustomed to the linoleum and rubber-tile flooring of the old *Queens* and, indeed, even the recent *Oriana* and the *Canberra*.

Above left: The Six Deck swimming pool, designed by Jon Bannenberg, had shower cubicles in red fibreglass tubes on either side. (Design Archives, University of Brighton)

Above right: Late afternoon sunshine strikes across the QE2's spacious aft lido decks. According to archived correspondence with Cunard and Captain Warwick, James Gardner was worried that the deck-chairs would look untidy unless some way was found to secure them in neat rows. On this point, Cunard and the Captain refused to be persuaded, insisting that passengers should be able to place the chairs wherever they liked, as shown here. (Design Archives, University of Brighton)

Below: The QE2's aft lido decks are crowded with sunbathers, enjoying the poolside ambience of Cunard's 'floating resort'. (Bruce Peter collection)

Right: 'Ship Shapes' highlighted by Crosby/Fletcher/Forbes' original publicity material not only included the exterior of the QE2 but also such small details as furniture, tableware, cutlery and fabrics. Nearly all of the original fixtures and fittings on the QE2 were bespoke designs and most, unfortunately, were disposed of during the Trafalgar House era of Cunard's shifting ownership. (Bruce Peter collection)

Right and below: When the QE2 was introduced, Cunard employed Crosby/Fletcher/Forbes to design the inaugural brochures. The cover of the 'White Brochure' controversially proclaims that 'Ships Have Been Boring Long Enough'. Alan Fletcher's graphic design was notably striking, with double-page spreads and the extensive use of modern 'lifestyle' photography. (Bruce Peter collection)

A New Advertising Identity

In order to sell the message of the QE2's modernism to as wide a public as possible (this was, after all, a national ship) Cunard employed Crosby/Fletcher/Forbes, the multi-disciplinary design agency master-minded by the architect Theo Crosby. Crosby had already been commissioned to design the Look Out Bar while one of his partners, Alan Fletcher, who was a graphic designer, produced all of the signage throughout the ship.

It was hence only natural that the graphic design brief should be extended to include Cunard's publicity material as well. Realising that sea travel was regarded as being increasingly *passé* in the age of jetliners and space exploration, Crosby/Fletcher/Forbes came up with the snappy and provocative slogan 'Ships Have Been Boring Long Enough' – which was bound to infuriate traditionalists. There was, however, more than a grain of truth in this pronouncement. As the well known New York travel writer, Ted Scull, recalls, 'the majority of the world's passenger fleet was distinctly average and ships like the *Canberra* really stood out because they were so much more daring and stylish than nearly all the rest.'[187] Thus, the first QE2 brochure to be released stated confidently:

'Whatever your preconceptions about QE2, she's bound to take you by surprise. It's like climbing into the most exciting thing to be launched since Apollo 1… With QE2's push-button bedrooms, high-up dining rooms, pop groups and cabaret artists, discotheques, acres of open deck, swimming pools, bars and shopping centre, Cunard have introduced a completely new way of thinking about cruise ships… The QE2 concept is a leisure that is not just relaxing but stimulating too!'

The brochures designed to promote the QE2 during the first few years in service were very stylish with bold graphics, bright colours and enticing lifestyle photography. Models wearing dark eye-shadow and dressed in Paisley-pattern shawls reclined on bright pink bedspreads, while foppish young men pouted in the middle distance. Meanwhile, beautiful people lined the cocktail bars or lounged around the swimming pools. Much emphasis was placed on promoting the ship as a relaxing leisure environment and, although when operating in trans-Atlantic service there were discreet class divisions, these were barely mentioned in the brochure imagery and texts. Instead, the liner was advertised as being:

'…A moving experience. Taking you gently from place to place. Through sun, sea and air. Into lazy, languid days and cool, moonlit evenings. A pleasure island… to indulge yourself, as you leisurely drift from place to place.'[188]

Nowadays, in complete contrast, Cunard actively promote a vertical hierarchy of classes, with the so-called 'Grill Classes' at the pinnacle – but the taste and aspirations of the upwardly-mobile evidently have changed considerably since the laid-back 1960s.

Bespoke Fixtures and Fittings

Although the QE2's designers went to a great deal of effort to give the ship a rigorously coherent and highly-refined aesthetic, suggestive of the 'high-tech' industrial methods and contemporary efficiency associated with the Modern Movement, the liner was actually almost every bit as bespoke and highly-crafted as her predecessors had been. Since the 1960s, of course, vast ranges of mass-produced and highly-standardised and sophisticated componentry for ship outfitting have been developed – meaning that today's cruise ships and ferries are largely prefabricated and finished off with items specified from catalogues. Four decades ago, such techniques were in their infancy and, indeed, the British ship supply industries were lagging behind Continental developments in this regard, meaning that if the QE2 were to have a futuristic style, and if her fixtures and fittings were to be sourced almost exclusively from British suppliers as the Government demanded, then almost everything would require to be specially made.

This situation had two effects: firstly, the QE2 set a new benchmark for British ship design and, secondly, nearly all British ships – and, indeed, many foreign ones – following in her wake were influenced by her precedent.

When the liner was delivered, the leading architecture and design journals – and several of the major broadsheet newspapers – published special

111

supplements, describing the QE2's design and many statistical superlatives in loving detail. These newspaper features also gave companies which had supplied the ship an opportunity to advertise because to be associated with the QE2 was regarded as being an honour and a sign of excellence. In the special QE2-themed edition of *The Architectural Review* in June 1969, Connolly Leather proudly proclaimed that 'Leather puts excitement into cruising', while Turners Asbestos expounded the fire-retardant qualities of their insulating panels and Concord Rotaflex stated that 'Lighting Has Been Boring Long Enough' – a witty reworking of Cunard's own QE2 publicity slogan. *The Times*, meanwhile, focused on the more domestic elements of the ship – such as the 5,000 'cosy, warm Moonweave blankets made in Bri-Nylon' and the '2,800 soft, cushiony Swanwic bath and shower mats tufted with Crimpolene.'[189]

It appeared, in fact, that almost the whole British ship and hotel supply industry had been mobilised

to produce vast amounts of highly-specialised items for the QE2 but, ironically, this was for the last time as never again would a passenger ship of such a scale and complexity be delivered from a British shipyard.

The Architectural Review was impressed by the high degree of co-ordination between the design elements and the scrupulous attention to detail. Indeed, a number of iconic items were made for the QE2 – most notably, the ship's furniture, for which Geoffrey Dunn (of H.G. Dunn's of Bromley) was appointed by Dennis Lennon to act as a consultant.

For the Columbia and Britannia Restaurants, the distinguished furniture designer Robert Heritage devised a remarkable chair, 1,300 of which were manufactured by Race Furniture. Heritage made use of pre-formed, formica-clad plywood shell components with foam-filled leather upholstery, mounted on two-legged aluminium frames, to provide great comfort to diners as well as practicality with regard to cleaning.

William Plunkett produced highly-distinctive lounge chairs for Jon Bannenberg's Double Room. For the Queen's Room, meanwhile, Michael Inchbald designed fibreglass 'Lurashell' armchairs, somewhat in the manner of Eero Saarinen's 'Tulip' range but perfectly complementing the light, futuristic design

of the ceiling and columns. Beresford and Hicks produced a standard stacking chair which could be used for special events throughout all the public rooms.

On 29 May 1969, HRH The Duke of Edinburgh visited the QE2 to present awards on behalf of the Council of Industrial Design – including an award for the Columbia and Britannia Restaurant furniture. Sadly, during various refits in the 1980s and 1990s, most of these chairs were thrown out and replaced by generic, catalogue-specified 'hotel' items of banal mediocrity.

All of the tableware was specially designed for the ship and most of it was made of Steelite, a new and (reputedly) almost unbreakable ceramic, developed by Ridgway Potteries. The Steelite range was designed by Lord Queensbury (David Douglas, 1929-) and consisted of 24 stackable items (as opposed to the more than ninety on the *Queen Mary* and *Queen Elizabeth*). An on-glaze gold decorative pattern was designed for the QE2 by Julia Chandley, a student of Queensbury at the Royal College of Art.[190] Silver-plated cutlery by David Mellor, cruet sets by Eric Clements and glassware by Waterford completed the stylish table settings. As with the lost furniture, most of these items have now gone from the ship but, not surprisingly, they are highly sought after by liner memorabilia collectors and, increasingly, by connoisseurs of modern British design in general.

Ships inspired by QE2

The group of designers employed by Cunard to draw up the QE2 made up a fairly small and intimate 'family' of London architecture, design and media establishment people which, bit by bit, had gained influence since the Second World War. Focused on the Council of Industrial Design's offices and on other creative centres, such as the Royal College of Art and the Designers & Art Directors Association, these men and women all knew each other very well and, to an extent, acted as mutual advocates within the wider British design scene. This situation meant that, even before the QE2's designs had been finalised, others involved in the scene already had a good idea of how the ship was going to look. Furthermore, in February 1968, the Council of

Above: The British Rail ferry **Vortigern**, *designed by Ward & Austin, entered service in the same year as the QE2 and with a remarkably similar standard of onboard design. For Cunard, the fact that a mere Dover Strait ferry should seek to emulate their prestigious flagship was problematic, but modernist ideology meant the application of a similar quality of design to all kinds of environments and experiences. (FotoFlite)*

Left: Here we see the **Vortigern***'s Tea Bar which, as with the QE2, made extensive use of GRP mouldings. (Bruce Peter collection)*

Below: The **Vortigern***'s First Class Lounge, featuring Eero Saarinen 'Tulip' chairs and remarkable GRP lighting fixtures against a dark ceiling. (Bruce Peter collection)*

Below left: The entrance hall of the British Rail Sealink ferry **St Edmund** *(1974), designed by Neville Ward, consisted of five inter-locking circular spaces, much like the Midships Lobby on the QE2. (Bruce Peter collection)*

Industrial Design had mounted an exhibition in The Design Centre in London's Haymarket to promote the liner as an icon of progressive British design to a wide public. As nearly all of Dennis Lennon's office was fully employed designing the ship herself, the exhibition work was given to Brian Beardsmore who, hitherto, had been dealing with nearly all of Lennon's other work.

Not surprisingly in the circumstances, the early imagery of the QE2's silhouette and, in particular, the interiors, proved to be highly influential. For instance, Neville Ward, of Ward & Austin, was inspired by the 'QE2 look' when designing interiors for a new multi-purpose cross-Channel ferry for British Rail, named the *Vortigern*. Externally, the railway's own naval architects, Tony Rogan and Don Ripley, emulated the QE2's funnel shape on the ferry which was also delivered in 1969 and which, ironically, entered service only two months after the delayed Cunarder. Most poignantly, the transport design commentator, Robert Spark, wrote an article for *Shipping World and Shipbuilder*, in which he directly compared the two ships.[191]

Of course, modernist rhetoric stressed egalitarianism – and the Council of Industrial Design's members were committed to the ideal of providing equally good design for all. For Cunard as a commercial business, however, it was problematic that a mere ferry should appear in any way similar to their grand flagship – a vessel largely conceived to attract the wealthiest and most discerning of travellers.

British Rail's subsequent *St Edmund* (1974) and *St Columba* (1977), also with Neville Ward-designed interiors, were even more heavily indebted to the QE2 – the former even had a circular entrance hallway with trumpet columns – but Scandinavian cruise and ferry operators also attempted to emulate the QE2's shipboard style. The Danish-designed, Finnish-built and Norwegian-owned cruise ships *Royal Viking Sea*, *Royal Viking Star* and *Royal Viking Sky* copied numerous aspects of the QE2's overall planning. As with the Cunard flagship, their hull decks were planned around central service cores with a preponderance of outside cabins. Furthermore, their galleys were located forward in the superstructure, their main restaurants amidships and the lounge spaces aft. Even their funnels were shorter, broader motor ship renditions of the QE2's iconic stack.

The Danish car ferry *Dana Regina* (1974) was also inspired by the QE2 – not least because the architect, Kay Kørbing, who designed the interiors, had visited the liner while she was fitting out in 1968. The subsequent *Tor Britannia* and *Tor Scandinavia* (delivered in 1975 and 1976 and also with interiors co-ordinated by Kørbing) equally shared the 'QE2 look.' All of these commodious vessels had spacious open-plan passenger accommodation with colour-coded staircases and matching furnishings in different areas of cabins to ease orientation. Moreover, their overall quality of finish, coupled with their remarkably wide ranges of leisure and entertainment facilities and their distinctive design details, all very directly reflected the precedent set by the QE2. The high-speed gas turbine cruise ferry *Finnjet* (1977) was yet another to show a similar approach to ship design and outfitting. Indeed, for at least a decade after the QE2 had first been publicised, there were few passenger ships which did not show signs of her great influence.

In Spain, meanwhile, a series of six so-called 'Canguro' ferries, built in the 1970s for Transmediterranea and Ybarra Line, had masts obviously copied from the QE2 (James Gardner certainly was aware of this situation and had the vessels photographed for his archive).[192]

Even as late as 1983, when the formerly Israeli turbine liner *Shalom* was converted into the Greek cruise ship *Royal Odyssey*, the naval architects Knud E. Hansen A/S once again turned to the QE2 to provide a benchmark for the required approach to the design and aesthetics. Given that, in the early 1960s, the *Shalom* had been held up by progressive design commentators as embodying the standards which Cunard should seek to emulate, this was a remarkable turn of events.

Unfortunately, neither British shipbuilding nor the British ship supply industries were able to capitalise on the QE2's great international acclaim. Most of the developments which the liner first introduced were refined and perpetuated by naval architects and interior designers based on the Continent – particularly in Scandinavia.

Above left: The **Royal Viking Star**, *the first of three luxurious Norwegian-owned cruise ships, had a similar layout to the QE2, with a central service core and cabins outboard of parallel corridors on the lower decks. More obviously the funnel is a smaller motor ship rendition of the QE2's famous stack. (Ivor Trevor-Jones)*

Above right: The Swedish **Tor Britannia** *and* **Tor Scandinavia** *also looked to the QE2 for inspiration – for example, in the tiered arrangement of the aft sun decks, with their glazed panelling, and in the general standard of design and decoration of the interiors, including colour-coded staircases and the design of cabin corridors. The* **St Edmund** *is in the background. (Bruce Peter collection)*

Left, below left and right: Kay Kørbing, who designed DFDS' **Dana Regina**, *had visited the QE2 and emulated both her layout and interior detailing. This was particularly evident in the Compass Nightclub, shown below. (Bruce Peter collection)*

(*Philip Deason*)

QE2
BRITAIN'S
GREATEST
LINER

WITH her turbine problems hopefully resolved, the *Queen Elizabeth 2* commenced her Cunard service on 22 April 1969 with an eight-day shakedown cruise to Las Palmas, Tenerife and Lisbon. Fortunately, this passed almost without incident (the discovery of a couple of stowaways on board while sailing down The Solent had necessitated an extra visit from the pilot cutter to apprehend these unwanted guests). Upon her return to Southampton, the Queen and the Duke of Edinburgh paid their first of many visits, spending several hours on board to marvel at the completed liner in all of her pristine glory.

Meanwhile, passengers were mustering in Southampton hotels in preparation for the maiden trans-Atlantic voyage to New York with departure on 2 May. Come the day, a deep low pressure passed over Southern England, bringing thick cloud and rain. Even this hardly deterred the thousands of revellers who packed the viewing galleries of the Ocean Terminal to wave the liner off, with rousing music provided by the Band of the Royal Corps of Transport. Streamers were thrown from ship to shore and, as per tradition, tugs used their fire-fighting cannons to send jets of water into the air. A flotilla of small craft followed in the liner's wake as she gathered speed and steamed serenely towards Calshot and the Isle of Wight, with her course set for Le Havre.

There, during a brief two-hour stay, the *Queen Elizabeth 2* received a tumultuous welcome – it seemed that almost the whole town had turned out on the promenade to spectate as she sailed past, following in the wake of such predecessors as the *Ile de France* and the *Normandie*. With her Continental passengers safely on board, the liner set sail for New York, leaving those who had spectated from shore to ponder the true merit, or otherwise, of the controversial new flagship.

As Cunard's publicity slogan had suggested, the QE2 certainly was anything but 'boring', as a vigorous correspondence in both the shipping press and the national press was to prove. In *Sea Breezes*, one Mr E. Armstrong wrote:

'The *Queen Elizabeth 2*'s 'funnel' [is] the most feeble monstrosity ever to disgrace the superstructure of a ship. It can truly be called a dreadful and atrocious sight and is enough to make Samuel Cunard turn over and weep. The pit-head gear of a coal mine is more graceful... The architects' intention seems to have been to wipe out the tradition of Cunard except for plastering the company's name on the superstructure... And the Directors, who obviously approve, stand indicted on the same count. The glorious red, black bands and black tops, revered on the North Atlantic for more than a century, have disappeared because of the whim of someone with a drawing board and a hangover...'[193]

To this correspondent, another amateur observer, Mr David Simpson, responded:

'Those who constantly refer to the "good old days" of the former *Queens*, the *Mauretania* and others are the very people who will cause the death of passenger liners. Having been present at the maiden departure of the QE2, I can truthfully say that I have never seen a ship so beautiful. The funnel, apart from being functional, is a masterpiece of 'free' design, and is an integral part of the ship. I hate to think of the QE2 with an eyesore, such as the funnel of the *Carmania*, stuck on top. As for Cunard's colours, the new ship does display them and, in my opinion, in a far more pleasing way than previous Cunarders.'[194]

The two positions were utterly entrenched and actually reflected a wider gulf in design opinion between traditionalists and progressives which cut right through all the strata of British society – from Royalty to the working classes. Many years later, the debate over the design of the new Sainsbury Wing of the National Gallery in London's Trafalgar Square provoked similar passions – with the design establishment supporting the competition-winning 'high-tech' solution by Richard Rogers and an unlikely coalition of traditionalists finding a voice in HRH Prince Charles, who described the design as being 'a monstrous carbuncle on the face of an old friend.'[195] Responses to the new *Queen Elizabeth 2* were remarkably similar but, in 1969, modernism won decisively whereas in the 1980s the traditionalists were victorious in the 'battle' for the National Gallery.

Ironically the new Cunarder, however, also represented the last hurrah for the Modern Movement in Britain. A number of seminal events in the 1960s – not least of which was the demolition of the Doric arch at London's Euston Station in 1961 – led to the birth of an increasingly vigorous and vocal conservation movement, dedicated to saving the past

*Left: Alexandra tugs gingerly manoeuvre the new **Queen Elizabeth 2** off her Ocean Terminal berth in Southampton. (Gallagher collection)*

Above: Notwithstanding the damp weather, crowds spectate as the QE2 is towed into Southampton Docks, following in the wake of numerous legendary trans-Atlantic predecessors. (Gallagher collection)

Below: The view towards Ocean Terminal from below the QE2's bridge when the liner arrived at Southampton for the first time. Crewmen, including a large contingent of chefs from the galley, spectate as the liner is gently nudged towards her berth by Alexandra tugs. (Gallagher collection)

Notwithstanding the torrential rain, curious spectators shelter under their umbrellas as the QE2 is manoeuvred away from her berth at the commencement of her maiden voyage to New York. (Bruce Peter collection)

in the face of relentless progress and modernisation. With so much, often unscrupulous, redevelopment affecting the appearance of British towns and cities, a backlash was inevitable and, to the traditionalist camp, the *Queen Elizabeth 2* was yet another example of 'inferior' modernist design replacing the 'stately' aesthetics of the past. Of course, the fact that the QE2 had had a difficult entry into service, suffering breakdowns and postponements, only seemed to reaffirm the sceptics' belief. To those reactionary naysayers, the liner was merely a floating version of the notorious Ronan Point high-rise flats which had partially collapsed following a gas explosion in 1968.

While some, apparently, remained immune to the QE2's great elegance and exquisite craftsmanship – largely because the ship did not look like the *Queen Mary*, it would appear – a far greater number were captivated by the relentless modernity and sophisticated technology of the Britain's glamorous new national flagship.

The *Queen Elizabeth 2* sailed from Le Havre to Ambrose Light, off New York, at an average speed of 28.02 knots, taking a respectable four days, 16 hours and 35 minutes to make the crossing, but carrying only 1,451 passengers out of a possible capacity of 2,025.

The QE2 may neither have been the fastest trans-Atlantic liner (that honour remained with the *United States*), nor the longest (the *France*), but she received one of the greatest welcomes that New York has ever afforded a liner. It was the beginning of an American love affair with the QE2 that was to last for forty years. The Mayor, John Lindsay, boarded the ship with other civic dignitaries before she sailed beneath the Verrazano Bridge to enjoy the final leg of the maiden voyage, while helicopters hovered above with press photographers eager to capture the liner's sleek silhouette against a background of Manhattan skyscrapers. Mayor Lindsay proclaimed that it was officially 'QE2 Day' in New York when he exchanged gifts with Sir Basil Smallpeice in the Queen's Room. 'With this ship,' Sir Basil told the assembled journalists, 'we are out of the transportation business and into the leisure business.'

Members of the press and public who visited the liner upon her arrival at Pier 92 in Manhattan were amazed by what they saw. Just as the *Ile de France* had brought the glamour and daring modernity of the 1925 Paris Exposition to America upon her maiden arrival back in 1927, over forty years later the new Cunarder brought London's fashionable West End across the Atlantic in all of its hip, swinging glory. *Time* magazine reported:

'On last week's maiden trans-Atlantic crossing of the *Queen Elizabeth 2* (one way fares: $490 to $3,000), the VIP list read like a page from the London telephone directory and the formal wear was mostly rented. With the weather still too cold to swim or sun, the passengers danced, drank, and rested. The most popular place on the ship was the cinema, which was packed to capacity for both afternoon and evening showings of first-run films.

The sleek vessel cut through choppy seas without so much as a tinkle of ice cubes in highball glasses. Computers charted a flawless course, and satellites monitored her position. "I'm sorry I have nothing dramatic to tell you," said the ship's Master, Captain William Warwick, a former relief Captain for both the *Queen Mary* and the first *Queen Elizabeth*, "but what's there to say when everything goes so well?"'[196]

Gradually, passenger numbers increased as Americans, in particular, flocked to book passages on Cunard's wonder ship. Peter C. Kohler recalls:

'QE2 was totally groovy when she first came out. In the publicity stills, everyone looked like Susannah York and Michael Caine. Even the crew – the stewards in those "turtleneck" (as Americans say) sweaters and ultra-suede jackets and the mini-skirted waitresses in the Coffee Shop, which had its own bistro-coloured brown earthenware crockery. And, of course, pre-decimal currency prices for egg and chips.

Every inch of this ship was conceived and executed to make a statement and yes, it was 'Ships Have Been Boring Long Enough!' And QE2 was sure not boring. The only things borrowed from the old *Queens* were literally the deck chair cushions (unzip the blue covers and there was that old zig-zag pattern!) and the steamer rugs. Even the flowers were hip: yellow daffodils in square glass vases. And orange-red shaggy bedspreads. The cutlery was gorgeous. All of the signage matched. And that intertwined QE2 logo was on everything including the most elegant 'flight bags.' No ship ever built had more luxurious carpet than that blue-black ink-coloured Axminster that clad the First Class stairways with the wonderful moulded balustrades in stark, contrasting white. Sublime. A word that hasn't been used in connection with ship interiors since.'[197]

Design and décor aside, the most important aspect by which liners were judged, then as now, was the quality of the cuisine and onboard service. Michael Cango, a New Yorker who started travelling on the QE2 in the early 1970s, recalls that the attention to detail in the arrangement of table settings and the food presentation was inherited from the *Queen Mary* and the *Queen Elizabeth*:

'I remember fondly having silver service in Tourist Class. They piped mashed potato borders on the serving tray and browned them. Looked delicious, but I was always too timid to ask to eat that. Of course, there was so much other wonderful food on which to dine. Tableside preparations were quite normal in Tourist Class, both on crossings and cruises. Part of our daily ritual was to pass the menus of the restaurants and compare what we were having with First Class. One day, we spotted a rather simple smoked salmon appetizer on the Columbia menu. Knowing that the two restaurants shared a galley and that it would be very simple for the steward to pick up a plate from the line, we asked if we might have the appetizer that we saw on the other menu... "Sorry Sir. That would be quite impossible."

At that time, the style of service was to take the dinner orders, then set out the silverware for the whole meal at once, before the first food came out. So, near the end of the trip, we decided to get even for the salmon incident, and challenge our stewards. We ordered something from every category on the menu. Cold appetizer, hot appetizer, soup, salad, fish course, main course, and whatever else we could. A heavy tray of silver came out and each place was set properly with forks, knives and spoons spanning the entire width of the table. The stewards didn't even flinch about this, and we all had a good laugh together on the last night as we tipped them generously for a really wonderful trip.'[198]

Yet, in contrast, Peter C. Kohler recalls that the QE2's galley fell some way short of the exacting standards of the rival French Line – and that the ship's design was partly to blame:

'The cuisine on most liners circa 1969 wasn't nearly as elaborate or as good as it is on most cruise ships today. QE2 menus from her maiden voyage show that two of the paltry three entrées for First Class were... lamb! In Tourist Class, the choice was limited enough for luncheon and dinner that both were printed on the same menu each day. Actually, this was quite common back then. There's a wonderful photo in *The Architectural Review*... showing 46 or so bottles of HP Sauce lined up and ready to go.

The singular worst aspect of QE2 cooking and directly relating to the design of the ship was the decision to co-ordinate all of the cooking and serving for officers, crew and both classes of passengers (and the grill) into one central galley – the largest ever constructed, by the way. This was done for all the right design, practical and efficiency reasons. But it immediately resulted in one thing: cold or tepid food. Hence, the provision of those awful, smelly meth braziers on all of the serving stations. I can close my eyes and still sniff that high school science lab smell now... And the food was often still barely warm and, of course, reheated several times when it finally reached the table. In addition, the stewards had godawful long walks and waits to get your food and, trust me, QE2 stewards delighted in telling you how far they had to go to get your toast they had forgotten.'[199]

Moreover, notwithstanding the 1960s desire for egalitarianism in terms of design and layout, the QE2's staffing continued to reflect Britain's established social hierarchies and so the liner, according to Kohler:

'...was at her Clydebank best in the lower recesses of Five Deck with a brace of foul-mouthed Scots engineers (they don't come in any other form) with their boilersuits unzipped as far as you can get (not a sight for the faint of heart) and their heads half-way into an open overhead service duct, trying to get running water into cabin 5043's washbasin instead of the wardrobe. Then, it was a case of counting the days it took for someone to wipe the greasy fingerprints off the ceiling panel.'[200]

Of course, the QE2's crew were all British (the National Union of Seamen would have countenanced nothing less) and, in that regard, the liner was little different from any other on the North Atlantic in being staffed entirely from her flag nation. Thus, passengers travelling in the first decade of service would have had a particularly British shipboard experience – and one somewhat different from today's cruise ships with their multi-national crews. Even so, a number of the QE2's original crew members remained with the ship until her withdrawal from active service in 2008 and, during the troubled 1970s, the QE2 enjoyed better industrial relations than many other British liners; indeed, she had a reputation for being a 'happy ship' on board which staff were proud to serve. Much credit for this goes to Captain Warwick who, as

*Styled externally by James Gardner and with interiors designed with the involvement of Tony Heaton, the **Cunard Ambassador** and **Cunard Adventurer** were moderately-sized cruise ships whose design was influenced by that of the QE2. (Bruce Peter collection)*

a career Cunard man, was a highly-respected figure – at once commanding, yet genial and, apparently, as much at ease entertaining Royalty as he was dealing with technical minutiae with members of his crew. His presence on the QE2 during her formative years did much to ensure the liner's early success and enduring reputation.

Beyond what passengers would have seen, however, the QE2's design enabled significantly greater economies of scale than her predecessors, meaning that, even when just over half full, the ship was still profitable. When Sir Basil Smallpeice addressed Cunard's shareholders in June 1969, he could

announce with satisfaction that, on the most recent eastbound crossing, the QE2 had brought 1,868 passengers from America, earning a profit of $700,000 from that voyage alone. At the end of October the same year, the liner was given her first overhaul in Southampton's King George V Dock and the turbines were found to be in excellent condition, after twelve round voyages to New York in all weather conditions. During that first summer season, the ship had carried 40,752 passengers, meaning that she had sailed on average 84% full and Cunard had repaid the British Government £2.5 million, or an eighth of the money borrowed to construct the ship.

In the era of the *Queen Mary* and the *Queen Elizabeth*, Cunard had always been quietly appreciative of the positive publicity brought by celebrity passengers being photographed aboard and published in the popular illustrated newspapers and gossip magazines on both sides of the Atlantic. The presence of important politicians, royals, aristocrats, business tycoons, film stars and sports personalities lent the great liners a special aura and glamour in the minds of the public – whilst celebrities, in turn, benefited from being photographed aboard the grandest ships. By the mid-1950s, however, Cunard had already lost some of their most famous passengers to the American Blue Riband winner *United States* – in fact, Bob Hope had joked about this situation when he arrived in Southampton aboard the new Yankee record breaker in 1952.

By the 1960s, many of the most distinguished celebrities – for whom speed and privacy were of the essence – had defected to the stratosphere and the new jetliners as crossing the Atlantic by ship became less desirable. Equally, business tycoons could ill afford five or six days at sea when they could instead spend just over six hours in a 'plane.

With the advent of the QE2, Cunard hoped to attract the glamour set to sail once more – but this time on leisurely cruises, where they could relax and be pampered with first-class service and all of the latest entertainment facilities. However, some of the greatest stars of the 1960s and '70s also enjoyed 'working holidays' on the QE2 to entertain the passengers. Of the many famous entertainers who performed during the liner's early career, the jazz pianist and bandleader Count Basie grew particularly fond of the ship –

indeed, he wrote at length about his QE2 experiences in his autobiography, *Good Morning Blues*:

'The four Caribbean cruises on the *Queen Elizabeth 2*... turned out very nicely all round. Our first QE2 began on the first Monday night of January 1970. We sailed from Pier 52 at the end of Fifty-Second Street on a ten-day cruise that took us down to Kingston, Jamaica; and Bridgetown, Barbados; and back by way of Charlotte Amalie, St. Thomas, in the Virgin Islands; and it was almost as much a vacation for us as for the regular passengers.

Each member of the band was provided first-rate accommodation for two. We worked only one set, which meant we had twenty-some hours free, so there was time for some sightseeing and shopping when we hit those ports of call with our wives. Naturally, most wives were very pleased to be able to go along on all of those cruises, and they had a wonderful time relaxing and getting all that first-class QE2 service, including the deck games, the movies, and the swimming pools, not to mention the food and drinks. It became an annual thing with them for five years. Incidentally, among the passengers on that first cruise were Sarah Vaughan and also Eubie Blake and his wife. Sarah was just taking a break from her busy schedule. But naturally, she did a couple of things with us, and she also took part in a few jam sessions in the Q4 Room...

Our set began at eleven and went until midnight. There were some passengers who wanted to dance and some who wanted to listen, and also some who were fans of ours.'[201]

Count Basie's modern, up-tempo swinging music, with its strong rhythms and shimmering riffs, would have perfectly complemented QE2's equally swinging interiors – and the experience of impromptu late night jam sessions in the Q4 Room with Sarah Vaughan on vocals must have been a very memorable experience for those who were there.

The New Cunard Cruise Fleet

One of the admiring American passengers on the QE2's maiden voyage was a Texan tycoon called Steedman Hinckley, who was Chairman of Overseas National Airways. Hinckley planned to enter the Caribbean cruise business and, in fact, had two sail-assisted cruise ships on order from the Rotterdam Drydock Company. So impressed by the new Cunarder was he that he decided to cancel the sailing ships and, instead, to construct two conventional motor cruise vessels, designed to resemble the QE2's style. Construction stopped abruptly in Rotterdam and this brought about the unusual situation of the shipyard invoking penalty clauses in the contract against Overseas National Airways for delays.

Meanwhile, Hinckley contacted James Gardner to bring some QE2 'magic' to bear on the new cruise ships which, otherwise, were being drawn up by the Copenhagen naval architects Knud E. Hansen A/S. When the first of the ships was nearing the time for launching, however, Overseas National Airways got into temporary financial difficulties and sold the two incomplete hulls to Cunard – who were only too happy to expand their cruising operations with new and economical motor ships. In his autobiography, Gardner gave his own version of how he came to style the superstructures of the new ships:

'Having made a redundant steam coastguard-cutter look like a yacht, a sticky problem put to me by a Texan tycoon, I was asked to play the same trick with liberty ship-style hulls, knocked out for ferries at a Rotterdam shipyard, again for an American client. After working on the QE2, this was comparable to switching from cutting Savile Row suits for the nobs, to running up off-the-peg togs for weekenders... First, I gave her a schooner-style prow, and the superstructure a sculptural form. Radar mounted over the wheelhouse and outriggers on the dignified funnel made masts, which went out with sailing ships, unnecessary. Horns for air vents, projecting port and starboard, gave her character, if nothing else. I was rather chuffed.'[202]

The ships' interiors were designed, in part, by Hinckley's son Albert who, in turn, employed Tony Heaton, freshly graduated from the Royal College of Art, to assist, having recently worked on the QE2's children's playroom, Coffee Shop and teenage disco while studying at the RCA.

Introduced in 1971 and 1972 respectively, the new *Cunard Adventurer* and *Cunard Ambassador* were unusual, but strangely beautiful craft and certainly about as atypical of Cunard's traditions as it would have been possible to imagine. The two ships were of

125

only 14,160grt, but they accommodated some 832 passengers in a compactly-ordered general arrangement, with cabins fitted into every one of the seven main passenger decks. These were small and fitted out like those on Scandinavian car ferries, with curtains to cover shelving, rather than the proper closets to which Cunard passengers were accustomed. Unlike the surviving members of Cunard's existing passenger fleet – the *Carmania* and the *Franconia* – the new cruise ships were profitable and they helped the Line to survive the economic turmoil of the 1970s.

While Cunard's new cruise ships became popular on short jaunts around the Caribbean, the *Queen Elizabeth 2* settled down and gained a peerless reputation as a trans-Atlantic liner and world cruise ship. While on a winter cruise in the West Indies on 8 January 1971, the Cunard flagship received a Mayday call from the stricken French liner *Antilles*.[203] The unfortunate vessel had struck a reef about half a mile north of Mustique, near St Vincent, and was holed in the engine room. Subsequently, escaping oil caught fire and the blaze spread throughout the ship. Fortunately, all 635 passengers and crew got away in the lifeboats and life-rafts, the majority being picked up by the *Queen Elizabeth 2* which steamed at full speed to the rescue. Upon arrival on the scene, the blazing *Antilles* was found illuminating the night sky. The QE2's crew were on full alert with the hospital readied to receive casualties and food and bedding laid out for those rescued. Passengers spectating from the ship's boat deck could feel the intense heat generated by the burning *Antilles* and, initially, there was great anxiety that some of the passengers might be lost or seriously injured. Fortunately, all were accounted for and 85 even decided to continue their cruise, booking available cabins on the QE2 and continuing to enjoy Cunard's hospitality where that of the French Line had come to a premature and abrupt end.[204]

While sedate winter jaunts around the sunny Caribbean hardly tested the QE2's hull design and powerful machinery, spring and autumn trans-Atlantic crossings were another matter – and the QE2, of course, proved to be an outstanding performer in even the worst weather. On one particularly notorious eastbound crossing in April 1972, the liner had to reduce speed to five knots as she hammered through 15-metre (50 ft) waves and a 100 mph gale. The actors Robert Wagner and Natalie Wood were amongst the passengers and, upon disembarkation in Southampton, Wagner described the storm to the waiting press as having been 'a great experience – it was very exciting.' The Captain, Mortimer Hehir, observed that 'It was the worst weather I have ever experienced... Nobody in the ship could recall winds of that velocity lasting so long. At times, there was nothing to be seen all round the liner but spume and spray. It was a fantastic sight.'[205]

The QE2 designer James Gardner had a similar experience on a different eastbound crossing, date unspecified, which he made in the company of his personal assistant:

'Mehitabel and I ventured a return trip from Boston (First Class at half-price, nice). The great ship had to plough through exceptionally heavy seas all the way across, the First Officer reporting it to be the most violent gale he had experienced in seventeen years. I became anchored in the corner of the card room by a landslide of tables, while Mehitabel found herself performing acrobatics in an entirely empty gymnasium, as a sixty-foot rogue wave knocked a hole way up in the ship's prow. To my relief, the funnel stayed upright. Mehitabel actually enjoyed the trip. What a ship – what a girl!'[206]

Throughout her career, the QE2 has proven to be an outstandingly robust 'sea ship' on countless occasions – indeed, she was one of the very last passenger liners to be built with the intention of coping with deep-sea trans-oceanic services, all year round. During the 1970s, shipbuilding costs increased so dramatically that, even if it had been desirable to build such a hull again, it would not have been affordable – especially during an increasingly turbulent economic and business climate. Other late entrants in ocean liner design were the German *Hamburg* (also of 1969) and the Norwegian *Vistafjord* (1973) – but these vessels only rarely made trans-Atlantic voyages and, instead, spent nearly all of their time on luxury cruises. Indeed, it was not until Cunard ordered the *Queen Mary 2* that another passenger ship was designed with a hull specifically shaped to make fast trans-Atlantic voyages.

Enter Trafalgar House...

Since the mid-1960s, the wider shipping world had been in a state of flux. Not only had this situation affected the established trans-oceanic passenger liner trades, leading to the development of new hybrid liner-cum-cruise vessels such as the QE2, but also cargo shipping had been deeply affected. As well as being a prestige operator of large passenger ships, Cunard were also major shippers of freight, with a substantial portfolio of ships and routes, trading all over the world. As well as sailing under Cunard's own flag, some cargo ships were run by the Brocklebank Line and others by the Port Line. These were so-called 'break bulk' vessels, carrying general cargo which was loaded and unloaded using vast workforces of stevedores. This system was inefficient, insecure and increasingly expensive as labour rates grew exponentially. The future lay with container shipping but, just as the 'high-tech' QE2 had been expensive to design and build, container ships were also relatively sophisticated and expensive. A good way to spread risk, however, was to join consortia of other shipowners, each providing only one or two large container ships of a standard design.

In 1965, Cunard joined the Atlantic Container Line consortium which otherwise consisted of Sweden's Broström Group, Wallenius Lines and Rederi Ab Transatlantic, the Holland America Line and France's Compagnie Générale Transatlantique. This firm then ordered a series of commodious and advanced ships which could carry containers, both driven on board and lashed to an internal freight deck, or stacked outboard, ahead of the superstructure. In addition, Cunard also modernised their fleet of oil tankers with larger and, hopefully, more efficient tonnage. As a result of these changes, the company accumulated rather a fragmented portfolio of ship types – tankers, bulk carriers, container vessels, two cruise ships, one trans-Atlantic liner (the QE2) and the remains of a pre-existing fleet of refrigerated general cargo ships, mainly run by the Port Line and Brocklebank subsidiaries. In order to find the best way forward and, perhaps, even to streamline their operations, Cunard sought the advice of the business consultancy, McKinsey. Their report stated that the QE2 was a 'one-off' ship in what was, more widely, a rapidly

declining trade – so the flagship would best be withdrawn and sold. Cunard, wisely, decided to ignore this poor advice; after all, the hybrid QE2 was a lot more flexible and with far greater profit potential than the other remaining trans-Atlantic liners under the French and Italian flags. The greatest fuel guzzler of them all, America's *United States*, had been withdrawn in 1969, but the *France* continued to trade, albeit with a large government operating subsidy. On the mid-Atlantic route from New York to Genoa and Naples, Italy still ran the recent, but conceptually antiquated, *Michelangelo*, *Raffaello* and *Leonardo Da Vinci* – also with generous subsidy. Of these ships, only the QE2 was a good commercial proposition – and continued to be so throughout her career.

Incidentally, at around the same time as it was attempting to advise Cunard, another of McKinsey's shipping clients, Denmark's Maersk Line, allegedly were being told not to enter the container shipping business. They too dismissed the report and grew to become the leading container line and, indeed, the world's biggest merchant fleet.

Not only was the shipping world changing rapidly in the 1960s, but so too was the world of business. A new generation of upwardly-mobile business tycoons was causing a stir in the City, and even the 131-year-old Cunard Line was not immune from being raided by just such an aggressive upstart. Trafalgar House plc had been established only in 1958. Founded by the buccaneering property speculator Nigel Broackes, this firm had an approach to business typifying what might now be described as 'proto-Thatcherism.' Broackes was a former Guards officer who was known to be a smooth but aggressive buyer of undervalued businesses and who sought to increase yields by whatever means necessary. His business partner, Victor Matthews, was a self-made man with a cockney accent and a reputation for blunt directness in his business dealings. During the Second World War he had served in the Royal Navy as an Able Seaman on Arctic convoys, thereafter beginning his business career in the building trade as an itinerant salesman of ceiling tiles for the fibrous plaster manufacturers, Clark & Fenn. Having bought a Brixton construction firm called Bridge Walker, he rode the 1960s wave in property development by buying up, then merging, small construction business.[207] Broackes and Matthews

127

*Top: A 1979 view of the **Queen Elizabeth 2** at Southampton, showing the external consequences of Trafalgar House's refitting work. The forward superstructure windows have been plated in and new penthouses have been added to the topmost deck. In addition, the boot topping was briefly painted with an experimental anti-fouling paint, then only available in blue. (Bruce Peter collection)*

Left and above: Two aerial views of the QE2 at sea during the latter 1970s, showing the extensive lido decks being put to good use as the ship glides through calm seas. (Bruce Peter collection)

had first met when the latter had been employed to renovate a block of flats which Broackes had purchased – and it was called Trafalgar House. Within four years, turnover had risen eight times to over two million pounds and Broackes bought a minority interest in Matthews' firm. For the next fifteen years, the two worked together to build Trafalgar House into a large conglomerate. Their roles were strictly divided: Broackes was the strategist, planning ambitious takeover bids, while Matthews ran the businesses. In 1980, Margaret Thatcher made Matthews a life peer, but the satirical magazine *Private Eye* constantly lampooned him as the spiv 'Lord Whelks' on account of his East End origins and his arguably dubious business activities.

Broackes' and Matthews' aggressively acquisitive methods were very much in tune with the era, as the conglomerate was becoming an increasingly popular corporate model from the 1960s onwards, with a number of large, multi-faceted businesses then being formed through mergers of existing smaller and more specialist companies. Some were notably successful – for example Grand Metropolitan – but others managed portfolios that were widely diverse and unable to achieve synergies between their many subsidiaries. In the longer term, Trafalgar House proved to be in the latter category. While it made Broackes and Matthews personally wealthy, it imploded in the 1990s and, with hindsight, its mercenary business tactics and short-termism hindered Cunard's development as a leading cruise line.

Six months after Cunard was acquired by Trafalgar House, Sir Basil Smallpeice retired as Chairman, his place being taken by Victor Matthews. Shortly thereafter, Matthews instituted a programme of redundancies and many of Cunard's experienced technical staff, including Dan Wallace and Tom Kameen, sought jobs elsewhere.

Not surprisingly, the new management quickly focused on the *Queen Elizabeth 2* in order to examine how the ship could be reconfigured so that more money could be extracted from the passengers. Instead of being regarded as an untouchable icon of British identity, the liner was now viewed in terms of profit yield per square foot of deck space.

Another significant, but opposing, factor was that a number of rival liners were gaining serious plaudits in the travel press by offering relaxed one-sitting dining for all of their passengers, whereas the QE2 had first and second sittings in her main Britannia Restaurant. In comparison, Norwegian America's highly-rated *Sagafjord* and forthcoming *Vistafjord* appeared to be superior in this respect. Furthermore, three other Norwegian shipping lines had recently joined forces to create a new up-market cruise brand, Royal Viking Line, and each had ordered a ship from the Finnish Wärtsilä shipyard for delivery in the 1972-73 period. As with the Norwegian America liners, the *Royal Viking Star*, *Royal Viking Sea* and *Royal Viking Sky* would offer commodious staterooms and one sitting for dinner. Moreover, their design was a near copy of many of the QE2's most innovative planning, technological and aesthetic innovations – a fact which must have been particularly galling for Cunard.

Thus, after only three years in service, the first of several major refits for the QE2 was planned. In order to advise on this work, Cunard approached the Copenhagen naval architects Knud E. Hansen A/S who had designed the Royal Vikings and also the *Cunard Ambassador* and *Cunard Adventurer*, and a contract for the conversion was awarded to Vosper Thornycroft of Southampton. In only 23 days, the QE2 would be reconfigured with two new decks, each containing ten penthouse cabins with private verandas, being inserted between the funnel and mast in the space previously occupied by the liner's sports deck. This, according to Cunard, had been under-used and was argued to be something of a 'dust bowl' when the ship sailed at speed. The naval architect Tage Wandborg, of Knud E. Hansen A/S, designed the new prefabricated aluminium cabin blocks to harmonise with the existing superstructure as best he could. On Boat Deck, Upper Deck and Quarter Deck, more radical alterations were planned. Cunard asked Dennis Lennon, the ship's original co-ordinating interior designer, to oversee the rebuilding work but, alarmed at what was proposed for the ship, Lennon withdrew, leaving the completion of the redecoration to others. Staff from Vosper Thornycroft sailed on the preceding trans-Atlantic voyage to carry out preparatory work.

To take Boat Deck first, the London Gallery, the ship's acclaimed showcase of contemporary art, was closed and replaced with a reading room and the adjacent shopping arcade was also cleared so that cabins could be built there. The 736 Club, the popular night club and casino, was also ripped out and a new restaurant called the Queen's Grill was established in its place. Unlike the rather understated existing Grill Room, which became known as the Princess Grill, the new establishment had Louis XV-style chairs and was ornamented with chandeliers and mirrors in gilded rococo frames. Travelling on the QE2 in 1975, Sir Hugh Casson wrote in his diary that 'The American Louis Quinze of the Queen's Grill Restaurant is a great disappointment architecturally.'[208] In what had been the Coffee Shop and the forward part of the London Gallery, a new grill kitchen was assembled. Aft on Boat Deck, the upper level of the magnificent Double Room was partially stripped of seating and a new shopping arcade was constructed – shops, apparently, being able to generate more profits than tables and chairs.[209]

In truth, the Double Room had, from the outset, been one of the QE2's least successful spaces and one which, despite the snazzy décor, actually harked back to an earlier era of shipboard planning. On the upper level, the seating gave a poor view of the entertainments below, as the floor was not terraced; furthermore, the bandstand was only large enough for a quartet rather than a full orchestra, and there was no possibility of presenting a stage show. For Americans, the new casino resorts of Las Vegas, Reno, Atlantic City and Miami Beach had shown how things could be done differently, with their large Copa rooms, containing terraced seating, facing full stage facilities. Although it was rebuilt several times, the purpose of the Double Room (latterly known as the Grand Lounge) was never fully resolved and it remained an unhappy hybrid of a ballroom, shopping arcade and show lounge without properly addressing any of these functions until the end of the QE2's long career.

On Upper Deck, immediately below, the forward Look Out lounge was eliminated and its windows plated over to form another kitchen. This was a particularly sad loss as the space was, hitherto, both very elegant and had given passengers wonderful panoramic views over the bow. Unfortunately, from the outset, its awkward location, ahead of the Britannia Restaurant, had made it difficult to find. To increase the restaurant's capacity, its central servery block was demolished and the escalator to the kitchen on Quarter Deck, below, was plated in, making the dining space completely open-plan. It would now be served by its own dedicated kitchen in the space left by stripping the Look Out. Moving down to Quarter Deck, the Columbia Restaurant was extended forward, swallowing up the grill room to port and galley space to starboard, and a new cocktail bar was fitted in an underused conference room, aft – but it was a poor replacement for the lost Look Out. Furthermore, the windows in the front and forward topsides of the superstructure were removed and, as a result, when viewed from bow quarters, the QE2 now had a much more 'plated in' appearance than before.

During 23 days in Southampton, not only were all of these tasks to be carried out but the ship was also to be fitted with a new bow thrust propeller and new stabiliser fins, as well as receiving a regular mechanical overhaul and repainting. To do all of this in so short a time-span was a tall order and, not surprisingly, the work was not quite completed on schedule. The QE2 sailed empty to New York, where frantic action took place to ready the interiors to receive passengers and the travel trade press.

Reporting on the ship from Southampton at the end of the 23 days and prior to the first post-refit crossing to New York, *Time* magazine's correspondent was not impressed. Commenting that 'the QE2 retained, in her original design, at least some of the proud aura of the days when Britannia ruled the waves', he went on to observe that the '$4½ million face-lifting, unveiled last week, seems to have turned the only Queen still afloat into a bit of a tart.'[210] He continued:

'The leather-panelled library, with its rosewood reading tables, has disappeared; in its place is a casino with gaming tables and one-armed bandits. The lounge area above the ballroom has become a shopping arcade. The best-located bar, which offered an intoxicating view over the ship's bow, has been turned into a kitchen. The forward observation platform, as well as the children's pool and play area and half the sheltered sports deck, have been taken over by 44 new prefabricated cabins... Dennis Lennon, who was chiefly responsible for the original interior design of the ship, quit after two weeks on the

*The **Queen Elizabeth 2**, at Nassau in the Bahamas during a Caribbean cruise in December 1980, now with her red boot topping restored. (Theodore W. Scull)*

new project. 'It was a national ship,' he explained. 'It wasn't something to play around with and turn into a honky-tonk.' James Gardner, the principal exterior designer of the original, said of the altered superstructure: 'We tried to give her lines a quiet dignity like the Mark III Bentley, but now lumps have been added on.'[211]

According to Brian Beardsmore, Lennon was indeed deeply hurt and bitter about what was done to the QE2 in 1972 – and understandably so. After devoting over three years to the project and having brought the best out of such a diversity of stellar design talent, it must have been very deflating to see destructive changes being made after his original interiors had received such great critical acclaim and after so short a time in service. However, the rebuilding was very much in line with Trafalgar House's more profit-orientated business strategy, as *Time*'s correspondent went on to explain:

'The Cunard Line, which expects the alterations to help increase the QE2's profits by 50%, seems prepared to weather the storm. But even the Line's Chairman, Victor Matthews, looked a little queasy after he toured the liner a few hours before she was due to depart Southampton for New York. 'This is a disaster,' he said, having peered through half-painted cabins with naked light bulbs hanging from their sockets and cables strewn across the floors. 'The ship looks as though a bomb has hit her.' The QE2's departure was delayed three days while workmen tried desperately to get her shipshape. Cunard were forced to cough up $250,000 in emergency shore accommodation or air fares home for 1,550 stranded passengers. After the liner finally weighed anchor this week, a clean-up party of 40 workmen was still aboard, hammering their way across the Atlantic.'[212]

It would not be the first time that the *Queen Elizabeth 2* attracted bad publicity in the wake of a major refit during Cunard's Trafalgar House era. Once the work was properly snagged, the liner settled down once again to give outstanding service, both on the trans-Atlantic run and as a cruise ship. From 1974 onwards, however, the QE2 would be the only remaining large passenger vessel regularly linking Britain, France and the United States in liner service because Valerie Giscard D'Estaing's Government in Paris decided to withdraw their subsidy to the *France* and to concentrate instead on sponsoring Concorde, which they felt was a more fitting symbol of modern French technical achievement. Thus, after her crew had made a final strike protest by holding a sit-in off Le Havre, the *France* was taken out of service in

October 1974 and moth-balled. The QE2 was now the world's largest passenger ship in operation – but she was not yet the last trans-Atlantic liner. The Italian Line struggled on until 1975 and the Polish *Stefan Batory*, as well as a variety of Soviet *Ivan Franko*-class liners, continued to link Europe and Canada well into the 1980s. Of course, none of these could aspire to offer the kind of luxury associated with the QE2, even though the cosy *Stefan Batory*, in particular, was much loved and enjoyed a very loyal following.

QE2 in the Media

As the world's biggest surviving liner and the British national flagship, during the 1970s the QE2 had a uniquely high media profile. Indeed, during this period of economic stagnation and rising unemployment, the luxury ship had become highly emotive. A voyage on the QE2 was perceived by many in Britain to be as desirable as it was unattainable – an experience only to be enjoyed vicariously through Alan Whicker TV documentaries. As Whicker put it, the liner was 'a space capsule drifting round the world in a delightful way.'[213]

Unfortunately, this high recognition status also attracted the attention of assorted terrorists, hoaxers, drug smugglers, extortionists and even dodgy third world dictators. In October 1971 a consignment of arms was found hidden in luggage offloaded in Cobh in Ireland and was clearly a gift to the IRA from American sympathisers. The following May, an extortionist called Cunard's New York office claiming that the liner would be 'blasted out of the sea' unless a $350,000 ransom demand was paid. Royal Marines bomb disposal experts were sent to the ship, which was *en route* to Southampton from New York. They were dropped into the sea by parachute from a Hercules aircraft and picked up by one of the QE2's launches.[214] Needless to say, no bombs were found and the FBI later arrested a lone extortionist in his New York shoe shop.[215] Understandably worried about security, Cunard had ended the time-honoured tradition of allowing visitors aboard for public tours of the ship in 1972.

Later, in April 1973, the liner was chartered to a Massachusetts travel agency for a special cruise from Southampton to Ashdod and Haifa in Israel to bring American Jews to celebrate the 25th anniversary of Israel's foundation. Security was very strict throughout the voyage and an exclusion zone was maintained when in ports of call *en route*. At the end of the charter, it appeared that there had been no detectable incidents but, the following year, Egypt's President Anwar Sadat alleged that Libya's Colonel Gadaffi had attempted to use an Egyptian naval submarine to torpedo the liner. At that time, Egyptian and Libyan warships were under joint command and Sadat revealed that he had vetoed Gadaffi's order and instructed the submarine commander to return to port in Alexandria. It appeared that Gadaffi had wanted to avenge the shooting down by Israel of a Libyan airliner over the Sinai desert in 1972.[216]

During a cruise to Bermuda, ironically on 1 April 1974, the QE2 suffered a major mechanical breakdown – her first serious technical trouble since the initial turbine problems during acceptance trials in 1969 – and the ship lost all power. Even the onboard services closed down, meaning that there was only emergency lighting, and neither the lifts, nor the air conditioning, nor the toilet system would work. With over 1,000 passengers on board, the QE2 was dead in the water.[217] Fortunately, the modern Norwegian cruise ship *Sea Venture* was on a three-day visit to Hamilton harbour (the ship sailed regularly on cruises from New York to Bermuda, along with her sister, the *Island Venture*). Cunard chartered the ship and she set sail for the stricken QE2, while frantic efforts were made to diagnose the problem and to restore power. By the following morning, the *Sea Venture* had arrived and the transfer of passengers could begin. Because the QE2 had no power, it was necessary to use only the *Sea Venture*'s lifeboats (those on the QE2 could be launched, but not winched back into their davits when the job was done because that required electricity). To transfer everyone took seven hours and, in the end, the 767-passenger *Sea Venture* was slightly overcrowded with the QE2's guests. Meanwhile, some 600 of her own passengers were temporarily stranded in Bermuda hotels while the rescue mission was under way.[218]

Cunard, meanwhile, chartered aircraft to fly the QE2's passengers home and the *Sea Venture* resumed her cruise once her own guests had re-boarded. A tug was dispatched to tow the disabled QE2 to Hamilton where, in deteriorating weather, she anchored offshore. The reason for the breakdown was that water being fed into the boilers had become contaminated with oil due to a ruptured feed pipe and this, in turn, had adhered to the inside of the tubes, preventing heat from being transferred evenly and causing them to distort and crack open. Consequently, the ship needed a partial re-tubing and a thorough clean of the boilers. Unable to tie up along the Front Street quay due to her great size, the liner was repaired offshore with new boiler tubes and other materials being ferried out in workboats. Once steam could be raised again, the liner limped back to New York, where further repairs were carried out by Todd's shipyard in New Jersey. Altogether, the debacle cost Cunard £700,000, wiping out nearly all of the profit for the 1974 season.

On 23 July 1976, while 80 nautical miles off the Isles of Scilly, the QE2 suffered a serious engine room fire, caused by a lubrication pipe rupturing and spraying oil onto the hot surfaces of the engine room, which ignited, causing a short but intense blaze that shot up the funnel casing and took twenty minutes to dowse. A 22-year-old engineer was seriously burned and the ship limped back to Southampton for repairs.[219]

Later that year, the QE2 hit the headlines again when IRA bombers attempted an assault whilst she was in dry-dock in Southampton, but police intercepted the IRA cell before they could carry out their mission. Two Southampton residents who worked aboard the liner were arrested and a third man, who had allowed his home to be used to store explosives, was also taken into custody. Fortunately, the QE2 escaped unscathed – although police did find that detonators had already been hidden on board as part of the plot.[220]

Through Turbulent Waters in the latter 1970s

When such glamorous 'high-tech' forms of transport as the QE2 and Concorde had first been mooted in the 1960s, there was the implicit suggestion that one day, not too far in the future, the kind of experience they promised would also be available to the masses. Such was the rate of technological progress – nuclear power, landings on the moon,

supersonic air travel – that it was surely only a question of time before almost everyone could experience the promised utopia.

Alas, by the mid-1970s the British economy was stagnating. Indeed, the sad circumstances surrounding the QE2's protracted outfitting and delivery were a premonition of serious underlying problems in the British industrial base. For shipping companies, including Cunard, worse was to follow. The 1973 oil crisis, which resulted from Arab protests against the ongoing Yom Kippur War, resulted in the quadrupling of the price of Gulf crude. Immediately, this had the knock-on effect of increasing costs for marine bunker fuel which, in turn, changed the

The Danish-built **Cunard Countess** *during her initial sea trials, when her funnel was painted white. Very quickly, she adopted the traditional Cunard livery. (Bruce Peter collection)*

economic basis of the passenger shipping industry. A great many hitherto-successful steam turbine liners were hastily withdrawn from service and consigned for scrap to Kaohsiung in Taiwan. Indeed, during the mid-1970s hardly a month went past without some famous and well-loved ship being pulled from service. Most of the combined P&O-Orient Line fleet disappeared (even the modern flagship *Canberra* was threatened) while famous lines such as Shaw Savill, Union-Castle and Canadian Pacific withdrew from the passenger trade altogether. By the mid-1970s, the Cunard passenger fleet was reduced to only three ships – the *Queen Elizabeth 2*, the *Cunard Ambassador* and the *Cunard Adventurer*. By the end of the year, Cunard were down to two as the *Cunard Ambassador* had been destroyed by fire and the wreck sold off for conversion into a livestock carrier.

Until the oil crisis, the international cruise industry had been growing confidently with many new liners entering service, mainly in the Caribbean. After 1973 the order book almost dried up but Cunard did, nonetheless, buy two new cruise ships. These had been ordered speculatively by a Miami-based shipbroker called Elie Schalit. Ironically, Schalit was a former arms smuggler who had been imprisoned by the British in Palestine before becoming involved in the illegal transport of Jews to Israel. His first vessel,

New duplex penthouses were added to the QE2's superstructure during her refit at Bayonne in 1977. These contained her most expensive accommodation - but further compromised her silhouette. (Gallagher collection)

named the *Exodus*, had been rammed by British destroyers while *en route* from France to Palestine. Schalit later moved to Florida where he founded the Freeport Cruise Line and, indeed, acted as a broker for several companies in the fledgling Miami cruise business – including Carnival.

The *Cunard Countess* and *Cunard Princess* were to have been the first two of eight identical sister ships constructed for Schalit's brokerage to sell on. MGM, the well known film and entertainment conglomerate, was to have owned the other six, but its management had a last minute change of heart about entering the

cruise business and they were never built. The ships were to have been positioned throughout the world – the Caribbean, the Mediterranean, even the Indian Ocean and the South Pacific – for what was expected to be a boom in long-distance air-sea cruising. The plan was to build the ships at the Burmeister & Wain shipyard in Denmark and then to outfit and complete them at the Industrie Navali Mechaniche Affine (INMA) yard at La Spezia in Italy.

The *Cunard Countess* was delivered in the summer of 1976 but the *Cunard Princess*, which was originally to have been named the *Cunard Conquest*, was delayed by a shipyard fire in April 1976 and was not introduced until March 1977. When Princess Grace of Monaco (formerly Grace Kelly) named the *Cunard Princess* in New York, Cunard announced that the liner was, in fact, 'the last cruise ship.'[221] For Trafalgar House, this was a self-fulfilling prophecy because, while the cruise industry began rapidly to expand from the early 1980s onwards, Cunard never again took delivery of a new passenger ship until being acquired by Carnival in 1998. Given their outstanding history and reputation, Cunard could undoubtedly have become one of the world's leading cruise lines – but, due to Trafalgar House's lack of vision, this did not happen.

Intriguingly, the *Cunard Countess* and *Cunard Princess* sailed their sea trials with white funnels but these had been repainted in traditional Cunard red and black by the time they actually entered service. Victor Matthews, apparently, preferred this traditional livery because he thought that it would have greater appeal to passengers and, thus, be more profitable for Cunard than the charcoal and white style introduced by James Gardner on the QE2. Thus, less than a decade after Cunard had been persuaded to ditch their heritage in favour of modernism, 'retro' design began to assert itself as it was realised that there was money to be made by evoking a romanticised 'lost golden age' of sea travel. It would only be a matter of time before the QE2 would follow suit.

In December 1977 the *Queen Elizabeth 2* was back in a New Jersey shipyard – this time Bethlehem Steel in Bayonne – for a scheduled winter overhaul. There, two additional new 'duplex' penthouse suites were added to the superstructure, squeezed in between the mast and the existing block on Signal Deck, dating from the 1972 refit. These, too, were prefabricated and became the liner's most exclusive and expensive accommodation – but they further compromised the dapper silhouette.

As Britain stagnated in the early 1970s and 'Swinging London' was consigned to history, America prospered and the completion of the World Trade Center in New York between 1970 and 1973 appeared to be a sign of its capitalist virility. Thus, the Britannia Restaurant was renamed 'Tables of the World', reflecting both a new international menu and the name of the exclusive 'Windows on the World' restaurant at the summit of the WTC. The space was hastily re-styled by Dennis Lennon who split it into five areas, each with its own 'themed' décor – reflecting rather clichéd and stereotypical views of Britain, France, Spain, Italy and the Far East. While this post-modern approach was very much in line with the mass market hotel and cruise ship interior design of the era, the new insertions looked tacky on the otherwise refined QE2 – and Tables of the World was heavily criticised. Indeed, within a decade, it was removed. Peter C. Kohler observes:

'Cunard essentially took the Britannia Restaurant and, without structurally altering it or changing the furniture or even much of the table plan, created six internationally-themed dining areas. The worst being the Asian one with fans arranged around the ceiling panels and also the French one (I think) which had outdoor sun umbrellas set on astroturf. The menus featured an "international" entrée each dinner, I think. Gradually, all of the gee-gaws went away or fell apart and, by the time I sailed westbound in 1979, some of the worst had gone. The service was dire. I think I tipped the steward a fiver, enough to show I hadn't forgotten to tip and that his service was perfunctory, rude and inefficient. QE2 circa 1979 was best avoided; she was suffering a depressing early midlife crisis.[222]

More than the tepid food, the insipid redecoration of the cheery Britannia Restaurant perhaps also signified a crisis of confidence in British identity – and the idea that New York, not London, was now the centre of all that was desirable. Kohler concludes ruefully that 'when Trafalgar House "Americanised" the QE2 by making her look like a down-market Hilton inside, I can't think of any American who

wanted that!'[223]

Nevertheless, the QE2 weathered both the turbulent North Atlantic and the economic squalls of the 1970s remarkably well. On 29 April 1979, the liner set sail from New York on her officially-designated 'Tenth Anniversary Crossing.' From being a calculated risk for Cunard in the 1960s, the liner was now well established as the biggest and most famous in operation anywhere.

In May 1980, however, the QE2 met an old rival sailing outbound down New York's Hudson River. The moth-balled CGT flagship *France* had been

Part of the controversial Tables of the World Restaurant, which replaced the Britannia's bright red, white and blue design with a series of rather ephemerally-decorated themed dining environments. (Peter Knego)

bought by the Norwegian cruise tycoon Knut Kloster and ingeniously converted from a quadruple-screw trans-Atlantic liner into the *Norway*, now the world's largest cruise ship. Although the QE2 had been robbed of her pre-eminent position, the two liners were hardly rivals any longer. The *Norway* had been rebuilt to cruise weekly from Miami to Caribbean ports, whereas the QE2 remained a proper trans-Atlantic liner and world cruise ship. The sight of these two surviving giants of passenger shipping was a stirring one – and a sure sign that the cruise industry was beginning to recover from its mid-1970s slump.

CHAPTER 8

THE FALKLANDS AND AFTER

QE2
BRITAIN'S
GREATEST
LINER

WHILE large ships such as the *Canberra*, the *Rotterdam* and the QE2, were making their annual world cruises in the early months of 1982, Argentinean scrap metal merchants landed illegally at South Georgia on 19 March to demolish an abandoned whaling station there, raising an Argentinean flag above their work site. The Falkland Islands, located 300 miles off the coast of Argentina, directly east from Rio Gallegos, and South Georgia, another 834 miles further to the east, together are a British Crown Colony, loosely associated with the British Antarctic Territory. Argentina has disputed the sovereignty of Las Malvinas, as the islands are known in Spanish, since the nation's independence in 1817.

The 1982 incident was played down by Whitehall at first, with only the nuclear submarine HMS *Spartan* being dispatched on 31 March to assist HMS *Endurance*, an ice-patrol vessel stationed in the region. Three days later, after there had been a full-scale Argentinean invasion of the Islands, Britain's Defence Secretary, John Nott, announced that a Task Force of up to 40 warships and a thousand commandos was being assembled to take the Falklands by force if no diplomatic settlement could be reached during the two weeks it would take the Task Force to make the 12,800-kilometre (8,000-mile) sea voyage.

While the Task Force's main body of naval vessels sailed from Plymouth on 5 April, a number of British merchant ships were requisitioned by the Ministry of Defence to join the fleet as soon as they could be converted and made ready for national service. Initially, these included the P&O flagship *Canberra* and educational cruise vessel *Uganda*, along with the *Norland* of North Sea Ferries and the line's cargo ships *Elk*, *Anco Charger* and *Strathewe*, as well as the *Atlantic Causeway* and the *Atlantic Conveyor* from Cunard's ACL subsidiary and the Cunard refrigerated cargo liner *Saxonia*. In total, forty-five merchant ships were called up. The British Government's ability to requisition and deploy merchant ships so quickly for an operation of this sort was the result of contingency plans drawn up in 1978 by NATO (the North Atlantic Treaty Organisation). With the Cold War continuing, NATO had planned for the expeditious acquisition of 300 suitable commercial vessels, belonging to its member nations, in times of national emergency.[224]

The QE2 was called up later, on Monday 3 May,

while approaching the British coast on a trans-Atlantic crossing from Philadelphia. The ship was needed to take additional troops and equipment to the South Atlantic to support units already mobilised aboard the *Canberra* and the *Norland*.

Perhaps the greatest anomaly of the Falklands Campaign was its heavy dependency on ships for moving troops and equipment. By the 1980s, trooping by sea was generally considered to be a thing of the past, superseded by the airlift capability of large and fast military transport aircraft and commercial airliners or cargo 'planes that could be chartered as needed. Yet, apart from the distances to be covered and sheer remoteness of the Falkland Islands, there was the greater problem of there being no airstrip there capable of landing large wide-bodied jet aircraft, nor anywhere close enough to be used as a staging point. There was no question of mounting any sort of D-Day-style amphibious assault from offshore. Ascension Island, the nearest possible jumping-off point on British territorial soil, is at about the same latitude as the Brazilian city of Recife, almost a week's sailing distance to South Georgia Island, itself still 1,390 kilometres (834 miles) east of the Falklands.

A quick conversion of the QE2 was undertaken in Southampton, primarily to install helicopter decks fore and aft and to make provision for refuelling at sea (RAS). Gardner's tapered windscreens and part of the Q4 Room were cut away from the after end of Quarter Deck to make way for a prefabricated helideck. As was done aboard the *Canberra* some weeks earlier, the ship's swimming pools, already capable of supporting the great weight of water that normally filled them, were used as foundations for the new decks, the big Sea King helicopters and whatever else that would land on them. The bottoms of the QE2's Quarter and One Deck pools were covered with thick steel plating, evenly distributing the weight exerted by a network of girders and trusses that supported the aft helideck. The forward helipad, also at Quarter Deck level, was built out over the bow whaleback and capstans, where its construction had the benefit of the ship's strengthening as a trans-Atlantic liner. As the QE2 lacked the bunker capacity to make a round-trip voyage to the South Atlantic without refuelling, feed pipes were installed so that she could refuel while under way by means of a connection inside the starboard-side baggage handling port on Two Deck, immediately forward of the Midships Lobby's gangway hatches.[225] Apart from these, few other structural changes were made.

Some of the ship's luxury furnishings, fittings and works of art, along with the grand pianos, casino paraphernalia, fine china and glassware, 17,000 bottles of Champagne and half a ton of caviar, were all taken ashore for storage. Carpeting in the public rooms, stairways, deck vestibules and many of the cabin corridors was covered with sheets of hardboard for protection from the heavier-than-usual wear and tear of her new battle-ready 'passengers' in combat boots. The names of those billeted in each cabin were neatly hand-lettered on the hardboard flooring outside its doorway by berthing officers before troops were embarked. Portable cots were set up wherever there was space for them in passenger and crew cabins, as well as the by-then-emptied Casino, Double Down Bar and parts of the promenade spaces on Upper Deck, to bring the ship's capacity up by fifty per cent.

After embarking some 3,000 personnel of the Fifth Infantry Brigade, including detachments of the Scots Guards, Welsh Guards and the Gurkha Rifles, along with their equipment and various military stores, including a large quantity of ammunition, the QE2 sailed from Southampton on Wednesday 12 May under the command of Captain Peter Jackson. The ship was staffed by a volunteer force of 650 British officers and crew, including 33 stewardesses and female pursers. Among these were some who had served aboard the old *Queens* during the Second World War. Senior bedroom steward Ted Worsley recalled that what worried him most this time was the great amount of ammunition and aviation fuel for the helicopters taken aboard in Southampton.[226]

As the ship made her way down The Solent, two Sea King helicopters alighted on her helidecks, where they were lashed down for the sea voyage. Once in the English Channel, the QE2 rendezvoused with the Royal Fleet Auxiliary tanker *Grey Rover* for a vital test of her RAS arrangements. As the QE2 slowed for the operation, the *Grey Rover* approached from astern, taking and holding a parallel position about 50 metres (150 feet) away from the Cunard liner's flank. A lightweight line was rocketed across to the QE2's bow

deck as 'messenger' for a heavier intermediate line, then pulled across, and its leading end brought along the ship's side to the open port on Two Deck. There, it served as a heaving line, over which was passed the 200 millimetre- (8 inch-) diameter flexible fuel hose to be connected to the newly-installed hydrant on board the QE2. Only a small amount of oil was pumped aboard, topping up the 5,969 tons already in the QE2's fuel tanks.

Though the ship was more crowded and noisier than usual, life on board was a strange mix of regular cruise activity and a more urgent sense of the mission at hand, with the constant pace of physical fitness and training for battle. The relentless pounding of soldiers' boots could be felt throughout the ship, as hundreds of men in full battle fatigues, with helmets, backpacks and automatic weapons, jogged in relays around Boat Deck from 06.30 in the morning onwards, while others engaged in firing practice from the ship's bow and stern. The Gurkhas practised getting from their accommodation on Five Deck to their emergency muster stations by various routes blindfolded, so that they would be able to escape if the ship were to be disabled and without power. As take-off and landing were being practised with the Sea Kings, rows of off-duty soldiers sunbathed on the open decks in the shadow of these activities as though the QE2 was on a regular Mediterranean cruise. Rather than the usual advice on sightseeing and shopping offered to passengers during cruise port lectures, mandatory briefings on Falklands terrain and topography stressed combat and survival in the inhospitable climate and rugged terrain of these remote Islands. In the deck vestibule outside the Columbia Restaurant, men gathered informally throughout the day to study and discuss the large detailed maps of the Islands, taped to the bulkhead where artist Helen Banynia's tapestries of the ship's launching had hung. Entertainment was a little different, though, with a notice advertising a 'Sod's opera', produced by servicemen for their shipmates, asking those attending to bring their own chair, if they could find one.

Room Service Supervisor Frances Milroy instructed her staff that military personnel berthed in cabins were responsible for their own bed linen, and that there was no objection if ship's staff made beds and changed bedding. Clean towels were only to be issued in exchange for soiled ones, as the laundry supervisor complained of diminishing returns on these. While there was untidiness in deck pantries where armed forces were free to make their own tea and coffee, these should, nonetheless, be kept clean and tidy.[227]

Following a brief refuelling stop at Freetown, Sierra Leone, on Tuesday 18 May and a call to load additional stores at Bridgetown, Ascension Island, two days later, the QE2 went onto an active war basis, in virtual radio silence, and her radar was switched off to minimise the chance of detection. All watertight doors below Five Deck were closed and the steel deadlights, fitted on all portholes below Three Deck when the ship was built, were lowered and secured. Military lookouts were posted on the bridge wings and near the funnel from dusk to dawn.[228] At night, the ship

*The QE2 is welcomed back to Southampton by HM The Queen Mother aboard the Royal Yacht, HMY **Britannia**. (Gallagher collection)*

was totally blacked out, with black plastic sheeting covering the large windows of the public rooms and cabin portholes darkened. Navigating Officer Philip Rentell, who had signed on for the mission and was appointed as Liaison Officer between the Royal Navy and Merchant Marine personnel, also served as Blackout Officer. After the 'Darken Ship' order was broadcast over the loudspeaker system each evening, he circled about the QE2 in one of the Sea King helicopters to ensure that no light was showing.

Cabins were the greatest problem, with lighted portholes having to be traced to individual rooms and their occupants ordered to return below and darken them.[229] As the ship approached South Georgia, she began to sail a zig-zag course further to evade enemy detection of her position and heading.

As the QE2 steamed towards South Georgia Island, the *Canberra* and the *Norland* had already started landing their contingents of 3 Parachute Regiment and Royal Marines Commandos at Falkland Sound and San Carlos Water on Friday 21 May. After completing their landing and de-storing operations, the *Canberra* and the *Norland* sailed on Tuesday 25 May to rendezvous with the QE2 at South Georgia. The Cunard flagship arrived in Cumberland Bay, South Georgia on the evening of Thursday 27 May, within sight of the *Canberra*, the *Norland*, HMS *Endurance*, HMS *Leeds Castle* and the 'small ships' – as they were referred to by BBC commentators –the *Cordella*, the *Farnella*, the *Junella*, the *Northella* and the *Pict*, standing by to transfer personnel to the *Canberra* and the *Norland*. The QE2's arrival was delayed by several hours as she had encountered thick fog and heavy pack-ice during the previous night and, therefore, had to reduce speed.

Within an hour of the QE2's arrival, transferring her embarked forces, their equipment and stores was commenced both by helicopter and ship. As the *Cordella* nudged alongside the big Cunarder's flank, the liner's Captain hailed her, asking: 'Which one are you?' to which the *Cordella* cheekily replied 'Which one are YOU?' The transfer operation continued through much of the next day, with the Welsh and Scots Guards contingents going to the *Canberra* and the Gurkhas to the *Norland* for transport into the war zone to join the fighting. As darkness fell later that day, 177 survivors from HMS *Ardent*, attacked and burned out by an Exocet missile on 21 May, transferred from the *Canberra* to the QE2 on their way home. Those aboard the *Canberra* packed her open decks to give these brave men a heroes' send-off. Royal Marines bandsmen gave them an impromptu farewell, playing Rule Britannia, A Life on the Ocean Wave and Hootenanny, which had become a sort of signature tune during the voyage south. Standing on the flight deck of their transfer ship, HMS *Leeds Castle*, in the white boiler suits given to them by the

Canberra's crew, the Ardent's men rejoined with a rousing chorus of the well known rugby Oggie song. Those on the Canberra's decks picked up the familiar 'Oi, Oi, Oi' refrain as their comrades-in-arms sailed off into the gathering darkness towards the QE2, with the song's final chorus ringing off the harbour's mountain cliffs in what was surely one of the whole campaign's more moving moments.[230]

The following day, survivors from HMS Coventry and HMS Antelope were brought aboard the QE2, while the liner simultaneously was offloading military stores and cargo to the RFA Stromness. As weather and sea conditions worsened during the day, it was learned that the tanker British Wye, 400 miles to the north, had come under attack and that Argentinean Intelligence had made high-altitude reconnaissance flights over the South Atlantic with a long-range Boeing 707 aircraft, flown at 18,000 feet, revealing the positions of ships in the area. The QE2 sailed for Ascension Island at 17.27 with 25 tons of ammunition still remaining in her holds. By this time, she was down to her last thousand tons of fuel as a rendezvous was arranged with the Royal Fleet Auxiliary tanker Bayleaf. At 09.00 on Wednesday 2 June, the QE2 slowed to ten knots and altered course to accomplish the fuel line hook-up in gale-force winds and heavy seas, as the Bayleaf approached her starboard stern quarter. While the tanker struggled to 'keep station' off the QE2's flank, 3,834 tons of oil were pumped aboard until the operation was finally halted to prevent further chafing of the fuel hose under such harsh conditions. The QE2 could proceed to Ascension at 25 knots.[231]

On board, the majority of the QE2's 640 'guests' were made comfortable in passenger cabins, with some of the more seriously wounded being cared for in the ship's hospital where medical officers observed that a number of them were 'lucky to be alive.' Many of the others were, however, wary of spending time on the ship's upper decks in the aluminium superstructure, having survived the white-hot conflagrations of alloy upperworks on the Royal Navy ships where they had just survived missile attacks. They asked if they could muster for emergency drills below, rather than in the public rooms, and were advised by Liaison Officer Philip Rentell that this was inadvisable while watertight doors on the lower decks were still being kept closed as a war precaution. After

the names of those killed in action were broadcast by BBC World Service radio, Ted Worsley found himself remembering many of these men and recalling their faces, 'my passengers' as he called them, when seeing their names still neatly lettered on the temporary hardboard, as though upon gravestones, outside the cabins these young soldiers had occupied when sailing south in such high spirits.[232]

As the QE2 made her way north to Ascension, word was received from the Ministry of Defence that, with her trooping mission accomplished, she was no longer needed in the South Atlantic and would best serve the Crown by bringing the survivors and wounded she was carrying directly home to Southampton. Some of the more serious cases were landed at Ascension on Friday 4 June, along with the 25 tons of ammunition still in her hold, before the QE2 set her bows northward again towards her home port of Southampton. As she steamed up The Solent on Friday 11 June, four weeks and two days after she had sailed, the liner received a memorable welcome from HM The Queen Mother, aboard the Royal Yacht Britannia, smiling and waving to those lining the QE2's decks as they acknowledged her good wishes with three resounding cheers.

Later, after everyone had disembarked and the ship was de-stored of all remaining military supplies and materials, the helidecks were removed and her interiors restored and refurbished for peacetime service. The refit was carried out pier-side in Southampton's Western Docks, where she was later joined by the Canberra following her return home on Sunday 11 July.

Among other messages festooned over the Canberra's deck railings, such as ''Allo mum,' 'Lock up your women, the boys are back' and 'Call off rail strike or we call an air strike,' one particularly large banner read 'Canberra cruises where QE2 refuses.' There was some mild resentment within Task Force circles that the Cunard flagship was spared the dangers of going into direct action. Other vessels, such as the Canberra and the Norland, were apparently deemed expendable and sent directly into the line of fire in San Carlos Water, where the Atlantic Conveyer was attacked and her Master, Captain Ian Harry North, was among those killed.

The QE2's refit was primarily remedial, with the

141

*Top and left: The newly-refitted **Queen Elizabeth 2** in her 'post Falklands' guise of pale grey hull and red and black funnel enters New York for the first time upon her return to civilian liner and cruise service. (Gallagher collection)*

Above: The QE2 glides through the English Channel in her new livery. The light hull colour did not flatter her appearance and, worse still, it showed every blemish. (Fotoflite)

most notable exterior changes being that, no doubt much to the chagrin of James Gardner, her funnel was painted in traditional Cunard red and black and her hull a light pebble grey. It is rumoured that the new hull colour was chosen by Cunard's Chairman Lord Matthews who, being an ex-Navy man, thought that his Falklands veteran would look becoming with the hull in a shade close to naval grey. Moreover, now fourteen years old and assumed to be approaching mid-life, it was felt that the ship needed to be re-launched in civilian service with a new identity. Ironically, the pale grey hull colour made the QE2 look middle-aged and portly (it will be remembered that, back in the 1960s, James Gardner had carefully delineated the original charcoal hull livery to avoid this effect). On board, teak decking and railings were replaced, carpets shampooed, artworks reinstated and the Q4 Room, which had been dismantled when the aft helideck was installed, was replaced by a new buffet restaurant called the Club Lido.

During the 1980s, major social shifts brought about by the Harvard Business School-influenced 'free market' economic policies of Margaret Thatcher and Ronald Reagan's Governments created an expanded middle class of prosperous, self-made individuals, anxious to translate their new-found wealth into social status. Whereas modernist design could most obviously be sold on the basis of its newness (and the QE2 was no longer new) a 'retro' experience could be sold on the basis of 'heritage value', however contrived or kitsch. Cunard hoped that, by promoting the QE2 in terms of the Line's 'glorious' past, the upwardly-mobile of 'eighties Britain and America would be attracted to sail trans-Atlantic and to take cruises. Interestingly in this context, Cunard decided to revert to the 1950s advertising slogan 'Getting There is Half the Fun!', which had been primarily associated with the old *Queen Mary* and *Queen Elizabeth*, to promote the 'new' QE2. The liner was beginning her long journey from modernism to 'retro' design, playing upon nostalgia for a 'lost golden age' of liner travel.

As things turned out, the pebble grey only lasted the remainder of the 1982-83 season, as it was found too difficult to keep clean. Unlike the majority of smaller cruise ships then in service, the QE2 still had to be berthed by tugs in New York against the Hudson's strong current, with the constant need for

touching-up of her shell plating above the waterline fore and aft. This situation was particularly evident when the 1983 world cruise was televised on *Whicker's World*.

Apart from scuff marks and rust streaks on the hull, the liner also suffered increasingly from boiler and turbine faults, often setting sail from Southampton under a pall of black smoke which suggested that mechanically all was not well. On Tuesday 7 September 1982, the liner was crippled by a mechanical failure in the English Channel at the

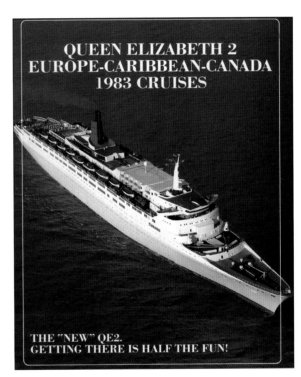

After the Falklands War, Cunard began to re-use their 1950s advertising slogan 'Getting There is Half the Fun!' to promote the renovated QE2. (Bruce Peter collection)

beginning of a voyage to New York. The disabled ship spent four days anchored off Falmouth while repairs were made, with nearly half of the 1,700 passengers aboard eventually being flown to New York at Cunard's expense. With repairs completed, the QE2 got under way again on Friday 10 September, fortunately averting the embarrassment of being passed the following day by the *Canberra*, returning to commercial service following her own post-Falklands refit. A December cruise was cancelled that year as the QE2 experienced more boiler trouble. Later, in June 1983, further mechanical woes led to the abandonment of one short cruise and two Atlantic crossings, costing Cunard £2.5 million in lost revenue, port fees and repair costs. It became evident that the starboard low-pressure turbine would require to be replaced and so the liner was withdrawn for 17 days to allow this work to take place, while she was berthed at Southampton. While this remedial work was being done, the hull was repainted in its original dark charcoal livery – but the red and black 'retro' funnel colours remained.

When the QE2 returned to service, further turbine problems soon began to plague the liner and another return trans-Atlantic voyage was cancelled, adding a further £1 million to Cunard's bill.[233] Finally, on 1 August, she set sail for New York with 1,750 passengers – and performed almost flawlessly. Even so, her machinery required careful nursing and, with the increasingly high fuel bills associated with turbine propulsion, Cunard decided that the liner would require either to be replaced prematurely or to be re-engined as a motor ship. While the former proposal initially was not rejected out of hand, in the summer of 1983 various shipyard representatives surveyed the liner with a view to drawing up a radical conversion plan.

In November 1983 the QE2 was dispatched to the Lloyd Werft shipyard in Bremerhaven for her annual dry-docking – a decision which predictably angered the British press, who indignantly protested that the work ought to have gone to a British yard (even although more than half of the £4.5 million contract's value went to British sub-contractors).[234] Lloyd Werft had an excellent reputation for ship repairs and conversions, notably the recent rebuilding of the *France* to the *Norway*. Apart from giving the QE2 a technical overhaul and repainting, the majority of the work concerned the construction of a retractable 'magradome' glazed roof, enclosing the upper of the two outdoor lido areas. As with the penthouse cabins added to the QE2's superstructure back in 1972, the magradome was entirely pre-fabricated from aluminium alloy and was assembled and tested ashore before being lifted in sections onto the ship.

The idea was to make a space which could, equally, be enjoyed inboard during inclement Atlantic weather and outboard in warmer climes. Home Lines' 1965 *Oceanic* had pioneered the concept and, subsequently,

the 1971-72 *Sea Venture* and *Island Venture* had also been so equipped. Of the new generation of cruise ships, Home Lines' *Atlantic* and DFDS Scandinavian World Cruises' *Scandinavia* also had magradomes. All of these ships sailed regularly from New York and so, clearly, the QE2 required to keep up with best practice. Sheltered from the elements, passengers could enjoy buffet luncheons or lounge around the pool but, with so many hard metal surfaces, such semi-enclosed spaces are very noisy as the sounds of chatter, splashing pool water, plates and cutlery reverberate around. Moreover, although the magradome fitted to the QE2 was designed as carefully as possible, the inevitable replacement of James Gardner's elegantly-tapered windscreens with solid metal plating further compromised the liner's silhouette.

The fact that Trafalgar House was prepared to invest in the QE2 signalled a growing belief in the development of the cruise business. Indeed, the wider industry was equally optimistic about the future and many cruise lines began to order new tonnage.

Instead of doing that, during the spring of 1983 Trafalgar House mounted a hostile bid for another famous British shipping conglomerate, P&O.[235] In total, Trafalgar House owned fifteen ships, including six refrigerated cargo liners that were laid up in Birkenhead Docks. Additionally, it had minority stakes in six Associated Container Transportation (ACT) vessels. P&O, in contrast, consisted of sixty-two ships and, as with Trafalgar House, had a large construction and property development portfolio.[236] Trafalgar House's bid for P&O was planned by Nigel Broackes, who hoped to realise shareholder value by merging the two conglomerates' varied interests. P&O argued that such a merger would not be in the national interest, given that Trafalgar House had a reputation for short-termism and under-investment and would probably require to dispose of P&O assets to finance the takeover. Thus, P&O mounted a robust defence, master-minded by its new Chairman, Sir Jeffrey (later Lord) Sterling, taking out full-page newspaper advertisements to warn investors to 'Stand by to repel boarders.' By the summer of 1983, Trafalgar House's bid had been referred to the Monopolies and Mergers Commission and, as a result of the consequent delay, Broackes lost momentum and Trafalgar House

Top: With her charcoal hull restored and now also sporting a 'magradome' glazed roof over her upper lido area, the **Queen Elizabeth 2** *is seen at Sydney in the mid-1980s. (Gallagher collection)*

Left: An aerial view, showing the QE2's reconfigured aft sun decks with the magradome roof enclosing the upper deck pool. (Gallagher collection)

Above: The magradome in its closed position, viewed from within. A welcome amenity in inclement weather, it was also very noisy as the glass and steel caused sound to reverberate. (Gallagher collection)

145

Above: The **Queen Elizabeth 2** *at Cape Town in the mid-1980s, during a world cruise. The addition of the magradome spoiled the flow of the glazed side screens of her aft decks. (Trevor Jones)*

Below left: The elegant **Sagafjord** *was a fine addition to the Cunard cruise fleet. The liner is shown here at Aruba. (Shawn Dake)*

Below right: While the **Sagafjord** *was mainly American-based, the* **Vistafjord** *tended to cruise from European ports. Here, she is seen in Copenhagen in the mid-1990s. (Bruce Peter)*

withdrew.[237] (Ironically, as we shall see, two decades on both Cunard and P&O Cruises became subsidiaries of the American cruise giant, Carnival Corporation.)Having failed to swallow P&O, Trafalgar House instead consoled itself by winning two notable Norwegian America cruise liners, the *Sagafjord* and the *Vistafjord*, from the Norwegian shipowner Leif Hoegh. Cunard's main luxury cruise rivals, the Royal Viking Line partners, were also strongly interested in the two ships but, eventually, Trafalgar House prevailed and the pair were handed over in October 1983. Their acquisition cost 83 million dollars.[238]

Built in 1965 and 1973 respectively, the *Sagafjord* and *Vistafjord* were, on paper at least, excellent fleet-mates for the QE2. Both were top-rated luxury ships, built for long voyages – but they had a very loyal following of wealthy passengers who booked cruise after cruise and who made it clear to Cunard that they did not want to see the ships changed in any way. Thus, Cunard created a subsidiary called Cunard-Norwegian America to run the pair under the Bahamian flag, but retaining their existing Norwegian officers and European crews.

At around the same time, Cunard won a British Government contract to operate a ferry service from Cape Town in South Africa to Port Stanley in the Falkland Islands, carrying workers and supplies for the construction of a new airport on the Islands. To run this service, Cunard's Cargo Division bought the handsome 19-year-old former DFDS North Sea ferry *England*, bringing the total passenger fleet up to six vessels. Although all were relatively modern and attractive, there were few commonalities between them. The QE2 was unique, being a very large steam turbine ocean liner flying the British flag, whereas the *Sagafjord* and the *Vistafjord* were medium-sized luxury motor ships, run effectively as a separate business, the *Cunard Countess* and the *Cunard Princess* were more 'mass market' cruise ships and the *England* was a small overnight ferry. While all of these ships were lucrative individually, as the cruise industry first rapidly expanded, then consolidated in the 1980s and '90s, Cunard's failure to develop a cohesive fleet under Trafalgar House became increasingly problematic.

Once the *England*'s charter to the Government ended in 1985, Cunard toyed with the idea of converting the ship for cruising, most likely from

Durban and Cape Town. However, increasing international outrage at South Africa's apartheid regime, in the form of trade sanctions, coupled with the *England* having a large number of cabins without private facilities, caused the idea to be abandoned. The vessel was laid up in Birkenhead and sold in early 1986. Cunard were down to five ships – but not for long. At the eleventh hour, the company took on charter a pair of modern and innovative yacht-style cruise ships, the 1984-built *Sea Goddess I* and *Sea Goddess II*. These sleek 4,253grt Norwegian-owned vessels could carry only 116 passengers, each in exclusive luxury, but their owner, A/S Norske Cruise, was on the verge of bankruptcy and it appeared that the shipbuilder, Wärtsilä in Finland, was about to repossess the ships. Indeed, Norway's Royal Viking Line, Cunard's main rival in the luxury cruise market since the early 1970s, had already entered negotiations with Wärtsilä with a view to acquiring the pair when, at the last moment, Cunard stepped in and arranged a charter with the owner, guaranteeing ongoing financial liquidity. As a result, Cunard had a fleet even more mismatched in terms of size and style than ever before. Indeed, the Line published no less than five separate brochures to publicise its various cruise operations.

Meanwhile, the QE2 steamed on as part of the Cunard cruise fleet, yet still very much alone in terms of size, power and *raison d'être*. Since 1983, Cunard had regularly chartered space on Concorde to carry QE2 passengers across the Atlantic, combining a supersonic air journey with a sea voyage in the opposite direction.[239] This winning concept of combining air and sea travel had first been pioneered by Cunard-Eagle Airways and BOAC-Cunard in the early 1960s and, by 1985, Cunard had become the most regular charterer of Concorde, even hiring the 'plane for a unique record-breaking flight to carry QE2 and *Sagafjord* cruise passengers from London to Sydney on 13 February, taking only 17 hours and just under four minutes.[240]

By this point, Lord Matthews had retired as Cunard Chairman, to spend his retirement decade living mainly in the Channel Islands, only returning to the mainland to indulge in his passion for horse racing; he died in 1995. His replacement, Alan Kennedy, was a former submarine commander.

147

CHAPTER 9

FROM STEAM TO DIESEL

BY 1986, the QE2 had clocked up more than 2.6 million nautical miles on her original steam turbine machinery in only seventeen years. This compares with 3.8 million miles logged by the *Queen Mary* during her 31 years of service from 1936 until 1967.[241] The QE2 had been driven much harder to pay her way, with more time spent at sea and port turnarounds reduced to just ten hours. During her early years, the QE2's trans-Atlantic schedule had included a two-day turnaround at Southampton and a full 24 hours in New York, until services were rationalised by Trafalgar House and a ten-hour turnaround was adopted as the standard for both trans-Atlantic and cruise service.[242] By 1986 she was, nonetheless, at about the middle of normal life expectancy for a ship of her type, and still structurally sound enough that she could be maintained to carry on for at least another twenty years. Probably closer to the truth was the fact that the cost of replacing her with a ship of similar performance and individuality was thought to be prohibitive. Moreover, the QE2 had developed a persona among her loyal following and in the eyes of the general public that would be difficult to replicate.

Up to this point, the ship had already undergone a number of refurbishments and refits, keeping her passenger facilities and services up-to-date in comparison with newer purpose-built cruise tonnage. Yet, perhaps the emphasis had been too much on passenger facilities and too little on the machinery. In December 1983, Cunard had invited representatives of several leading shipyards and marine engine manufacturers from Great Britain, Germany, Korea, Japan and The Netherlands to a three-day conference in London for presentation and discussion of an overall specification for a complete re-engining of the QE2. While the participants were given a fairly free hand over the choice of approach in their tenders for the conversion, the winner of the conversion contract would have to demonstrate that their solution would bring no increase in noise and vibration over that of the ship's existing steam turbine machinery. The job also involved further upgrades to the passenger spaces and an extensive revitalisation of galleys and other working areas, officers' and crew accommodation.[243]

Of the three most probable propulsion alternatives, low-speed diesels running at the propeller speed,

which would have been the simplest solution mechanically, were rejected as the engines themselves would be too high, with an inherent need to extend the machinery spaces upwards and resulting in an inevitable loss of revenue-earning cabin space on Five Deck. Medium-speed engines, while being small enough to fit into the existing engine spaces, would have presented complexities with the reduction gearing and clutch mechanisms needed for optimum running, both at 28.5 knots for trans-Atlantic service and at lower cruising speeds. Ultimately, a diesel-electric power-plant installation, with variable-speed drive motors energised from a common power source that would also meet all of the ship's electrical needs, was found to offer the best possible alternative with the greatest degree of flexibility. Only the drive motors would need to be lined up with the propeller shafts, five metres to either side of the centreline and angled downwards towards the stern by 1.5 degrees, leaving the arrangement of the remaining machinery to be determined by the existing spaces that would have to accommodate it. The diesel-electric approach also best suited Cunard's requirements for a system that would offer the greatest fail-safe possibilities, with the diesel alternator sets divided between two separate engine compartments, formed from the original boiler and engine rooms, and with the possibility for the ship to function normally with at least one engine off-line for maintenance or repair at any time.

In the final stages of tendering, after the Japanese and Korean contenders were eliminated and the British and Dutch yards declined to bid as they lacked the expertise and facilities to undertake such a large conversion, competition was reduced to being between three German yards – Howaldtswerke Deutsche Werft (HDW) in Kiel, Blohm + Voss in Hamburg and the Bremerhaven-based Lloyd Werft. HDW eventually declined to bid as they had other major projects scheduled at the time, leaving the final competition to the two remaining yards.[244] A DM 312 million (£180 million) contract was signed with Lloyd Werft on 24 October 1985, the work to commence on 26 October the following year and the QE2 returning to service 179 days later on 25 April 1987.

The yard was subject to stiff penalties at different levels for failure to complete the project as scheduled, and for other deficiencies that might arise from the conversion. These included late delivery of the ship or hand-over with work remaining to be completed, failure to meet the contract speed and exceeding the noise or vibration levels of the ship's existing steam turbine installation. While late delivery was a situation that could always be overcome in time, the issues of performance, noise and vibration could well have been beyond anybody's power to resolve, other than by redoing the whole conversion. This contract was the greatest challenge the yard had ever accepted, yet it was undertaken in a spirit of determination to assert Lloyd Werft's high standing as world-leading specialists in ship repair and conversion work.

Tracing their origins to the Technicher Betrieb (Technical Works), formed in 1886, with its engineering workshops and dry dock, Lloyd Werft's forebears had provided ship maintenance and repair facilities to the North German Lloyd and their affiliates since 1899, when the Kaiserdok at Bremerhaven was completed and first used by the express Atlantic liner *Kaiser Wilhelm II* in 1899. The Technicher Betrieb continued to grow and flourish through the first half of the twentieth century, with ships such as the Blue Riband liners *Kaiser Wilhelm der Grosse*, *Deutschland*, *Bremen* and *Europa* being serviced there, together with other military and civilian ship repair work. The facilities survived fairly well intact through both World Wars. When the North German Lloyd and HAPAG lines were merged, becoming HAPAG-Lloyd in 1970, the yard's name was accordingly changed to Hapag-Lloyd Werft GmbH, with DM 50 million being spent on upgrading of its facilities in Bremerhaven. Later taken over by Bremer Vulkan AG, the name was changed to Lloyd Werft, Bremerhaven GmbH in 1984.

Apart from its wide variety of other work, the yard developed a strong speciality in passenger ship and ferry repair and conversion. The former Moore-McCormack liners *Argentina* and *Brasil* were extensively rebuilt for cruising as Holland America's *Veendam* and *Volendam* in 1972, and the lengthening of the *Royal Viking Star*, *Sea* and *Sky* between 1981 and 1983 was also done there. During the winter of 1979-80, the former *France* underwent what was then the most extensive conversion of its type as she was transformed from an express trans-Atlantic liner into the cruise ship *Norway* at Hapag-Lloyd Werft. The

QE2 would be no stranger to Lloyd Werft, having had her Quarter Deck swimming pool and lido enclosed and covered with a retractable glass roof as a major part of her refit at the German yard in late 1983. During the QE2's re-engining stay in Bremerhaven, she would be accompanied by the *Canberra*, undergoing her annual refit at the same shipyard. Virtually no other yard could support its bid with so great a diversity of experience to undertake such a complex conversion within so short a time-frame.

During those 368 days, from the contract being signed until the QE2's arrival in Bremerhaven, a vast amount of detailed work had to be done in preparation for the conversion. One of the first tasks was to set up project teams to organise and manage this vast project, from the outset of its detailed design and technical planning to programming and scheduling the numerous steps in the conversion processes themselves. Many of these could be done concurrently, while others would be vitally interdependent. Engines, generators, drive motors, propellers and other large specialised items would all have to be ordered well ahead of time, and their deliveries assured to coincide with the times they would be needed at the yard. Steel would need to be purchased and cut ahead of time.

Following a similarly detailed approach to that which went into the ship's original technical planning, a one-twentieth-scale plastic and Plexiglas model was made of the ship's entire engine spaces, including all machinery, equipment, ducts, vents, plumbing, wiring and fittings, right down to the smallest possible details. Coloured plastic was used for the machinery and other components, while the steelwork, including a number of relocated bulkheads, was shown in clear Plexiglas. Detailed isometric drawings were also made for the prefabrication of pipes, ductwork and other services to assist various suppliers with the production of these assemblies beforehand. The objective was to use as much as possible of the 179-day conversion period for the installation of completed systems and assemblies, including the steelwork, directly aboard the ship, rather than for their fabrication at the yard. During her 1986 season, shipyard technicians travelled aboard the QE2 carefully to study and survey those parts of the ship that would be affected and altered during the conversion and to determine

Above: The vast void created in QE2's hull once the boilers, turbines and associated equipment were removed begins to be filled with new steelwork to support her new diesel engines, one of which is being fitted in the background. (Lloyd Werft)

which items of auxiliary equipment could be retained.

As a whole, the conversion was to be a pan-European effort, the engines being built at Augsburg in southern Germany. The nine generators, two propulsion motors and their switchgear would come from Britain, while the propellers were to be made in The Netherlands. Electrical switchboards were to be manufactured in Norway and the engine exhaust gas boilers would come from suppliers in Sweden. Extensive model testing of the new propellers was carried out at the Maritime Research Institute Netherlands (MARIN) tank at Wageningen, about 80 kilometres inland from Rotterdam. As a larger funnel would be needed to carry the exhausts from nine engines, models of the QE2 with a considerably fatter version of Gardner's original design had to be thoroughly wind-tunnel-tested at the Institut für Schifftechnik in Hamburg.[245]

Lloyd Werft's approach – developed in collaboration with the suppliers of the engines, generators, propulsion motors, propellers and various auxiliary systems – was to replace the QE2's existing steam turbine machinery with a modern power station-type diesel-electric generating plant, its primary function being to power the electric motors that drive the propellers. This set-up was precedented by the German Kraft durch Freude cruise ship *Robert Ley* of 1939, the world's first large diesel-electric passenger ship. Subsequently, diesel-electric propulsion had rarely been used for large passenger ships, the Swedish ferries *Visby* and *Gotland* of 1972-73 being among the more prominent examples. After the QE2 conversion, however, diesel-electric became one of the most popular propulsion modes for cruise ships of the 1990s and 2000s.

The generating plant would also distribute electrical power, through step-down transformers and secondary switchboards, to all other ship's services, from large items, such as the steering gear, anti-rolling stabilisers and bow thrusters, through further step-down stages, for ventilation and air conditioning, galleys and laundries, along with all lighting and domestic services right down to the 115-volt shaver sockets in cabin bathrooms. The heart of the installation was an aggregate of nine MAN-B&W

model 9L58/64 9-cylinder medium-speed diesel engines, each one driving a water- and air-cooled brushless GEC synchronous generator yielding 10.625 kilowatts of electricity at 10,000 volts / 60 cycles per second AC (Alternating Current). These were arranged with their generator ends facing one another in two adjacent compartments, with four engines in the forward space and five aft.

Principal users of the maximum 95,625 kW output from all nine generator sets were, of course, the two main propulsion motors, connected by way of the main switchboards from which power was also to be distributed to meet all of the ship's electrical needs. The two 44 megawatt main propeller motors were powered directly from the main switchboard at 10 kilovolts. When running at their full speed of 144 revolutions per minute, these were synchronised to the 60-cycle alternating current frequency of the generators. For start-up and low speed running, motor speed was controlled by synchro-converters that, in effect, converted the 10-kV 60-cycle current from the switchboards to a pulsed variable synthesis of alternating current (AC). By lowering the current's frequency, i.e. its number of cycles per second, the motors could be started without an excessively large initial power surge, and their speed regulated to as little as 72 rpm at an effective power level of around 11 mW at start-up and for manoeuvring runs.[246] With the motor speed controlled by the frequency of its alternating power source, rather than by attenuating the voltage or current, there was no inherent loss of torque at lower speeds.

Another key aspect of the conversion was the installation of new five-bladed controllable-pitch (CP) propellers. The advantage of these, especially in electrically-powered ships, is that a constant shaft speed can be maintained for maximum running efficiency of the drive motors, with the ship's sailing speed being regulated by adjusting the angle (pitch) of the propeller blades. This also aids overall manoeuvrability, providing a more immediate source of reverse power than would otherwise be possible in mechanically-coupled turbine or diesel installations where an auxiliary reverse-power turbine, or reverse gearing, must be engaged. The highly-skewed blade design of the new propellers lowered the exertion of pressure pulses while running, significantly reducing

the level of vibration in the after part of the ship caused by her original six-bladed propellers.[247] Free-spinning vane propellers, known as Grim wheels from their inventor, Professor E.H. Otto Grim of Hamburg, were originally shafted directly aft of the new propellers, designed to harness energy normally lost in the slip-stream and, in effect, give the ship an added push, with a marginal fuel economy of perhaps two to four per cent.[248] While running astern at 19 knots, a number of the blades from these sheered off and the Grim wheels were later removed altogether.[249]

On Monday 20 October 1986, the QE2 sailed from New York to Southampton, making Cunard's last trans-Atlantic crossing under steam and ending a chapter in the history of steam navigation that had begun with the Line's inauguration of regular steamship service. Yet, for the QE2, her conversion and change of designation from SS (steam ship) to MS (motor ship), as diesel-powered ships' names are prefixed, was to signify a new beginning and a life-giving extension of her service career for, at least, another twenty years.

After landing her passengers and de-storing in Southampton, the QE2's arrival in Bremerhaven the following Monday, 27 October, marked the start of a relentless 179-day countdown of her scheduled time in Germany. Rather than being set up in quayside buildings, shipyard and owners' project offices, complete with secretarial and support staff, were located directly aboard the QE2 in the larger cabins on One and Two Decks, taken over and temporarily refurnished for the purpose. This was done to maintain the most immediate exchange of information and highest level of contact with the project's progress. As issues would inevitably arise, effective decisions had to be reached on the spot and work continued without being delayed by formality and bureaucracy. As in the *France*-to-*Norway* conversion and other significant works, this very 'hands-on' management approach supported Lloyd Werft's motto *Vertrauen ist gut, Kontrolle ist besser* (Confidence is good, control is better).[250] Each day, as shipyard workers entered the yard and filed aboard the ship, they passed beneath large notice boards clearly keeping them ever mindful of how many days remained to complete the conversion – 74 DAYS TO

GO - 73 DAYS TO GO – and so on, as the relentless countdown continued.

The Neptune floating oil rig service crane *Hebe 2*, with her jib length of 170 metres and maximum lifting capacity of up to 500 tons, was chartered to help with handling the major items to come off the ship and, later, for the new machinery and equipment that would replace them. For the stripping-out stage, the *Hebe 2* was moored on the outer side of the pier, alongside Graving Dock II where much of the conversion work was done, with her jib able to make the 110-metre reach over the pier and the winter building hall to the QE2, beyond in the graving dock. Two additional cranes, each with an eight-ton lifting capacity for handling smaller items, were installed aboard the ship on platforms erected at Signal Deck level above the outer Boat Deck promenades and lifeboat davits, directly adjacent to the opened boiler casing. A temporary hatch cover was fitted over the casing, so that it could be closed when not being used.

The 12.6 metres of clear fore-and-aft space needed later for lowering the nine engines aboard was created by cutting away five metres of the deck vestibules and stairways, immediately forward of the casing down as far as Two Deck where the casing widened to accommodate the original boiler exhaust uptakes. The drive motors, at 295 tons apiece, and the 220-ton diesels were lifted aboard while the QE2 was afloat at the quayside, with the *Hebe 2* secured closer in and her jib's outreach thereby shortened to about 30 metres, so as to take advantage of the higher lifting power needed to handle these. Handling and positioning of the new machinery inside the QE2's engine spaces was contracted to the Netherlands firm Lastra, which erected special track systems to assist hydraulically with manoeuvring such large and heavy items as these within the confines of the QE2's machinery compartments. Remarkably, an entire truck with a telescopic rotating crane was one of the first items to be lowered aboard. Once the machinery installation and structural work on the exposed uptake shaft was completed, and the crane truck and other handling gear lifted ashore, the exhaust assemblies, of 130 and 140 tons each, and a new funnel were lifted in place with the assistance of the Schuchmann crane *Thor*, with her 85-metre

vertical-lift capability.

The re-engining also entailed a considerable amount of structural work throughout the 67-metre stretch of the QE2's lower decks (between hull frames 105 and 178) that had been her original three machinery compartments. After the steam machinery and its supporting structures were stripped out, the ship was in a fragile state, with all three compartments laid open where bulkheads were to be relocated and other supporting elements rearranged to accommodate the new machinery. Once the foundation structures for the drive motors and the vibration-absorbing resilient diesel engine mountings were complete, the machinery could be manoeuvred into position and the new bulkheads and other supporting pieces erected as this progressed. Where the original turbine, boiler and auxiliary spaces had occupied three adjacent watertight compartments of similar length, the re-engined spaces were divided into two main diesel alternator rooms. Each was 20 metres in length, with smaller compartments aft for the drive motors. Auxiliary machinery was located below and the new engine control room was above on Seven Deck.

Thanks to the relatively low headroom needed for the diesel alternator sets, a heat- and sound-absorbing shell was fitted above and around the engine spaces up to the ceiling level of Seven Deck. Above this, the uptakes from all nine engines, along with the exhaust-gas-heated boilers, silencers and other equipment, were housed inside a rigid metal framework that was resiliently mounted inside the QE2's original boiler casing in such a way that there was a mere 'hand's breadth' of 80 mm between this and the ship's structures, so as to avoid exhaust noise and vibration being transmitted to the passenger spaces and decks. Fabricated in two parts beforehand, with all its pipework and tubing already installed, this looked something like a rocket launching gantry from Cape Canaveral as it was lowered into the ship's boiler casing in two parts, with the apparent ease of a lady's lipstick being slipped into its case. These same exhausts brought about the need for a funnel of considerably greater girth. While the overall concept of the tall exhaust pipe, air uptakes cowl and wind scoop was retained, its original slender form thus acquired a considerable middle-aged spread. With a continuation of the original funnel's effectiveness, assured by the wind-tunnel testing carried out beforehand in Hamburg, its broader form had, in effect, grown into the traditional Cunard colours, first added in the ship's post-Falklands refurbishment.

The one aspect of the QE2's conversion where there was no way to determine the extent of work involved beforehand was for repairs needed to the superstructure. During the seventeen years the ship had already been in service, the superstructure had begun to show signs of fatigue from its alternate function as a load- and stress-bearing counterpoint to the hull. The aluminium alloy had weakened and cracked, especially from the corners of the forward-and aft-most large Quarter and Upper Deck windows where bending and twisting strains of the ship's movement had the greatest effect. While, to some degree, these stresses were anticipated in the spacing of large openings fore and aft of the web-frames and in their shape, with widely-rounded corners and bowed edges top and bottom, sustained seasonal

trans-Atlantic service had apparently taken a greater toll than perhaps anticipated. A proposal to retrofit expansion joints in the superstructure shell was ruled out, with the damaged plating being reinforced and new windows fitted, adding about 60 tons of alloy.

The conversion time-frame was also taken as an opportunity further to refit and upgrade the passenger accommodation. Structurally, this involved adding eight more de luxe penthouse veranda suites lifted atop Signal Deck in two already-built and completely-outfitted aluminium deckhouse sections, filling a remaining space between the existing penthouses and the funnel's base structure.

During the re-engining, the liner's interiors were also refurbished – but mainly in insipid pastel shades, typical of the 1980s, enlivened here and there by occasional Art Deco flourishes. These alterations reflected the fact that, during the latter 1970s and '80s, modernist aesthetics of the kind favoured in the 1960s had gradually fallen out of fashion. Partly, this change in public perception can be accounted for by the cycle of taste but, undoubtedly, it was also an

Above: Viewed from behind a mound of scrap steel removed from the QE2's engine room, the liner has reached the stage of having her new funnel fitted. Note also the additional penthouse cabins. (Gallagher collection)

Top left: During the winter of 1986-87, the conversion of the QE2 from steam to diesel made rapid progress. Surrounded by icy water and shrouded in canvas sheets, work continued practically 24 hours a day. (Lloyd Werft)

Left and above: The liner looks rather strange with the new exhaust pipes for her diesel plant exposed to view. This structure was pre-fabricated and lifted aboard with great precision by crane. (Lloyd Werft)

Below: Once the new, broader funnel was lifted in place, the QE2 looked much better. In this scene from early 1987, there remained a great deal of fitting-out work to be completed. (Lloyd Werft)

indirect consequence of intrusive (and sometimes corrupt) redevelopment on *terra firma*, coupled with the apparent failure of large-scale social housing schemes, ruining the image of modernism in architecture and design as a whole. Meanwhile, a growing conservation body positively revelled in the design forms which the modernists hated – namely eclectic Victoriana and Art Deco.

Moreover, modernism of the variety originally applied to the QE2 required to remain uncluttered by subsequent additions and existing fittings to be replaced with exact replicas in order to retain the intended visual effects and colour palettes. Over the years, the QE2's interiors had, instead, been compromised by successive changes, meaning that much of their original *élan* had already been lost. Besides, notwithstanding the Council of Industrial Design's apparent belief that an understanding of modernist design as being 'good' was a universal 'given', in reality any such appreciation actually required a certain level of visual literacy and aesthetic sophistication on the part of users. Many passengers, who had probably paid above the odds to sail on the QE2, simply could not understand why 'less' was in any way 'more', and thus the liner was found to be insufficiently ornate to meet the expectations of popular bourgeois taste in the 1980s. Consequently, during the ensuing decade Cunard expended a great deal of money and effort to make the ship better reflect the preconceptions and aspirations of the majority of passengers who now apparently wished to wallow in nostalgia, enjoying a romanticised version of Cunard liners of the past, albeit while benefiting from the latest technology and servicing.

Viewed in the context of the QE2's design history and ownership, it was, however, ironic that the ship should be progressively retro-styled to emulate the Art Deco 'golden age' of liner travel. Only twenty years previously, Cunard had proudly trumpeted the demise of that very style, declaring of their existing Art Deco fleet that 'Ships Have Been Boring Long Enough.' More poignantly, in 1980, Cunard's parent company Trafalgar House had bought the famous Firestone Factory which was a landmark on London's Great Western Road. Designed by Wallis, Gilbert & Partners and completed in 1928, it had arguably boasted England's finest Art Deco façade. Over the

August Bank Holiday weekend in 1980, the new owner carried out a sudden demolition before the building could be listed, clearing the site for a property development. It was a cynical act of vandalism and, evidently, Trafalgar House's senior management had instructed that the fine tiled entrance portico should be destroyed first.

In contrast to Cunard's many alterations to the QE2 since the early 1970s, Holland America Cruises had been scrupulous in maintaining their 1959 flagship, the *Rotterdam*, in immaculate original condition, carefully replacing worn items with exact replicas of the initial designs. Right until the end of the *Rotterdam*'s cruising career in 2000, in fact, the liner remained a beautiful showcase of 1950s Dutch design expertise and shipbuilding craftsmanship whereas, by the latter 1980s, the QE2's equally distinctive 1960s modernism was increasingly compromised by subsequent changes. Yet, the *Rotterdam* retained a very loyal following right until the end, largely on account of her unique style. Perhaps these differing approaches can be attributed to wider cultural differences between Holland America's genteel respect for the past and Trafalgar House's more aggressively short-termist business methodology. Maybe also the *Rotterdam*'s less radical 1950s modernity, with its extensive usage of real wood veneers, withstood the cycle of taste better than the QE2's original snazzy 'Swinging London' look. (Indeed, one may speculate that, in the mid-1960s, Lady Brocklebank and Sir Hugh Casson perhaps imagined that the Cunard flagship would have been similar to the *Rotterdam* or the *Canberra* in terms of onboard style).

A 16-metre superstructure extension, aft on Boat Deck, provided for an expanded shopping arcade at the original Double Room's upper level, featuring fashion boutiques for Louis Feraud, Louis Vuitton, Christian Dior, Dunhill, Gucci, Bally and others. Pompously renamed the Grand Lounge, the Double Room itself was reworked by the architect Iain Pattie in an effort to turn it into a suitable venue for cabaret entertainment. Pattie was a London-based Scot who had graduated from Dundee in the early 1970s and who subsequently established himself in the capital, specialising in international hotel and hospitality design – a fast-growing business in the 'seventies and

157

'eighties. Interestingly, all subsequent major interior refitting work on the QE2 was undertaken by London Scots – namely Alex McCuaig of Met Studio and John McNeece.

Unfortunately, Bannenberg's magnificent curved staircase was sacrificed to increase the size of the stage and replaced by two quadrant stairways, bracketing an enlarged, though still hopelessly inadequate, replacement of the room's original bandstand at the forward end. Although this achieved a significant improvement to the room's terraced seating and sightlines towards the entertainment, the whole stage arrangement was reworked seven years later in the 'Project Lifestyle' refit of 1994, with Pattie's quadrant stairways scrapped altogether in favour of a wider proscenium stage with small dressing areas for players worked into its wings.

The original Double Down Bar, aft on Upper Deck, was expanded, becoming the Yacht Club, with a wave-effect slatted ceiling and the addition of a Shimmel Perspex piano with a bar surround and high stools. The room was extended into the enclosed promenade space aft, and connected at either side directly to the indoor circulating promenades. The aft foyer spaces thus became redundant and were converted into a Teen Club, with large-screen TV and video games, to starboard, and an Adult Club, set up as a reading and card room with table-top games, to port. These two rooms were designed also to use their adjacent promenade spaces as part of the activities they hosted, and to integrate closely with the Yacht Club as an overall family recreation area where people of all ages could feel welcome. The outdoor sports deck, aft of these, was equipped with what was claimed to be the first automatic golf simulator to be installed aboard a ship.

On Quarter Deck, the Queen's Room was refurbished with the original wood-blocked end bulkheads being redone in lighter veneers. While the original Michael Inchbald furniture was becoming chipped and worn, its replacement with Le Corbusier/Charlotte Perriand 'Petit Comfort' leather and chrome cube chairs – in what was described as adding an 'interesting contrast' to the room's existing curvilinear trumpet columns and latticed ceiling – was an unfortunate misfit. [251] Like the Grand

Lounge's quadrant stairways, these too were ditched at the next refit opportunity. What was originally the Britannia Restaurant, latterly known as the Tables of the World, was changed yet again to the Mauretania Restaurant and decorated in 1920s *jazz moderne* style. Unfortunately, this had to be divided into two separate fire zones with the addition of a solid bulkhead which followed the line of an existing web-frame, dividing the room's aft-most alcoves. Throughout the ship, furniture and carpets were replaced, mainly in rather bland 1980s pastel shades.

As part of an extensive modernisation of all catering facilities throughout the ship, the buffet areas in the Club Lido, aft on Quarter Deck, were greatly expanded to make the area more flexible as an informal food service facility, especially popular for breakfast and lunch-time dining, as well as for the midnight buffet. Other work included renewal of soft furnishings in all passenger cabins and modernisation of the crew accommodation. The new arrangement of exhaust uptakes and engine-room ventilation shafts allowed for the inclusion of a lift-shaft in the original engine casing, at long last providing the QE2's engineers with direct lift access from their accommodation on Signal Deck to the upper reaches of the machinery spaces on Six Deck, without having to pass through other parts of the ship.

Extensive sea trials were run from 8 to 15 April 1987, during which the new machinery was put to the test, technical adjustments made and the computerised control systems that would ensure the whole ship's efficient operation in service were commissioned. Measured mile runs were made in the Skagerrak, with a maximum ahead speed of 33.1 knots recorded, corrected to 31.9 knots with allowances made for the prevailing weather. The QE2's new controllable-pitch propellers, and the automation used to control them, showed better manoeuvring capabilities than she was capable of before the conversion. The ship could make a full stop from a speed of 30 knots in only 3 minutes and 38 seconds over a distance of only 1.2 statute miles, and could reach a maximum speed of 19 knots going astern in an additional 12 minutes, going faster that way than many ships can proceed ahead at full speed. With her original machinery, the QE2 had taken 6 minutes 10 seconds, over a distance of 1.7

The new funnel is carefully lowered into position, already fully painted in Cunard colours. (Gallagher collection)

Top left and left: In the public rooms and cabins, a great deal of work was undertaken. Here, the new Grand Lounge, filling the space previously occupied by the Double Room, is being assembled with the frames for an expanded shopping arcade taking shape at its Boat Deck level. (Iain Pattie)

Above: In everyday service, QE2's passengers are used to experiencing an immaculate ship. During complex refitting work, the scene is more one of organised chaos. In the after end of one of the liner's Upper Deck arcades, rolls of carpet await installation. (Iain Pattie)

Below: With the wall panelling already in place, electrical work is completed before the suspended ceiling is installed in the Grand Lounge. Modern passenger vessels contain great complexities of hidden servicing. (Iain Pattie)

statute miles, to make a full stop from 30 knots. A sustained 12-hour run at her 28.5-knot trans-Atlantic service speed indicated fuel consumption to be significantly reduced to 295 tons per 24 hours. A further reason for keeping the ship at sea for a week was to ensure that contract workers – who were consequently trapped on board – exerted themselves as hard as possible to complete as much of the interior outfitting as they could without being tempted by the distractions of night life ashore. This was only partially achieved, however, as subsequent events showed.

The entire conversion and re-engining were enormous technological successes. This was especially significant for the shipbuilding industry as cruise lines such as Royal Caribbean and Vlasov-owned Sitmar were beginning to construct larger cruise ships in tonnage ranges that had once been exclusively in the domain of express North Atlantic and colonial liners. The commercial potential for such large ships in full-time cruise service, albeit at speeds typically of less than 20 knots, had already been abundantly proven with Lloyd Werft's earlier *France*-to-*Norway* conversion. Carnival's 70,367-ton *Fantasy*, delivered in 1990 as the first of an eight-ship series, used diesel-electric propulsion, following the precedent of the re-engined QE2 though controlled by the simpler synchro-converter system, thought to be more suitable for Carnival's sedate speed of operation. Apart from saving fuel, another great advantage of diesel-electric propulsion for passenger ships is far greater redundancy than with a steam turbine plant, or a direct-drive diesel installation. When, in June 1992, the QE2 suffered a severe breakdown of one of her diesel engines, which seized and fractured, the liner did not immediately have to be withdrawn from service as the remaining engines allowed her to maintain her scheduled speed. Indeed, the damaged engine was not replaced until January 1993.

As the major cruise companies inevitably progressed to larger ships with greater operating ranges and more speed and flexibility of service, diesel-electric propulsion generally became the mode of choice, with synchro-conversion chosen as the preferred means of controlling motor speeds. In some instances, including Celebrity's *Millennium* class,

the diesel has given way to the aviation-style gas turbine as a power source for generating electricity. Cunard's new *Queen Mary 2* uses a hybrid combination of both diesel and gas turbine power to fulfil the diverse needs of both her trans-Atlantic and world cruising roles.

After being handed back to Cunard in Bremerhaven on 25 April 1987, the QE2 set sail for Southampton, achieving a remarkable 33.8 knots *en route*. After festivities in her home port, including a visit by HRH The Princess of Wales, she departed for New York on her first trans-Atlantic crossing as a motor ship. The voyage was not without its problems as some interior refitting work was incomplete, with the result that shipyard workers had to sail with the ship, and many new and unfamiliar hotel staff were still being trained, meaning that the onboard service was often patchy and certainly not of the usual high Cunard standard.[252] Bryan Appleyard, reporting for *The Times*, observed:

'It is impossible to find an American who does not feel that Cunard has violated his constitutional rights, while the Brits just murmur bitterly into the ear of every passing officer. Orange-overalled workmen of every conceivable nationality are constantly removing panels to fiddle with pipes and wires, and the condition of the lowest-class decks, in the bowels of the ship, has to be seen to be believed. By Friday, every news service in the world was calling the ship about the 'disastrous' maiden voyage. The best were the German radio stations - 'Iss eet troo ze Cherman shipyard wass to blame?' The company line was that it was nobody's fault, and it was getting better all the time. Press officers had been scouring the ship to find contented passengers to talk to the BBC… In fact, a general wave of 'We're all in this together' feeling had swept over the ship. Crew and passengers were moaning together, while sunshine and an exceptionally calm sea had begun to introduce a degree of euphoria. Even the joke about Fawlty Towers afloat was now being cracked by staff members as well.'[253]

The main reason for this latter problem was that Cunard had decided to break what it saw as the stranglehold of the National Union of Seamen by sacking 800 hotel and catering staff and offering to re-employ them via an external contractor on lower pay rates. Although around three-quarters reluctantly accepted this deal, despite strong union objections, the situation was bad for morale. Nonetheless, by employing more 'international' staff at lower pay, Cunard were merely following standard practice throughout the cruise industry. With her 'retro' styling and lower-wage crew, the QE2 had gone from being a modernist liner to a post-modern ship, selling a romanticised view of Cunard's past, albeit in the context of the social and fiscal realities of 1980s free market economics.

The liner arrived in New York on 4 May, welcomed with fire-fighting tugs spraying red, white and blue jets of water into the air, and by the Mayor, Ed Koch, who attended a gala luncheon in the new Mauretania Restaurant.

Between late March and early June 1989, the QE2 was temporarily withdrawn from cruise service for a special charter to the Japanese city of Yokohama, which was celebrating the 130th anniversary since its foundation and required extra up-market hotel capacity. The QE2 was berthed in the city for seventy-two days, filling the slot in the liner's cruise calendar normally occupied by the annual world cruise; instead, a one-off cruise voyage from Los Angeles to Yokohama via Australia was offered. The charter fee was £250,000 per day, meaning that a great many visitors would have to spend a lot of money to recoup the cost of the operation. Although 69,000 people stayed overnight, and a further 180,000 day visitors dined and shopped on board, the project still lost the charterer money – but was lucrative for Cunard, earning the Line £18 million in fees.

Following this success, Cunard secured a second, longer charter for the first six months of 1990. A consortium of Japanese businesses had joined forces to hire the ship, to act not only as a hotel and convention centre at the World Exposition in Osaka but also to undertake a series of ten short cruises to Hong Kong and other nearby ports. Again, the fee was £250,000 per day – and this netted Cunard £50 million. A third Japanese charter was mooted for 1991, bringing about speculation that Cunard might withdraw the liner from trans-Atlantic service altogether. After all, such charters might be lucrative but, in removing the ship from service, the regular

business of the line was disrupted and frequent passengers might have begun to transfer their loyalty elsewhere. Hence there were no subsequent charters of this kind and, thereafter, the QE2 remained constantly and successfully in liner and cruise service.

In July 1990 the QE2 made a series of commemorative voyages to celebrate the 150th anniversary of the first ever sailing by Cunard's pioneering trans-Atlantic mail steamer *Britannia* in 1840. On 17 July, the QE2 sailed eastbound from New York in four days, six hours and 57 minutes at an average speed of 30.16 knots – her fastest ever Atlantic crossing.[254] Next, she sailed from Southampton on a five-day cruise to Cobh, Liverpool, Greenock and Cherbourg. At Cobh, her arrival coincided with the opening of a new ro-ro cargo terminal, where she berthed and entertained the Irish Taoiseach, Charles Haughey, to luncheon. Huge crowds gathered to watch her leave and an estimated one million spectators gathered in Liverpool as she motored slowly up the Mersey the next day, anchoring opposite the Cunard Building. That evening, a special fireworks display rounded off a memorable visit. At Greenock, more large crowds assembled on the promenade and, on board, a large group of pensioners from the John Brown shipyard toured 'their' ship and enjoyed lunch. After a brief call at Cherbourg on 26 July, the QE2 headed for Spithead, where she anchored the following day. There, she was joined by the *Vistafjord* and by the modern ro-ro container vessel *Atlantic Conveyor*, a replacement for the ship of the same name which had been lost in the Falklands War. All three Cunarders were to take part in a special commemorative Royal Review of Cunard and Navy ships by HM The Queen and HRH The Duke of Edinburgh. Surrounded by yachts, pleasure craft and sightseeing excursion boats, HMY *Britannia* left Portsmouth, accompanied by the Trinity House Vessel *Patricia* and by the Type 22 frigate HMS *Broadsword*. Even British Airways joined in the salute to Cunard for 150 years of Atlantic crossings, sending a Concorde, a 747 and a 767 from Heathrow to make a special fly-past. Then, The Queen and The Duke of Edinburgh transferred to the QE2 by Royal Barge, while the assembled ships dispersed, and the Royal Party returned to Southampton aboard the

Top: The refurbished Queen's Room, showing the contrast between Michael Inchbald's original ceiling design and the newly installed 'Petit Comfort' chairs. (Shippax Archive)

Left: The completed Grand Lounge, looking towards the enlarged bandstand and the new staircases. In comparison with Jon Bannenberg's treatment of the Double Room, the space is somewhat bland in character, reflecting the 1980s fashion for pastel shades. (Bruce Peter collection)

Above: The new Yacht Club, showing the wavy ceiling and the perspex grand piano. (Bruce Peter collection)

*Above: Fresh from re-engining, the **Queen Elizabeth 2** looks majestic as she motors through the English Channel. (Fotoflite)*

liner which was newly under the command of Captain Ronald Warwick, the son of William Warwick who had stood by the liner while under construction and had commanded her during her first years in service. This short voyage was actually the first time that The Queen had sailed on the QE2 and the whole day, which was rounded off with another firework display, brought excellent publicity to Cunard and further enhanced the QE2's increasingly prominent position as a media icon.

For her annual refit in December 1990, Cunard sent the ship to Blohm + Voss in Hamburg, one of the unsuccessful bidders for the 1987 re-engining contract. There, a new grill room was constructed in space formerly occupied by part of the Columbia Restaurant on the starboard side of Quarter Deck. Seating only 106, this meant that the liner now had five restaurants, four of which were First Class and three of which were also grill rooms. The casino and Club Lido were refurbished and, predictably, all three spaces were decorated in a pseudo-1930s style by Graham Fahye, a hotel interior designer who had previously worked for Hilton in the Middle East.

This meant that yet more bespoke original fittings were consigned to skips, to be replaced by generic 'catalogue' items of the type used in countless chain hotels the world over. Of course, the modern requirement for fireproofing, which had led to the QE2 being finished largely in synthetic materials in the first place, meant that the new 'retro' Art Deco spaces required to be panelled in fake wood veneers, which could never emulate the lustre and fine craftsmanship of the *Queen Mary* or the *Queen Elizabeth*.

Meanwhile, Trafalgar House itself was fragmenting, with serious losses in its engineering and construction divisions. The cruise division was also suffering reduced profits as a result of the Gulf War – and so the troubled conglomerate decided to cut costs wherever it could. Having demolished unionised British labour in the hotel and catering departments, it emerged in August 1991 that Cunard were planning to replace 140 British deck and engine room crew with contract labour. This caused political outrage and provoked Labour's transport spokesman, John Prescott, himself a former Cunard steward and National Union of Seamen agitator, to accuse the Line of showing 'contempt for taxpayers who subsidise its vessels', continuing that the removal of British seafarers from the QE2 would be 'the final nail in the coffin of British merchant shipping.'[255] Cunard protested, once again, that they were merely following standard international practice in the wider cruise industry and, of course, John Major's Conservative Government did not intervene, insisting that this was a matter for Cunard to resolve.

In early August 1992 the QE2 had been scheduled to make a cruise from New York to Bermuda, but this had to be cancelled when Cunard failed to achieve the necessary licences from the Bermudan authorities. Instead, the liner was rescheduled to undertake a short cruise to St John's, Newfoundland and Martha's Vineyard. Unfortunately, after sailing from the island on the evening of 7 August, the QE2 grounded on a reef. An experienced US pilot, Captain John F. Hadley, was on the bridge with Captain Robin Woodall and his officers. The liner was being navigated with great care to avoid the

shallowest waters. Even so, once clear of the many small craft around Martha's Vineyard, the speed was increased to 25 knots and, some time later, two serious bouts of vibration were felt throughout the ship. At first, the officers thought that this was due to a mechanical problem but, actually, the QE2 had touched the bottom, causing extensive damage to the hull. Although the chart had suggested that there was sufficient depth, when a ship sails at speed the displacement causes a 'bowl' to be created in the water around the hull, lowering the ship and reducing the depth below the keel. In shallow water this phenomenon, known as the 'squat effect', is intensified.

When oil pollution was sighted around the ship, the Captain immediately informed the US Coast Guard, who sent out a boarding party in the early hours of the morning and an oil protection boom was put in place. The next day, it was decided that the passengers would have to disembark by tender, returning by train and bus to New York, and once flood water had been pumped overboard under

Another fine view of the renovated liner in the English Channel in her 1987 'maiden season' as a motor ship. The addition of blocks of penthouses to her upper decks in 1972, 1977 and 1987, as well as satelite beacons, has greatly changed her appearance. (Fotoflite)

165

Coast Guard supervision the stricken liner proceeded to Boston, to be dry-docked by the General Ship Corporation for a survey and temporary repairs.[256] It was only then that the true extent of the damage to the hull was realised, with an area of keel plating 125 metres long by 25 metres wide gouged, dented, buckled and fractured and severe damage to the port bilge keel. Indeed, it was remarked that the mightily robust double-bottomed hull construction had saved the liner from being declared a Constructive Total Loss and that, in similar circumstances, a lesser

HRH Princess Diana is escorted into the Grand Lounge during a children's party in Southampton prior to the first trans-Atlantic crossing under diesel power. (Bruce Peter collection)

cruise ship would probably have been written off.

The Boston yard had neither the manpower nor the materials to carry out permanent repairs and so, after the QE2 had been patched up, she set sail for Blohm + Voss in Hamburg, returning to Southampton on 3 October. During the summer, the liner had missed nine Atlantic crossings and two cruises. Two months later, she was back at Blohm + Voss for her scheduled annual overhaul, at which time yet more internal changes took place, involving the creation of a new health spa in the former Six and Seven Deck gymnasium and indoor pool spaces

and the retro-styling of the Midships Lobby, which was over-laid in synthetic burled walnut. On the technical side, a damaged engine was replaced.

In 1993, Cunard expanded their cruise fleet by chartering three recently-constructed vessels from the Swedish-Finnish Effjohn International subsidiary, Commodore Cruise Line. Effjohn was a shipping conglomerate, formed through the amalgamation of the Finland Steamship Company (EFFOA) and the Stockholm-based Johnson Line. Although its core activity was the operation of large cruise ferries in the Baltic Sea, carrying Swedes and Finns *en masse* on short tax-free shopping and drinking trips, it had inherited the US-based Commodore and Crown Cruise Lines through the Johnson Line business, as well as cargo liner services from Sweden to South American ports. The *Crown Monarch* (built 1990), *Crown Jewel* (1992) and *Crown Dynasty* (1993) were medium-sized, Spanish-built vessels of fairly insubstantial construction and all three were taken under charter by Cunard in 1993, being marketed principally in the United States. Later, in 1994, Cunard purchased the one remaining member of the Royal Viking Line fleet, the top-rated *Royal Viking Sun*, for 170 million dollars, along with rights to use the 'Royal Viking' brand name. Built by Wärtsilä in Finland in 1988, the *Royal Viking Sun* certainly was a fine cruise ship but, yet again, there appeared to be few synergies with Cunard's many other vessels and cruise brands. Certainly, the *Royal Viking Sun* was very different in appearance and style from the graceful *Sagafjord* and *Vistafjord* but, equally, a far superior ship to the three chartered from Commodore. Of course, she had even less in common with the QE2 and this situation of speculative chance investments, without any apparent deeper strategy, was reflected right across all of Trafalgar House's business areas. Sir Nigel Broackes, the Trafalgar House Chairman was, it seemed, to investors, more enthused by the thrill of acquiring businesses than by taking the trouble to devise a structured and stable long-term business strategy.[257]

In 1993, 26% of Trafalgar House's shares were bought by Hong Kong Land Co, a subsidiary of the prosperous Jardine, Matheson & Company, belonging to the Keswick family. Hong Kong Land quickly ousted Broackes as Chairman, replacing him with their own Alan Clements. Yet, Clements struggled to make sense of Trafalgar House's sprawling business empire and, within a year, Nigel Rich became Chief Executive Officer, accusing Trafalgar's previous management of 'inadequate leadership' and 'weak financial disciplines.'[258]

Cunard soldiered on against this rather unsettled corporate background. The *Crown Monarch* was sold by Effjohn to Far East interests in 1994 and the *Crown Jewel* and *Crown Dynasty* left the fleet in 1995 and 1997 respectively. With the sale of the *Cunard Princess* in 1995 and of the *Cunard Countess* in 1996, this meant that Cunard were down to only four large-ish cruise ships at a time when the wider industry was expanding aggressively. In particular, two mass market cruise corporations – Carnival and Royal Caribbean – were beginning to expand apace from their initial Caribbean territories, fuelled by the 1990s economic boom and able to purchase brand-new fleets of glittering, economy-of-scale tonnage. When Norwegian Caribbean's SS *Norway* had re-entered service in 1980, following conversion from the *France*, the QE2 had been knocked into second

place in terms of size, if not reputation. Since the latter 1980s, practically every new Carnival and Royal Caribbean cruise ship had been considerably bigger than the Cunard flagship and neither Cunard nor Trafalgar House appeared to have foreseen this situation, which had been predicted by cruise industry analysts. Although Cunard was one of the most famous names in cruising – and ought, by rights, to have been a leading player in the 1990s – in reality the Line was contracting and, apart from the *Royal Viking Sun*, possessed an ageing fleet, unchanged since 1983. Carnival, in contrast, had started out with a mature fleet in the early 1970s but, by the 1990s, was leading the industry with a massive new building programme.

The best Cunard could do was to give their flagship, the QE2, a further refurbishment. This undertaking was code-named 'Project Lifestyle' and was initially developed by Met Studio, a London-based corporate design agency without any existing experience of shipboard design. The firm was commissioned because its founder, Alex McCuaig, was an acquaintance of Cunard's recently-appointed

The QE2 is manoeuvred by tugs in the Hudson River in New York at dusk in November 1987 at the commencement of another voyage. (Andrew Kilk)

Moran tugs guide the QE2 to her Manhattan berth in this classic New York scene. (Andrew Kilk)

*The **Queen Elizabeth 2** at anchor in the River Mersey during a visit to Liverpool. The ferry **Royal Iris** is carrying sightseers. (Richard Danielson)*

Chairman, John Olsen. Olsen had come to the Line from the Cathay Pacific airline, for whose parent company, the Swire Group, Met Studio had previously carried out design work. Cunard's wider management, allegedly, were sceptical about Met Studio's ability to oversee a major and complex refurbishment without specialist knowledge and so Olsen was persuaded to team McCuaig up with the cruise ship interior designer John McNeece, who had recently designed and supervised renovations of the *Cunard Countess* and the *Cunard Princess*. (It will also be remembered that McNeece had been suggested by the Council of Industrial Design as a potential interior designer for the Q4 in early 1965). The contract was to be split fifty-fifty between the two firms, with Met Studio producing the overall theme and rationale for the renovation and McNeece's company creating a planning strategy, detailed designs and assisting with the application of the relevant SOLAS (Safety Of Life At Sea) regulations.

With the QE2 now successfully operating as a motor ship and with a cheaper 'international' crew, the entry level prices of sailing on the liner had not greatly increased for a decade, whilst the top penthouse suites remained the preserve of the seriously wealthy; a far broader social range of 'guests' was now to be found on board than when the

ship had originally been conceived and, furthermore, throughout the wider cruise industry, lower brochure prices were being offset by more aggressive generation of onboard revenue through the prominent placement of bars, shops and casinos (a situation which had mandated the QE2's initial 1972 refit). Thus, the concept of 'adjacencies' – meaning the careful placement of retail outlets to generate 'synergetic' revenue-gathering effects – had become industry jargon informing modern cruise ship planning, and McNeece was a leading expert in this particular field.

With McNeece mainly in a technical support role, Alex McCuaig prepared an overall concept for the projected QE2 refurbishment, and this was unveiled to Trafalgar House's directorate in February 1994. This sought to 'research into expectation levels of the existing customer mix' and to 'identify the shortfall in delivery measured against the above.' The resulting plan was 'to create a new cohesive flow pattern through the ship to bind together the various individual treatments and to produce a manageable new *lifestyle* on the ship from which important commercial advantages will ensue' – 1990s 'corporate speak' for bringing a semblance of visual coherence while extracting more money from passengers without them noticing.[259] It was estimated that a thorough-going refurbishment of the QE2's passenger areas would cost in the region of £40 million, over and above the £4.7 million needed for a standard scheduled overhaul.

The document explained to Trafalgar House that 'the creation and delivery of new expectations will centre around the definition of an onboard quality lifestyle. By drawing together and extending the QE2's heritage and unique characteristics, this lifestyle will emerge… The design will allow the unique aspects of the QE2 product experience to be enhanced and then provide a basis for a strong product-orientated message to the market.'[260] To achieve this somewhat vague and ambiguous aim, Met Studio proposed to create an 'unspoken aspirational hierarchy' across the three main public room decks. In reality, what this translated into was the careful gradation of activities in terms of their relative 'exclusivity' and 'sophistication.' The idea was to achieve the most effective 'adjacencies' to encourage greater onboard spending by passengers. Boat Deck was to house the most up-market spaces, with those on Upper Deck and Quarter Deck being more populist. Ironically, this was a partial reversal of the QE2's original planning strategy which, from the outset, had the most exclusive accommodation on Quarter Deck and the shops, discotheque and teenage areas on Boat Deck, where any rolling motion would be slightly accentuated due to the height above the water.

Otherwise, the plan involved a further dismantling of remaining elements of the original 1960s design and their replacement with as seamless a *homage* to the 1930s as Trafalgar House's shrinking budget would allow. For example, Met Studio's report criticised the circular Midships Lobby – a space praised by *The Architectural Review* in 1969 for its 'stunning effect' – for failing 'to achieve a dramatic entry signature' and proposed cutting a void to the deck above, making a double-height atrium space. The Queen's Room, apparently, 'lacked the elegant ambience appropriate to its name and location and will be redecorated to emphasise the royal heritage of the *Queens* (meaning, presumably, the *Queen Mary* and *Queen Elizabeth*). Furthermore, Gaby Schreiber's double-height Theatre auditorium was to be split horizontally with a large casino in the stalls and a smaller auditorium on Boat Deck, above. The QE2's remaining genuine 'heritage and unique characteristics' were thus to be trashed in order to achieve the aim of emphasising these very aspects.

Perhaps fortunately, the budget for the 'Project Lifestyle' refit was slashed to £32 million, meaning that the most ambitious elements, described above, were to remain unrealised. Moreover, Alex McCuaig and John McNeece – both of whom were strong-minded – allegedly had a rather strained working relationship, the latter finding the former to be 'unnecessarily aggressive and with an unfortunate tendency to use coarse language.'[261] Additionally, the protocols for communication between Cunard's senior management, the Line's project managers, the two design agencies, the QE2's Captain and officers and the shipyard were unclear, meaning that it was difficult for each party to grasp the others' agendas and to reach quick decisions.

In New York, a large team of contractors boarded the ship and began work by removing around 1,500 pieces of original furniture.[262] These bespoke items, mainly dating from the time of the QE2's construction, were distributed via middle-men to thrift shops and stripping continued from the time the liner left New York on 13 November 1994 until she arrived at the Blohm + Voss shipyard. There, during twenty days, many public areas and all cabins were to be renovated.

McNeece re-upholstered the cabins in 'traditional dusky hues', all bathrooms were replaced and the majority of public rooms and connecting spaces were refurbished. The original Princess Grill remained largely intact, but the Midships Lounge became the Chart Room and the restaurants were reconfigured. Nominally First Class passengers would, in future, dine in a new Caronia Restaurant on Upper Deck, whilst the Mauretania Restaurant was moved to the former Columbia's space on Quarter Deck; also on Upper Deck, a new Crystal Bar (serving Champagne) was created and, at the more populist end of the scale of 'unspoken aspirational hierarchy', a rather kitsch 'English Pub' called 'The Golden Lion' replaced the Theatre Bar, looking for all the world like a provincial branch of Wetherspoon's. Throughout the re-panelled foyer and public room corridor spaces, a 'Heritage Trail' of Cunard

*The **Queen Elizabeth 2** motors past the World Trade Center in Manhattan in September 1996, painted in her short-lived 'Project Lifestyle' livery with red, gold and blue stripes on the superstructure. (Andrew Kilk)*

Top left: The Queen's Grill on Upper Deck following the 'Project Lifestyle' refit. (Bruce Peter)

Above: The Caronia Restaurant, which subsequently became the Mauretania without being substantially altered. (Bruce Peter)

Left: The Britannia Grill. (Bruce Peter)

Below: The Midships Lobby, re-panelled in faux Art Deco style. (Bruce Peter)

memorabilia was installed (the ship already had a small Cunard history display) and this proved popular with passengers.

More controversially, Met Studio also devised a new colour scheme for the exterior, consisting of a navy blue hull with red, gold and blue 'go faster' stripes, applied half-way up the superstructure where the bi-metallic joint between the steel and aluminium sections occurred. The Cunard name, forward on the topsides, was moved down and a lion rampant motif applied above. Needless to say, this fiddly design, which may have looked satisfactory when viewed in two dimensions on a computer screen, actually appeared rather tacky when applied to the ship, especially as it only emphasised the increasingly patched appearance of the ageing aluminium alloy upper works.

The project involved both shipyard workers and British sub-contractors, who were to be accommodated alongside the QE2 on a chartered cruise ship, the *Enchanted Isle*, which was hired from Effjohn, having previously served as a hotel ship in St Petersburg. Meanwhile, allegedly without informing McNeece, Cunard's senior management had apparently authorised the QE2's own officers and crew to replace steelwork and plumbing in the cabin areas (there was serious corrosion of steel plating below bathroom floors due to long-term water damage). This aspect of the project, plus a new ring main in the corridors, was not accounted for in McNeece's planning strategy – and it was his 14-strong fit-out snagging team that had constantly to re-inspect areas that had already been deemed complete. He recalls:

'There were huge pressures on Cunard's already stretched project managers who appeared to lose control. No sooner had blocks of cabins and corridors been carefully refurbished than QE2's own crew members began to dismantle them again to replace the plumbing and electrics – and this caused damage to the new ceilings, wall finishes, furniture, fittings and carpets and delays to the overall project. Later, one week before the work was due to be completed, the *Enchanted Isle* charter expired and so the sub-contractors were transferred to hotels and guest houses in Hamburg. Of course, they hit the town and this brought a decrease in productivity

during the closing stages, including some instances of sabotage, presumably in the hope that their contracts might be extended to make good the damage.'[263]

Although the ship was far from complete, John Olsen signed off the contract documentation and the liner set sail for Southampton with steelwork for the new Yacht Club and the extended lido buffet area still in the process of being welded in place and much of the rest of the passenger accommodation essentially a construction site.

After returning to her home port, the QE2 had a Royal visit by HRH Prince Andrew on 17 December (the day she was due to sail for New York), but the outfitting work was still far from being finished. Cunard managed to contact 300 passengers to inform them that the ship was not ready, but a further 160 had to be told at the terminal and, exacerbating the Line's woes, the Marine Safety Agency's inspector placed a capacity limit of 1,000 due to the unfinished state of the accommodation.[264] As space was required for 400 building contractors, this meant that only 600 passengers finally set sail for New York, whereupon the QE2 ploughed straight into a force 8 storm, resulting in seasick workers and more delays. When the liner finally arrived in New York, twelve hours behind schedule, on 23 December, the US Coast Guard boarded and found enough violations to fill a six-page report, barring the ship from sailing again until these safety issues were properly resolved.[265]

Meanwhile, passengers had used their new-fangled video cameras to take footage of the mounds of builders' debris and old mattresses piled up around the ship, and of the various leaking pipes, gaping holes and backing-up toilets.[266] Inevitably, the British tabloid press had a field day at Cunard's expense.

Yet, throughout the incident, Trafalgar House remained ominously silent as they figured out how to cope with this latest crisis. Passengers were, however, generously compensated and, strangely, the extensive media coverage did get over the message that the QE2 had been refurbished; once the work was properly completed, bookings did eventually increase by 15%. As a result of the debacle, however, John Olsen was subsequently forced to resign as Cunard's Chairman.

(Philip Maxwell)

CHAPTER 10

ENTER CARNIVAL

QE2
BRITAIN'S
GREATEST
LINER

DURING the mid-1990s, Trafalgar House's losses in the engineering sector had increased to £154 million and a further £12 million was written off in a failed 1995 bid for the Northern Electric generating and supply company. Having been so aggressively acquisitive during the 1970s and '80s, the Group was now, itself, ripe for acquisition to be broken up. Indeed, in March 1996 the expansive Norwegian engineering, construction and shipbuilding group, Kværner, bought Trafalgar House for £904 million.[267]

Kværner were principally interested in Trafalgar's construction division and in aspects of its engineering businesses. Certainly, they had no interest whatsoever in operating a cruise line and so it was clear that Cunard was, effectively, up for sale.

1996 proved to be a miserable year for Cunard. In February, the *Sagafjord* suffered a serious engine room fire while cruising off the Philippines. Towed to Singapore, then to Sembawang, for repair, the liner never re-entered Cunard service but was, instead, chartered to a German firm, Transocean Tours, taking the name *Gripsholm*. (The reason for this was that Transocean had initially attempted to charter the old Swedish American liner *Gripsholm* of 1957 from Regency Cruises, but that firm had gone bankrupt and so the *Sagafjord* was seen to be the next best option, given that brochures had already been printed and distributed). Cunard were therefore down to three very diverse ships – the QE2, the *Vistafjord* and the *Royal Viking Sun*.

Later, that April, the *Royal Viking Sun* ran aground on a coral reef near to Sharm-El-Sheikh in the Red Sea during the latter stages of a westbound world cruise. The Egyptian authorities had then arrested the ship for causing damage to the coral and, initially, refused to release her until Cunard paid £16 million in compensation.[268] In the end, the ship was released after only a couple of million dollars had been transferred.

In November 1996, the QE2 was given a further refit, this time undertaken by A&P in Southampton in the King George V dry-dock. Once again, Met Studio was engaged to design the scheme and a generous twenty-four days were reserved to ensure that there would be no repeat of the 'Project Lifestyle' debacle. In order to compete at the high end of the cruise industry, it was felt necessary to reduce the liner's passenger

capacity from 1,870 to 1,500 – principally to allow the Mauretania Restaurant to provide a single sitting dining experience, like the Caronia Restaurant and the grill rooms. The Mauretania Restaurant was refurbished, again in an Art Deco idiom, and the ship's top penthouse suites were expanded and redecorated by annexing adjacent suites. Around three-quarters of the work carried out, however, was technical to bring the ship into line with forthcoming SOLAS (Safety Of Life At Sea) regulations. Fortunately, due to the forward thinking of the original layout, many of the anticipated SOLAS 1997 safety features – such as the provision of an active sprinkler system throughout – had been incorporated in the QE2's design from the outset.

Meanwhile, under Lord Sterling's Chairmanship, P&O Cruises had been in perpetual expansion. Apart from the evergreen *Canberra*, the line operated the *Victoria* (ex *Sea Princess*, ex *Kungsholm*, built by John Brown's in 1966) and had recently taken delivery of the first of two new ships for the British market from Meyer Werft in Germany – the *Oriana*, delivered in 1995, later joined in 2000 by the *Aurora*. P&O's Princess Cruises Division was growing at an even greater pace. Back in 1984, the line had taken delivery of the *Royal Princess* from Wärtsilä in Finland, then it had bought Sitmar Cruises in 1988, continuing with a series of very large so-called 'Grand Class' ships from Fincantieri from 1998 onwards. Surely, there was no reason why Cunard, under Trafalgar House, could not have done likewise?

If the expansion of P&O's Cruise Divisions had been impressive, it was as nothing compared with that of their US and Norwegian counterparts, Carnival and Royal Caribbean. Carnival, in particular, had grown rapidly into the world's leading cruise line and, having swallowed up Holland America in 1989, Seabourn in 1992 and Costa Crociere in 1997, the Corporation was well placed to snap up Cunard as well – but was Cunard worth having? The Line had only three disparate ships but an outstanding reputation and, in an increasingly mediated world of corporate branding in which social status could best be gained through being associated with the right names, that counted for a great deal. Put simply, if Carnival were to be taken seriously at the luxury, as well as the mass market, end of the cruise spectrum, it would need to buy an existing brand with an aura of 'heritage' upon which

*Above left: The **Caronia**, ex **Vistafjord**, was QE2's Cunard fleet-mate during the first few years of Carnival ownership. Here, she is seen on the River Forth. (Bruce Peter)*

Above right: Carnival quickly decreed that Cunard ships should be painted in the Line's traditional livery and so the 'Project Lifestyle' colours were removed. Here, the QE2 is shown in the short-lived paint scheme. (Fotoflite)

Left: The QE2 arrives at Sydney during a world cruise. The famous Opera House and Harbour Bridge form an impressive backdrop to the iconic liner. (Gallagher collection)

Below: With firefighting tugs sending plumes of water into the air, the QE2 glides slowly down Southampton Water. (William Mayes)

Top: The 'new' Caronia Restaurant on Quarter Deck was installed in 1999, decorated in an ersatz Edwardian style which clashed with the design of much of the remainder of the ship. (Cunard)

Above left: The hallway outside the Caronia Restaurant, in contrast, retained its 1960s design, albeit with the bulkheads re-panelled in simulated wood veneer. (Miles Cowsill)

Above: The Princess Grill, formerly the Grill Room, has kept much of its exclusive and luxurious 1969 design. The chairs originally were in the Britannia Restaurant. (Bruce Peter)

Left: The Chart Room, formerly the Midships Bar, is also still recognisable from its 1960s origins. (Miles Cowsill)

to build. (Interestingly, a similar situation occurred in the automotive industry at about the same time, with mass market manufacturers like Ford purchasing luxury brands, such as Jaguar and Aston Martin). Cunard, though neglected by Trafalgar House, had a similar cachet and so Carnival bought the business from Kværner for 500 million dollars on 3 April 1998.

One passenger aboard the QE2, sailing westbound in early April 1998, was the cruise ship naval architect Stephen Payne, who was acting as Cunard's guest lecturer on passenger shipping history. Payne had first encountered the QE2 as a nine-year-old when his family visited the brand-new ship in the late spring of 1969, shortly after the maiden crossings to and from New York. As the tour group was guided on a circuit through the liner's public rooms, young Stephen was absolutely fascinated by all that he saw to the point that it ultimately set the direction of his adult life and career. Yet, with the British shipbuilding industry then in serious decline and passenger shipping also waning, his teachers tried to persuade him otherwise. Ignoring their well-intentioned advice, he enrolled in the Ship Sciences and Naval Architecture programme at Southampton University, where, as his study project, he designed a passenger ship based on a hypothetical specification given to him by P&O.

After serving in the Royal Navy and working a short while with Marconi, Payne finally joined the firm Technical Marine Planning in London as a practicing naval architect. There, he was heavily involved in Carnival's cruise ship building programme. As Carnival continued to expand, their ship design work and technical services were brought in-house, with Payne ultimately rising to the position of Chief Naval Architect.

Upon arrival in New York on the QE2, Payne was met by Carnival's senior management, who wanted him immediately to begin work to plan the liner's eventual successor, the *Queen Mary 2*. At last, Payne would be able to fulfill his childhood dream of designing the biggest trans-Atlantic liner yet seen.

Carnival's origins could be traced back only to the mid-1960s when Ted Arison, an Israeli businessman who had retired to Florida but could not resist a business opportunity, set up a ro-ro ferry service from Miami to Nassau in the Bahamas and to Montego Bay in Jamaica. Arison chartered a modern Israeli ferry called the *Nili* from Somerfin Lines of Haifa, which was marketed to American holidaymakers as the *Jamaica Queen*. The idea was to transport freight trailers to and from these Caribbean ports while, simultaneously, carrying tourists on short cruises. Arison's business was a success – but the ship's owner, Somerfin Lines, went bankrupt in 1966 and the *Nili* was arrested. Through his friend, the shipbroker Elie Schalit, Arison made contact with the Norwegian shipowner Knut Kloster who had recently attempted to introduce a ferry service of his own between Southampton, Lisbon and Gibraltar, using a new Norwegian-built ship called the *Sunward*. Due to political difficulties with Spain over Gibraltar and foreign exchange problems, this was a failure, meaning that Kloster had a suitable spare ship and Arison had an urgent need, and so the two joined forces to form the Norwegian Caribbean Line. This expanded rapidly in the latter 1960s, but Kloster and Arison later fell out. With help from Schalit, Arison established his own line, intending to convert the former Israeli Zim Lines passenger-cargo liner *Theodor Herzl* into a cruise ship to be named the *Carnivale*. Although the work was begun, this never happened and, instead, Arison bought the much more substantial sale-listed Canadian Pacific flagship liner, *Empress of Canada*, which he introduced on short cruises from Miami in 1972 as the *Mardi Gras*. After a somewhat rocky start – the ship grounded outside Miami on the maiden voyage – Carnival became well established as a provider of inexpensive, down-to-earth, fun party cruises. By the latter 1970s, the line had three ships – the others being the *Carnivale* (ex *Empress of Britain*) and the *Festivale* (ex *Transvaal Castle*). Moving into the 1980s, Carnival began building their first new cruise ships and each was carefully designed to maximise revenue. With such a fleet, Carnival successfully rode the 1980s leisure and entertainment boom, and so lucrative was their Caribbean operation that it paid for new buildings out of profits earned by the existing fleet. By the 1990s, they had a substantial war chest to invest by purchasing existing cruise lines and, moreover, by that stage, the industry was also beginning to consolidate.

Under Carnival, Cunard's new CEO was Larry Pimentel, an experienced travel industry executive. A graduate in Business Administration of the Californian State University, but with family roots in Hawaii, he initially ran the Classic Hawaii Tour Company for eight years before moving into the cruise industry. From 1992 he was President and Chief Operating Officer of Seabourn, another up-market line in the Carnival empire.

Pimentel made several quick changes to Cunard. Most urgently, the Line's shore-based operations were improved with more efficient booking systems. Secondly, the *Royal Viking Sun*, the *Sea Goddess 1* and the *Sea Goddess 2* were transferred to Seabourn. Thirdly, the QE2 was repainted in the traditional Cunard livery she had carried from 1984 until the 1994 'Project Lifestyle' refit – Met Studio's 'go faster' stripes being removed much to the benefit of the liner's external appearance. This took place during an extensive £30 million refit at the Lloyd Werft shipyard in Bremerhaven in November 1999. The entire hull and superstructure were grit- and hydro-blasted, removing caked-on layers of paint and returning the ship to a pristine external state, not equalled since her 1987 re-engining. On board, the cabins, restaurants and crew accommodation were refurbished – bringing the liner into excellent condition to enter the new Millennium. Once again, the main dining rooms were swapped over with the former Caronia on Upper Deck becoming the Mauretania Restaurant without substantial alteration and the former Mauretania, below, being completely rebuilt, this time in an ersatz Edwardian style, as the new Caronia Restaurant. Being a firm believer in maximising profits, Cunard's new owner was unimpressed by the fact that the QE2's capacity had been reduced and so it grew to 1,778 – after all, why turn potential passengers away?

At the same time, the *Vistafjord* was renamed the *Caronia* and, also painted in full Cunard colours, she raised the British flag to considerable acclaim. Cunard now had a two-ship fleet – but Pimentel had ambitious plans to build a new flagship trans-Atlantic liner as an indirect replacement for the QE2. This mammoth project rapidly gained momentum and the new liner entered service in December 2003 as the *Queen Mary 2*, the largest passenger ship the world had yet seen, but subsequently eclipsed by other new cruise ships. From the outset, the new *Queen Mary 2* was a post-modern 'retro' ship and the product of very different thinking and values from the *Queen Elizabeth 2* in her original modernist form. Indeed, one Cunard Director tellingly commented on the cumulative outcome of the QE2's

many refits, observing that 'finally, we have the ship the way we want her.' Similarly, the *Queen Mary 2* is, essentially, a 'tissue of quotations' of Cunard's Edwardian and inter-war past, albeit contained in a hull and superstructure packed with the very latest technology and thinking with regard to twenty-first century passenger ship design. No doubt Lady Brocklebank would warmly have approved!

In 2001, Pam Conover replaced Pimentel as Cunard's CEO. Conover was a very successful shipping financier and cruise line executive who had enjoyed a meteoric rise through Carnival Corporation's corporate structure. Born near London, she grew up in Thailand where her father ran a trading company. Conover was accepted to study geography and anthropology at the University of London but instead opted to move directly into banking, starting out as a cashier for Wells Fargo in the City of London. In 1979 she moved to the bank's New York office, leaving in 1981 to work as assistant treasurer of the United States Line, once a famous passenger liner company but latterly involved mainly in the container trade. In 1985 she joined Citicorp, where she became involved in ship finance. This first brought her into contact with Carnival, who were then commencing their 'Fun Ship' new-building programme that Conover helped to facilitate. In 1994 she moved to Carnival when they bought a stake in the Greek Potamianos family-owned Epirotiki cruise line. After one year, due to differences in management philosophy between the profit-driven, entrepreneurial Carnival and the patriarchal Greek line, the companies went their separate ways – and Conover moved to Carnival's headquarters in Miami, becoming their Vice-President of Strategic Planning.

With Carnival committed to yet more new ships, some of which were intended to join the Cunard 'brand', clearly time was running out for the now venerable, yet much-loved *Queen Elizabeth 2*.

Ever since the mid-1990s, the many new, purpose-built, 'economy of scale' cruise ships entering service had begun to displace older 1950s-60s tonnage. One of the first major liners of the era to be scrapped was P&O's famous *Canberra*, which departed for Gadani Beach, near to Karachi in Pakistan, in October 1997. Back then, however, there were very few digital cameras – certainly amongst the poor tribesmen whose dangerous job it was to demolish the ship, and so the

*Left: The **Queen Elizabeth 2**, **Queen Victoria** and **Queen Mary 2** at Southampton on 22 April 2008. (Cunard)*

*Above: During the January 2008 parallel crossing with the **Queen Victoria**, the **Queen Elizabeth 2** slices through heavy swells en route to New York. (Steve Swanson)*

*Below: The **Queen Mary 2** and the **Queen Elizabeth 2** berthed together at Fort Lauderdale. (Cunard)*

*The **Queen Elizabeth 2** berthed at Flåm in Norway in the summer of 2003. (John Peter)*

Canberra practically disappeared without trace, demolished far away from her home port and recycled to provide steel for the accelerating Asian construction boom. Since then, many more old liners have been dispatched to the Indian sub-continent for breaking, with the scrap merchants of Alang in India being particularly acquisitive. Gradually, the environmental movement took notice of the pollution and danger to public health caused by this industry and, with the advent of digital cameras and internet communication, poignant images of old cruise ships being torn apart began to filter back to Europe and America, troubling the socially conscious and depressing former crew members and passengers who remembered the ships in happier times. Things came to a head when, via several middle-men, the once-magnificent SS *Norway* arrived for breaking at Alang in August 2006. Greenpeace had already forced the French Government to turn back an old aircraft carrier, the *Clemenceau*, which was also headed for Alang's beaches and, following that success, the environmental campaigners took legal action to prevent the scrapping of the *Norway*. For two years thereafter, the once grand liner, originally Charles De Gaulle's *grand projet* and the pride of France, lay mouldering on the beach, with plenty of web images regularly being posted to the internet.

Clearly, in such circumstances, selling the QE2 for scrap would be unthinkable – but ships exist only to make money for their owners and, as soon as they are deemed obsolete, they are sent for recycling. An unused ship is a liability and, without intensive maintenance from an extensive and expensive professional crew, decay quickly takes hold. Cunard thus had a challenge to find something positive to do with their famous flagship which, thanks to her advancing years and illustrious history, now had such an aura that crowds turned out to spectate wherever she sailed.

Meanwhile, with the *Queen Mary 2* in service, Cunard retired the QE2 from regular trans-Atlantic crossings and, instead, used the ship almost exclusively for cruising, based mainly in Southampton. Sailing at speed through the big Atlantic swells was placing too much of a strain on the ageing aluminium superstructure, and so more gentle routeings were selected for the dowager QE2. There were still, however, occasional trans-Atlantic sailings included as

legs of world cruises – and these attracted great followings of liner enthusiasts. More imaginative still was a memorable tandem eastbound crossing, leaving New York on 25 April 2004, during which the *Queen Elizabeth 2* and the *Queen Mary 2* sailed at speed, side-by-side, allowing passengers to spectate from one ship to the other for six wonderful days.

Quite unexpectedly, and after top secret negotiations, Cunard announced on 18 June 2007 that the *Queen Elizabeth 2* had been sold to Istithmar, the investment wing of Dubai World, for 100 million dollars. Chaired by Sultan Ahmed bin Sulayem, this firm is essentially a property developer, presently engaged in the construction of a vast resort on a man-made island, shaped like a palm frond and accessed by causeway from Dubai's Persian Gulf coast. The purchase of the QE2, it was hoped, would lend the scheme a prestigious attraction with 'heritage value' – while, equally, taking a potentially troublesome liability off Cunard's hands. Thus, with the QE2's medium-term future apparently secured, Cunard could make the most of celebrating the liner's final year in service, giving the ship a worthy, rousing send-off after so lengthy and distinguished a career.

On 15 September 2007, the QE2 set off on a special round-Britain cruise to commemorate the fortieth anniversary of her launching at Clydebank on 20 September 1967. Later, in January 2008, the QE2 sailed trans-Atlantic from Southampton to New York in the company of Cunard's second large new cruise ship of the Carnival era, the *Queen Victoria* (delivered in 2007). This time, both ships met serious swells and so passengers who avoided seasickness were able to take very dramatic photographs. It was also possible to compare the differing behaviours of their very different hull configurations. The rather bluff, Italian-built *Queen Victoria*, essentially a standard 'economy of scale' Carnival 'Vista' class cruise ship, crunched through the waves with some occasional slamming motion, whereas the purpose-built 'Atlantic greyhound' QE2 pitched gracefully – her bulbous bow and stern occasionally lifting clean out of the water as she motored towards New York.

Cunard also organised several memorable harbour meetings of their three-strong fleet. On 20 February 2007, the QE2 and the *Queen Mary 2* met in Sydney Harbour and, the following year, the QE2 and the

Queen Victoria spent three days in Sydney – these events drawing hundreds of thousands of onlookers to admire the ships. Fittingly, the most ambitious parade of Cunarders took place in their home port of Southampton on 22 April 2008 when all three liners were brought together for the first time. Later, on 2 June, the QE2 received a farewell visit from HM The Queen, who was also celebrating the 55th anniversary of her Coronation. On board, she met past and present Captains, officers, senior Cunard managers and long-serving members of staff.

The wider marketing framework for Cunard's image today consciously evokes the 'spirit' of the line's history – with the QE2 enjoying a very prominent 'heritage' role. Of course, this is a very different situation from the Line's attitude to the old *Queen Mary* and the *Queen Elizabeth* in the latter 1960s, which were rejected by Cunard as having been 'Boring Long Enough.' Whereas Crosby/Fletcher/Forbes' graphic design for the QE2 back then fixated on the future, today Cunard is 'branded' very much in terms of the past.

In the QE2's final season, the Line's website (burgundy background, gold details, fonts with serifs and cursive script) described the vessel as being 'A legendary liner adored the world over...an iconic favourite, an undisputed legend of the seas.' It continued that her 'immortal story...spans forty years, crosses continents, circles the globe and inspires generation upon generation... *Queen Elizabeth 2* exudes an ageless glamour that appeals to seasoned voyagers the world over. No wonder so many celebrities have revelled in her ambience of relaxed sophistication and gracious hospitality.'[269]

Of course, the fascination with famous names and faces mirrors the very contemporary phenomenon of 'celebrity culture' – as also seen on reality TV shows, in glossy gossip magazines and throughout the tabloid press. In that sense, the QE2's marketing is highly reflective of the aspirations of our present era, in which a cash-rich public goes in search of social status by 'buying into' notions of heritage and tradition – and, with her forty-year-plus career, the QE2 can perhaps fulfil such desires better than most other cruise ships.

Beyond that, what does QE2 nowadays represent as an object deemed worthy of preservation – at great cost? Well, after so many refits and radical alterations,

the liner no longer represents any particular era or the work of any distinct group of designers, fired up by a specific ideology. Instead, the ship could better be seen as an archaeological site, containing layers and accumulations of styles, representing changing British and American bourgeois taste of the past half-century. Fragments of the original 1969 QE2 remain – the trumpet columns and lattice ceiling in the Queen's Room, Misha Black's tiny synagogue and much of the Princess Grill. Other fragments, such as staircase balustrades and cabin corridors remain, but in mutilated form. On top, there are many accretions, dating from successive refits since the early 1970s, making the ship fascinating territory for design

Anticipating an ocean voyage, passengers gaze seaward from the QE2's forward viewing deck at Southampton in June 2008. (Miles Cowsill)

historians and sociologists alike. Writing about a visit to the old *Queen Mary*, now a museum and hotel ship at Long Beach in California, the architect Terry Farrell observed that the liner, 'like the uncovered Pompeii, conveys as much about society and its values at a point in time as it does about a form of transport.'

The QE2, in contrast, reflects changes in aspiration over a forty-year span – a fascinating reminder of luxury ocean travel in the latter twentieth century and a great survivor in the otherwise ephemeral cruise industry.

CHAPTER 11

NEW WATERS

QE2
BRITAIN'S
GREATEST
LINER

ON 30 September 2008, the *Queen Elizabeth 2* set sail from Southampton on her farewell Round Britain cruise, calling at Cork, Dublin, the Isle of Man, Liverpool, Belfast, Greenock, South Queensferry (for Edinburgh) and Newcastle. At each port, vast crowds and flotillas of small craft came to pay their respects to Britain's greatest liner. There were fireworks displays and fire-fighting tugs sent water jets high into the air. On 10 October, the liner set sail for New York on her final trans-Atlantic crossing, taking six days in each direction. There too, she was given a memorable send-off. After a final Mediterranean cruise to Piraeus, via Lisbon, Cagliari, Naples, Messina, Dubrovnik and Zakinthos, she returned to Southampton on 11 November. That same evening, she left on her delivery voyage to Dubai. En route, she called at several familiar ports – including Civitaveccia, Valletta and Alexandria – arriving at her new home on 27 November.

Meanwhile, her new owners, Istithmar, worked frantically to find out how best to convert their forty-year-old acquisition from an ageing ocean liner into a modern luxury hotel, capable of withstanding comparison with the finest in the world.

Although much loved by her devoted cruise clientele, the QE2 was designed for ocean voyages and was never intended to be a static object. Thus, although she has many commodious staterooms, she has a much larger number of small cabins which, however beautifully outfitted by Clydebank's joiners in the latter 1960s, would be regarded as being very perfunctory as up-market hotel rooms – especially in the context of Dubai, which can boast some of the most elaborate hotels in the world. Moreover, the gap in aspiration between the European and American passengers who enjoyed QE2's rather cosy atmosphere and the expectations of Dubai's jet-setters provided an extra challenge. Clearly, to be successful in her new role and setting, the QE2 would have to change radically – perhaps even more than she had done between 1969 and 2008. This, in turn, would, of course, be bound to enrage the liner's existing world-wide fan base, who are generally conservative by instinct.

The QE2 makes her final visit to Liverpool on 3 October 2008. (Ian Collard)

Faced with such a dilemma, both Istithmar and Cunard agreed that absolute silence was the safest course of action until a conversion plan could be developed and an appropriate design solution accepted. Even so, internet discussion groups were rife with rumours. Perhaps the entire aluminium superstructure aft of the bridge would be reconfigured to provide staterooms with balconies, as found on modern cruise ships? Or maybe the funnel would be removed and replaced by a glazed facsimile, containing exclusive penthouses? At the opposite extreme, it was rumoured that the liner might even be maintained in such a way as to make occasional short voyages around the Persian Gulf – this notwithstanding the very real problems posed by new marine safety regulations to be imposed in 2010 prohibiting ships of QE2's vintage from continuing in service without major technical modernisation. The wildest rumours even suggested that the QE2 might somehow even be restored to her original 1969 form – even although such a *homage* to the Modern Movement would be unlikely to be understood or appreciated by her *nouveau riche* Dubai clientele any more than it was by the majority of her passengers during the Cunard era.

The conversion of the liner to suit her new role is estimated to take a minimum of two years – probably longer – and the design solution is yet to be finalised at the time of going to press. In Dubai, the QE2 will have a static role as a hotel and attraction. The feasibility of retaining and enhancing at least some of the QE2's original design elements is being given serious consideration. Whatever final design solution emerges, however, the 'new' QE2 will necessarily be a very different vessel from the one which sailed from Southampton for the last time in November 2008. In addition to the many physical changes required to adapt her successfully for her new role, there will also be significant cultural changes to the ship. Much of what made the QE2 special when in Cunard service was the unique ambience created by her officers, crew and passengers. When they disembarked in Dubai to fly home, the 'old' QE2 ceased to exist, but the 'new' QE2 was yet to emerge.

*On her one and only visit to the Isle of Man, the **Queen Elizabeth 2** passes Onchan Head at 07.10 on 3rd October 2008 as she turns for Liverpool. (Miles Cowsill)*

The final departure from New York. (From an original painting by Robert Lloyd)

Above and below: The QE2's final visit to Greenock on the Clyde was memorable for the large crowds who came to pay tribute to the liner. Throughout, there was warm autumn sunshine and numerous yachts and small craft were also in attendance. (Miles Cowsill)

REFERENCES

1 The *Mauretania* first captured the Blue Riband in 1907 from the *Lusitania*. She subsequently re-captured it in 1909.

2 'Sir Percy Bates at a luncheon for the Institute of Marine Engineers in London', <u>Dumbarton Herald</u>, 30 March 1940.

3 'Mammoth order for Clyde is in the offing to replace the two 'Queens' of the Atlantic: Super-liners Ahoy! – and Cunard talks it over with John Brown's, <u>The Scottish Daily Express</u>, 9 April 1959, p 1.

4 Arthur J. Davis, 'The Architecture of the Liner', <u>The Architectural Review</u>, April 1914, p 99.

5 Kenneth Frampton, <u>Modern Architecture: A critical history</u>, Thames and Hudson Ltd, London, 1987, p 221.

6 Baird Dennison, '534 And All That,' <u>The Architects' Journal</u>, 25 January 1934, p 156.

7 Neil Potter and Jack Frost, <u>The Elizabeth</u>, George G. Harrap, London, 1965, p 20.

8 Le Corbusier, <u>Towards a New Architecture</u>, Rodker, London, 1931, p 93.

9 John Heskett, <u>Industrial Design</u>, Thames & Hudson, London, 1997, p 186.

10 Becky Conekin, 'Fun and Fantasy, Escape and Edification: The Battersea Pleasure Grounds' in Elain Harwood and Alan Powers (eds), <u>Twentieth Century Architecture 5: Festival of Britain</u>, Twentieth Century Society, London, 2001, pp 127-139.

11 Philip Long and Jane Thomas (eds), <u>Basil Spence: Architect</u>, National Galleries of Scotland, 2008, p 55.

12 Clive Harvey, <u>The Saxonia Sisters</u>, Carmania, London, 2001, pp 10-24.

13 Frank Jackson, 'The New Air Age: BOAC and design policy 1945-60', <u>Journal of Design History</u>, Oxford University Press, Oxford, Volume 4 Number 3, 1991, pp 167-85.

14 'The Passenger Ship: Backward or Forward', <u>The Architectural Review</u>, November 1960, p 367.

15 See Brian Haresnape, <u>British Rail 1948-1978: A Journey by Design</u>, Ian Allan, Shepperton, 1979 and Brian Haresnape, <u>Sealink</u>, Ian Allan, Shepperton, 1982 for detailed descriptions of the British Rail Modernisation Plan.

16 See Philip Dawson, <u>British Superliners of the Sixties: A design appreciation of the Oriana, Canberra and QE2</u>, Conway Maritime Press, London 1990, for a detailed description of the *Oriana* and the *Canberra*.

17 John Betjeman, <u>Ghastly Good Taste, or, a depressing story of the rise and fall of English Architecture</u>, Alan Blond, London, 1933.

18 See Guy Oliver, 'The House of Michael Inchbald', <u>Country Life</u> No 15, 2003, pages 92-98 for a description of Inchbald's interior design work.

19 'Questionnaire: Sir John Brocklebank – Chairman of Cunard', <u>Shipping World and Shipbuilder</u>, 28 January 1965, pp 282-283.

20 Ibid.

21 <u>The Turboliner Michelangelo of 46,000 g.r.t.</u>, Italia Navigazione, Genoa and Ansaldo Shipyard Ltd, Genoa-Sestri, 1965. Giuseppe Zuccoli, President of the Italian Line, wrote in his foreword that 'British plans [to build a new Cunard flagship] tarried a bit but have recently come to a point, so winding up their research brought up to date in the meantime; this British research has not overlooked – and by our consent – our own layout and arrangements for the subdivision of classes and passenger accommodations on board, acknowledging their validity.'

22 Interview with Tony Benn by Bruce Peter by telephone, 21 April 2008.

23 Peter C. Kohler, posted to the Yahoo! Web discussion group Liners List on 14 April 2008.

24 Ibid.

25 From a conversation with David Trevor-Jones regarding his family's perception of QE2 on 12 April 2008.

26 'A Week at Sea or a Week at Butlins', <u>Shipping World and Shipbuilder</u>, 28 January 1965, pp 390-391.

27 Unpublished and incomplete memoirs of Graham Strachan held at Glasgow University Archives.

28 Neil Potter and Jack Frost, <u>QE2: The Authorised Story</u>, George G. Harrap, London, 1969, p 87.

29 Ibid, p 17.

30 Neil Potter and Jack Frost, <u>QE2: The Authorised Story</u>, George G. Harrap, London, 1969, p 19.

31 Ibid, p 18.

32 Ibid.

33 James Gardner, <u>The ARTful Designer: Ideas off the Drawing Board</u>, Centurion, London, 1993, p 285.

34 Ibid.

35 James Gardner, <u>The ARTful Designer: Ideas off the Drawing Board</u>, Centurion, London, 1993, p 288.

36 Unpublished and incomplete memoirs of Graham Strachan held by Glasgow University Archives.

37 Letter from Roy Turner, formerly Vickers-Armstrongs' Naval Architect, sent to Ian Johnston, dated 5 December 1996.

38 'New 'Queen' vital to Clydebank', The Glasgow Herald, 11 August 1961, p 1.

39 Mr John Brown was not related in any way to John Brown & Company and the fact that his name was the same as that of his employer was a coincidence.

40 John Brown's hull would have cost £2.15 million more to build although its machinery price was £0.35 million lower.

41 Interview with Roy Turner by Ian Johnston by telephone, 5 November 1996.

42 Ibid.

43 Neil Potter and Jack Frost, The Elizabeth, George G. Harrap, London, 1965, p 22.

44 Interview with Norman Gilchrist by Ian Johnston by telephone, 3 November 1996. Gilchrist was Chief Draughtsman at Swan, Hunter & Wigham Richardson and, in 1961, in charge of the tender drawings for Q3.

45 Stephen Garrett, 'Amid-Ships', The Architectural Review, September 1961, p 155.

46 'The New Queen', Time, 1 November 1963.

47 Neil Potter and Jack Frost, QE2: The Authorised Story, George G. Harrap, London, 1969, p 36.

48 'Dan Wallace: Cunard Naval Architect', Q4/9, Cunard press release, dated 4 April 1967.

49 'Tom Kameen: Technical Director, Cunard Line', Q4/10, Cunard press release, dated 4 April 1967.

50 UCS 1/107/405, Salholm tender document, 31 May 1963, National Archives of Scotland.

51 Letter from Lord Aberconway to Ian Johnston, dated 23 September 1998.

52 Interview with Tom Kameen by Ian Johnston by telephone, 19 November 1996.

53 John Brown & Co Ltd, Report and Accounts 1966, Lord Aberconway's statement, page 16.

54 In February 1966, 5861 men were employed in the Shipyard and 1855 in the Engine Works. UCS1/5/101. Report of 25 Feb 1966, National Archives of Scotland.

55 UCS 1/107/405, Draft letter by Robin Williamson dated 31 January 1966, National Archives of Scotland.

56 UCS 1/107/405, Table of losses.

57 John Brown & Co Ltd, Report and Accounts 1966, page 16.

58 UCS 1/5/101, Report, 25 February 1966.

59 Japanese Shipyards, Board of Trade 1965. A report on the visit of the Minister of State (Shipping) in January 1965.

60 Sir John Brocklebank's message to staff, March 1962. Document in QE2 folder, University of Liverpool Archives.

61 Ibid.

62 Arnold Kludas, Die Großen Passagierschiffe der Welt Band V, Gerhard Stalling Verlag, Hamburg, 1974, pp 84-87.

63 Ian McCallum, 'Ship Interiors', The Architectural Review, February 1956, pp 133-140.

64 Frank O. Braynard, The Big Ship: The Story of the ss United States, Mariner's Museum, Newport News, Virginia, 1981, p 50.

65 Anne Wealleans, Designing Liners: A History of Interior Design Afloat, Routledge, London, 2006, p 146.

66 Interview with Brian Beardsmore by Bruce Peter by telephone, 23 April 2008. See also The Independent, no. 1417, 27 May 1991, p 27 for Lennon's obituary.

67 Diana M. Byrne, 'Jon Bannenberg 1929-2002: A look at the rule-breaking originality of the pre-eminent yacht designer', Power & Motor Yacht, August 2002.

68 Interview with Brian Beardsmore by Bruce Peter by telephone, 23 April 2008.

69 See Ashley Hicks, David Hicks: Designer, Scriptum Editions, London, 2002 for a description of Hicks' career.

70 Information on Gaby Schreiber's career in the form of notes for a lecture for the Design History Society entitled 'Plastics to Planes: Gaby Schreiber, Consultant', given on 16 March 2004, was kindly provided by Dr Jane Pavitt of the University of Brighton. See also Edward Timms and John Hughes (eds) Intellectual Migration and Cultural Transformation: Refugees from National Socialism in the English-speaking World, Springer, Vienna and New York, 2003, Ulrike Walton-Jordan 'Although He is Jewish, He is M&S: Jewish Refugees from Nazism and Marks & Spencer from the 1930s to the 1960s' in Anthony Grenville (ed), Refugees from the Third Reich in Britain, The Research Centre for German and Austrian Exile Studies, 2002, pp 128-129 and Frank Jackson 'The New Air Age: BOAC and Design Policy 1945-60', Journal of Design History, Vol. 4, No. 3 (1991), pp 167-185.

71 Interview with Alan Irvine by Bruce Peter by telephone on 13 May 2008.

72 Interview with Lord Snowdon by Bruce Peter by telephone on 9 May 2008.

73 'Make Q4 British Ambassador', The Times, 1 March 1965, p 10.

74 The Times, 30 April 1965, p 18.

75 Directors' report to the 142nd meeting of Council held on 21 May 1965, Design Archives, Brighton College of Art and Design.

76 See Sir Basil Smallpeice, Of Comets and Queens, Airlife Publishing, Shrewsbury, 1981 for a detailed account of Smallpeice's business career.

77 James Gardner, The ARTful Designer: Ideas off the Drawing Board, Centurion, London, 1993, p 289.

78 Ibid, p 291.

79 Neil Potter and Jack Frost, QE2: The Authorised Story, George G. Harrap, London, 1969, p 127.

80 José Manser, Hugh Casson: A Biography, Viking, London, 2000, pp 167 and 251.

81 Originally, Gaby Schreiber had been commissioned additionally to design a Tourist Class cocktail lounge, veranda lounge and library – but when Q4 was re-planned from a three-class to a two-class liner, these spaces were dropped.

82 Ibid, p 128.

83 Interview with Brian Beardsmore by Bruce Peter by telephone, 23 April 2008.

84 Interview with Alan Irvine by Bruce Peter by telephone, 13 May 2008.

85 Originally, Michael Inchbald had been allocated to design the grill restaurant when Q4 was being planned as a three-class ship.

86 See Bryan Robertson, John Russell and Lord Snowdon, Private View, Thames Nelson, London, 1965, pp 180-181.

87 Elizabeth Beloe is sometimes referred to in period sources as Elizabeth Mower-White. She was the daughter of the actor, Wilfred Mower-White, and she married a teacher and educationalist called Michael Beloe towards the end of her studies at the Royal College of Art. Originally, Jon Bannenberg had been allocated the design of teenage rooms for all classes when Q4 was being planned as a three-class ship.

88 'Interior design: public rooms for a variety of uses and tastes', Design, April 1969, p 71.

89 Interview with Tony Heaton by Bruce Peter by telephone, 22 April 2008.

90 Interview with Brian Beardsmore by Bruce Peter by telephone, 23 April 2008.

91 Ibid.

92 James Gardner, Elephants in the Attic, Orbis, London, 1983, p 128.

93 Interview with Brian Beardsmore by Bruce Peter by telephone, 23 April 2008.

94 Interview with Tom Kameen by Bruce Peter by telephone, 6 June 2008.

95 Neil Potter and Jack Frost, QE2: The Authorised Story, George G. Harrap, London, 1969, p 129.

96 Ibid.

97 D. N. Wallace, Shipping World and Shipbuilder, January 1969, p 87.

98 'Queen Elizabeth 2: A ship with a past...and a future', Shipbuilding and Shipping Record, January 31, 1969, p 146.

99 Shpbuilding and Shipping Record, January 31, 1969, p 160.

100 Sir Hugh Casson, Special QE2 Supplement, The Times, 29 April 1969, p iii.

101 Interview with Sir Hugh Casson by Philip Dawson at his home in Holland Park, London, 15 September 1982.

102 Comment recounted to Philip Dawson when sailing from Southampton to Cherbourg on board the QE2 in June 1982.

103 Kenneth Agnew, 'Concept to Cunarder: The Building of the QE2', The Architectural Review, June 1969, p 412.

104 'Queen Elizabeth 2: A ship with a past...and a future', Shipbuilding and Shipping Record, January 31, 1969, pp 160-161.

105 Neil Potter and Jack Frost, QE2: The Authorised Story, George G. Harrap, London, 1969, p 176.

106 'Queen Elizabeth 2', The Motor Ship, January 1969, p 505.

107 Ibid, p 508.

108 Kenneth Agnew, 'Concept to Cunarder: The Building of the QE2', The Architectural Review, June 1969, p 417.

109 Ibid, p 418.

110 J.T. Palmer, 'The Queen Elizabeth II Superstructure: Welded Fabrication of 1,100 tons of Alcan aluminium', Welding and Metal Fabrication, January 1968, pp 2-19.

111 Kenneth Agnew, 'Concept to Cunarder: The Building of the QE2', The Architectural Review, June 1969, p 418.

112 'Queen Elizabeth 2: A ship with a past...and a future', Shipbuilding and Shipping Record, January 31, 1969, p 146.

113 Neil Potter and Jack Frost, QE2: The Authorised Story, George G. Harrap, London, 1969, p 39.

114 The Shipbuilder and Marine Engine Builder, Canberra Souvenir Number, 1961, p 67.

115 Interview with Stephen Payne by Philip Dawson by telephone, 5 June 2008.

116 'Queen Elizabeth 2: A ship with a past...and a future', Shipbuilding and Shipping Record, January 31, 1969, p 147.

117 Ibid, pp 148-149.

118 'Queen Elizabeth 2', The Motor Ship, January 1969, p 508.

119 Kenneth Agnew, 'Concept to Cunarder: The Building of the QE2', The Architectural Review, June 1969, p 417.

120 Vincent Mulchrone, 'The World's Finest Ship', Queen Elizabeth 2: Pride of British Industry, Pitkin Pictorials, London, 1969, p 7.

121 Sir Hugh Casson, 'A Ship is an Island', The Architectural Review, June 1969, p 408.

122 'The structure: every inch counts', Design, April 1969, p 42.

123 Ibid.

124 James Gardner, The ARTful Designer: Ideas off the Drawing Board, Centurion, London, 1993, p 298.

125 Edward C. Pyatt, National Physical Laboratory – A History, Mauve Publications, London, 1983, p 199.

126 James Gardner, The ARTful Designer: Ideas off the Drawing Board, Centurion, London, 1993, p 302.

127 Ibid, p 296-297.

128 'Interior design: public rooms for a variety of uses and tastes', Design, April 1969, p 72.

129 Ibid, p 73.

130 Ibid, p 64.

131 Interview with Don Sibebottom by Philip Dawson by telephone, 24 April 2008.

132 John Brown & Co Ltd, Report and Accounts 1966, page 16, National Archives of Scotland.

133 UCS 1/8/88 and UCS 1/8/89 ///, National Archives of Scotland.

134 Figures courtesy of Graeme Smith CA, supplied to Ian Johnston.

135 James Gardner, The ARTful Designer: Ideas off the Drawing Board, Centurion, London, 1993, p 294.

136 Ibid p 296.

137 Much has been written about the supposed controversy surrounding the liner's launch name. HM Queen Elizabeth II was actually only the first Queen Elizabeth of Scotland and so there was some consternation that a Scottish-built liner should be named with the suffix 'II.' On the other hand, it was a unique honour for Cunard to have their flagship bearing the name of the reigning monarch. The name finally applied to the hull Queen Elizabeth 2 was appropriately modern and much more in keeping with the spirit of the era than a name ending with a Roman 'II.'

138 The Times, Thursday 21 September 1967, p 11.

139 'The Uninvited – or how Mr Bannenberg missed the party', The Daily Express, Friday 22 September 1967, p 2.

140 Ibid.

141 UCS 1/5/102, Minutes of John Brown & Company (Shipbuilders) Ltd, 20 December 1967, National Archives of Scotland.

142 UCS 5/1/5, Executive Committee minutes, 22 April and 27 May 1968, National Archives of Scotland.

143 UCS 5/1/5, Executive Committee minutes, 2 September 1968, National Archives of Scotland.

144 UCS 5/1/2 Minutes, 11 September 1968, National Archives of Scotland. It was also agreed that if labour troubles arose in docking the ship at Greenock, she would be taken to Belfast and docked there.

145 UCS 5/1/2, Minutes, 11 September 1968, National Archives of Scotland.

146 D42/B10/3, Minutes of Cunard Board, 22 October 1968, University of Liverpool Archives.

147 D42/B10/3, Minutes of Cunard Board, 27 November 1968, University of Liverpool Archives.

148 Graham Strachan described the damage: 'Each high-pressure turbine, consisting of 13 rows of blading through which the steam expanded giving up its energy to driving the turbine, had suffered considerable damage. The 9th stage was completely stripped in the starboard turbine and partially stripped in the port with partial stripping of the 10th and cracking observed in the 8th and 10th stages of the port rotor. Further cracking was later discovered in some other rows when the rotors were closely inspected.' Unpublished and incomplete memoirs of Graham Strachan held by Glasgow University Archives.

149 Of over 200 steam turbines designed by Pametrada, QE2's were the only ones to fail due to this cause. See R.F. Darling, 40 Years of Progress, A History of the Wallsend Research Station 1945 -85, British Maritime Technology, London, 1985.

150 The Scottish Sunday Express, 9 February 1969, p 1.

151 Unpublished and incomplete memoirs of Graham Strachan held by Glasgow University Archives..

152 Letter to Ian Johnston from Tom Kameen, 5 December 1996.

153 Unpublished and incomplete memoirs of Graham Strachan held by Glasgow University Archives. Despite this public statement, Sir Arnold indicated privately that he thought JBE were guilty of gross negligence and offered, short of appearing as a witness, to 'render whatever assistance he could to Cunard and their legal advisors in establishing this point.'

154 This was made up as follows; basic cost of hull £19,716,172 plus escalation costs of £3,093,673. Basic cost of machinery £4,741,370 plus escalation costs of £511,252.

155 Cunard Line brochure 1969, pp 4-5.

156 Sherban Cantacuzino, 'QE2 Interiors', The Architectural Review, June 1969, p 426.

157 'Interior design: public rooms for a variety of uses and tastes', Design, April 1969, p 54.

158 Drusilla Beyfus, 'How to Design a 'Floating Resort', The Weekend Telegraph Magazine, 7 April 1967, p 23.

159 Neil Potter and Jack Frost, QE2: The Authorised Story, George G. Harrap, London, 1969, p 141.

160 Sherban Cantacuzino, 'QE2 Interiors', The Architectural Review, June 1969, p 452.

161 Vincent Mulchrone, 'The World's Finest Ship', Queen Elizabeth 2: Pride of British Industry, Pitkin Pictorials, London, 1969, p 14.

162 Ibid.

163 Ibid.

164 Sherban Cantacuzino, 'QE2 Interiors', The Architectural Review, June 1969, p 448.

165 Vincent Mulchrone, 'The World's Finest Ship', Queen Elizabeth 2: Pride of British Industry, Pitkin Pictorials, London, 1969, p 10.

166 Ibid p 3.

167 Ibid.

168 'Interior design: public rooms for a variety of uses and tastes', Design, April 1969, p 68.

169 Robert Melville, 'QE2 Interiors', The Architectural Review, June 1969, p 447.

170 Vincent Mulchrone, 'The World's Finest Ship', Queen Elizabeth 2: Pride of British Industry, Pitkin Pictorials, London, 1969, p 10.

171 Ibid, pp 15-16.

172 Vincent Mulchrone, 'The World's Finest Ship', Queen Elizabeth 2: Pride of British Industry, Pitkin Pictorials, London, 1969, p 16.

173 Sir Hugh Casson, Special QE2 Supplement, The Times, Tuesday April 29 1969, p iii.

174 'Interior design: public rooms for a variety of uses and tastes', Design, April 1969, pp 62-63.

175 Neil Potter and Jack Frost, QE2: The Authorised Story, George G. Harrap, London, 1969, p 145.

176 Vincent Mulchrone, 'The World's Finest Ship', Queen Elizabeth 2: Pride of British Industry, Pitkin Pictorials, London, 1969, p 16.

177 'Interior design: public rooms for a variety of uses and tastes', Design, April 1969, pp 63-64.

178 Sherban Cantacuzino, 'QE2 Interiors', The Architectural Review, June 1969, p 426.

179 Sir Hugh Casson, Special QE2 Supplement, The Times, 29 April 1969, p iii.

180 D. N. Wallace, Shipping World and Shipbuilder, January 1969, p 88.

181 'Queen Elizabeth 2: A ship with a past...and a future', Shipbuilding and Shipping Record, January 31, 1969, p 146.

182 Kenneth Agnew, 'QE2: Design for future trends in world travel', The Architects' Journal, 9 April 1969, pp 985-996.

183 D. N. Wallace, Shipping World and Shipbuilder, February 1969, p 88.

184 Philip Dawson, Cruise Ships: An evolution in design, Conway Maritime Press, London, 2000, p 44.

185 Sherban Cantacuzino, 'QE2 Interiors', The Architectural Review, June 1969, p 460.

186 Ibid, p 461.

187 Neil Potter and Jack Frost, QE2: The Authorised Story, George G. Harrap, London, 1969, p 153.

188 From a lecture entitled 'Ocean Liner Twilight' by Ted Scull at the Ocean Liner Society's Ship Show at the National Hotel, Bloomsbury, London on 20 October 2007.

189 'Pleasure Island' (Cunard brochure, published in 1971).

190 QE2 Special Supplement, The Times, 29 April 1969.

191 'Interior design: public rooms for a variety of uses and tastes', Design, April 1969, p 57.

192 Robert Spark, 'Design in Ships of Contrasting Size and Function', Shipping World and Shipbuilder, October 1969, pp 7-11.

193 These photographs are filed with other QE2 material from Gardner's personal collection at the Design Archives in the University of Brighton.

194 Sea Breezes, February 1969, p 159.

195 Sea Breezes, July 1969, p 496.

196 HRH Prince Charles, in his address to the Royal Institute of British Architects on the occasion of its 150th Anniversary Royal Gala Dinner at Hampton Court Palace on 30 May 1984. See http://www.princeofwales.gov.uk/speechesandarticles/a_speech_by_hrh_the_prince_of_wales_at_the_150th_anniversary_1876801621.html.

197 'Hotel at Sea', Time, 16 May 1969.

198 Peter C. Kohler, posted to the Yahoo! Web discussion group Liners List on 14 April 2008.

199 E-mail sent by Michael Cango to Bruce Peter, April 2008.

200 Peter C. Kohler, posted to the Yahoo! Web discussion group Liners List on 14 April 2008.

201 Ibid.

202 Count Basie and Albert Murray, Good Morning Blues, Da Capo, New York, 1985, pp 355-356.

203 James Gardner, The ARTful Designer: Ideas off the Drawing Board, Centurion, London, 1993, pp 304-305.

204 'Antilles runs aground in Caribbean; Queen Elizabeth 2 goes to aid passengers', The Times, 9 January 1971, p 1.

205 Sea Breezes, March 1971, p 164.

206 Carol Thatcher, Eric Flounders and Michael Gallagher, QE2: Forty Years Famous, Simon & Schuster, London, 2007, p 124.

*The **Queen Elizabeth 2** gets under way from Southampton for Bilbao on 15 June 2008. (Miles Cowsill)*

207 James Gardner, <u>The ARTful Designer: Ideas off the Drawing Board</u>, Centurion, London, 1993, p 303. Here Gardner appears to exaggerate as no evidence can be found substantiating his assertion that the QE2's bow was badly holed by a rogue wave.

208 The QE2 architect Alan Irvine remembers meeting Matthews in his role as a ceiling tile salesman in the mid-1950s. Interview with Alan Irvine by telephone by Bruce Peter on 13 May 2008.

209 Diary from Sir Hugh Casson's personal papers, stored at the Victoria & Albert Museum, London.

210 'QE2 more suited to cruising role', <u>Shipbuilding and Shipping Record</u>, 24 November 1972, pp 27-32.

211 'Anchor's Awry', <u>Time</u>, 20 November 1972.

212 Ibid.

213 Ibid.

214 'Whicker's World: QE2', BBC TV, 1983.

215 'Extensive security operation launched after mid-Atlantic bomb threat', <u>The Times</u>, 19 May 1972, pp 1-2. See also 'A Queen's Ransom', <u>Time</u>, 19 May 1972.

216 'QE2: Man charged by FBI', <u>The Times</u>, 22 May 1972, p 1.

217 President Anwar Sadat, interviewed by telecast by the BBC on 16 July 1974, reported in *Time* magazine on 29 July 1974.

218 'QE2 – Boiler trouble halts cruise', <u>The Times</u>, 3 April 1974, p 1.

219 'Passengers transferred to Norwegian liner', <u>The Times</u>, 4 April 1974, p 1.

220 'QE2 turns back after fire in engine room', <u>The Times</u>, 24 July 1976, p 3.

221 'Southampton explosives conspiracy: six men face charges; jury told of plan to blow up the QE2', <u>The Times</u>, 12 October 1976, p 2.

222 Bruce Peter, <u>Knud E. Hansen A/S: Ship Design Through Seven Decades</u>, Forlaget Nautilus, Copenhagen, 2007, pp 232-233.

223 Peter C. Kohler, posted to the Yahoo! Web discussion group Liners List on 14 April 2008.

224 Ibid.

225 'The Queen is Hailed', <u>Time</u>, 17 May 1982.

226 Captain Ronald W. Warwick, <u>QE2: The Cunard Line Flagship, Queen Elizabeth 2</u>, Norton, New York, 1988, p 115.

227 John Maxtone-Graham, <u>Tribute to a Queen: The Rededication of Queen Elizabeth 2</u>, Berlitz, Springfield, NJ, 1987, p 100.

228 John Maxtone-Graham, <u>Tribute to a Queen: The Rededication of Queen Elizabeth 2</u>, Berlitz, Springfield, NJ, 1987, p 100.

229 Captain Ronald W. Warwick, <u>QE2: The Cunard Line Flagship, Queen Elizabeth 2</u>, Norton, New York, 1988, p 119.

230 John Maxtone-Graham, <u>Tribute to a Queen: The Rededication of Queen Elizabeth 2</u>, Berlitz, Springfield, NJ, 1987, p 100.

231 Lt Cdr JL Muxworthy, RN (Ed.) <u>Canberra: The Great While Whale Goes to War</u>, Peninsular & Oriental S.N. Co., London, 1982, pp 77-79.

232 Captain Ronald W. Warwick, <u>QE2: The Cunard Line Flagship, Queen Elizabeth 2</u>, Norton, New York, 1988, pp 124-125.

233 John Maxtone-Graham, <u>Tribute to a Queen: The Rededication of Queen Elizabeth 2</u>, Berlitz, Springfield, NJ, 1987, p 103.

234 'QE2 has second refit', <u>The Times</u>, 23 July 1983, p 2.

235 'QE2 due in Bremerhaven for two-week refit', <u>The Times</u>, 28 November 1983, p 14.

236 Trafalgar House buys stake in P&O', <u>The Times</u>, 19 May 1983, p 17. 'Has P&O met its Trafalgar?', <u>The Sunday Times</u>, 29 May 1983, p 63.

237 'Trafalgar House Takeover Bid for P&O', <u>Ships Monthly</u>, August 1983, pp 11-13.

238 'Why Nigel Broackes Stops Laughing', <u>The Times</u>, 15 July 1983, p 7.

239 'Trafalgar House to buy Norwegian cruise liners', <u>The Times</u>, 12 May 1983, p 25.

240 'Cunard to treble use of Concorde charter', <u>The Times</u>, 8 November 1983, p 3.

241 'Concorde makes flight in record time', <u>The Times</u>, 15 February 1985, p 9.

242 Neil Potter and Jack Frost, <u>QE2: The Authorised Story</u>, George G. Harrap, London, 1969, p 81.

243 Interview with Stephen Payne, Chief Naval Architect of Carnival Corporate Shipbuilding, by Philip Dawson by telephone, 2 June 2008.

244 Dipl.Ing. Peter Bahr, Dipl.Ing. Anwar Elahi, Dipl.Ing. Dieter Haake, Dipl.Ing. Georg Klinge, Dipl.Ing. Werner Lüken, Dipl.Ing. Klaus Rugel, 'Umbau Queen Elizabeth 2 auf der Lloyd Werft, Bremerhaven, in nur 179 tagen', <u>Hansa</u>, Nr 12, 1987, p 725.

245 Ibid, p 726.

246 Ibid, p 726.

247 Ibid, p 744.

248 Interview with Stephen Payne, Chief Naval Architect of Carnival Corporate Shipbuilding, by Philip Dawson by telephone, 2 June 2008.

249 John Maxtone-Graham, <u>Tribute to a Queen: The Rededication of Queen Elizabeth 2</u>, Berlitz, Springfield, NJ, 1987, p 106.

250 Captain Ronald W. Warwick, <u>QE2: The Cunard Line Flagship, Queen Elizabeth 2</u>, Norton, New York, 1988, p 145.

251 Dipl.Ing. Peter Bahr, Dipl.Ing. Anwar Elahi, Dipl.Ing. Dieter Haake, Dipl.Ing. Georg Klinge, Dipl.Ing. Werner Lüken, Dipl.Ing. Klaus Rugel, 'Umbau Queen Elizabeth 2 auf der Lloyd Werft, Bremerhaven, in nur 179 tagen', <u>Hansa</u>, Nr 12, 1987, p 727.

252 Ibid, p 742.

253 'QE2 – Widespread problems on first voyage after refit', <u>The Times</u>, 1 May 1987, p 1.

254 Bryan Appleyard, 'All at sea on the ocean wave', <u>The Times</u>, 4 May 1987, p 9.

255 'QE2 begins celebrations to mark 150th anniversary of Cunard shipping line by cutting 99 minutes off the best time for Atlantic crossing', <u>The Times</u>, 23 July 1990, p 2.

256 'Reports that Cunard is to replace remaining British crew members of QE2 with Filipinos spark political dispute', <u>The Times</u>, 3 August 1991, p 2.

257 'Holed QE2 limps to port after evacuation of passengers', <u>The Sunday Times</u>, 9 August 1992, p 1.

258 Broackes was knighted in 1984 for his work as Chairman of the Docklands Development Corporation to encourage the redevelopment of London's Docklands.

259 Erik Ipsen, 'Kvaerner Is Close to Bidding for Troubled Group : Lifeline for Trafalgar House?', <u>International Herald Tribune</u>, 28 February, 1996.

260 'Refurbishment and development proposals for Queen Elizabeth 2', Met Studio/McNeece, February 1994.

The QE2 at the Spithead Fleet Review in 1977. (Ambrose Greenway)

261 Ibid.

262 Interview with John McNeece by Bruce Peter at his home on 16 May 2008.

263 '1,500 pieces of furniture too old or battered for liner undergoing refurbishment spread across NY thrift shops', <u>The Times</u>, 21 November 1994, p11.

264 Interview with John McNeece by Bruce Peter at his home on 16 May 2008.

265 '300 passengers booked for first trans-Atlantic journey on QE2 since refurbishment stranded because of faulty plumbing in cabins', <u>The Sunday Times</u>, 18 December 1994, pp 1 and 24.

266 'Cunard faces further embarrassment after US Coast Guard in NY order safety repairs before vessel allowed to sail', <u>The Times</u>, 24 December 1994, p 1.

267 'Passengers on board unfinished QE2 display Dunkirk spirit but insist voyage no laughing matter', <u>The Times</u>, 22 December 1994, p 4.

268 'Kvaerner says it will raise £1 billion from sale of Trafalgar House's non-core assets after company accepts its £904 million takeover bid', <u>The Times</u>, 5 March 1996, p 25.

269 'Egyptian Govt demands £16 m in damages from Cunard cruise liner which collided with protected Red Sea coral reef', <u>The Times</u>, 11 April 1996, p 2.

270 Cunard Line website, www.cunard.co.uk.

271 Terry Farrell, 'Place: A Story of Modelmaking, Menageries and Paper Rounds', <u>Terry Farrell - Life and Work - Early Years to 1981</u>, Laurence King, London, 2004, p 72.

*Profile drawings of the **Queen Elizabeth 2** in her 1969 condition, top, as delivered from Upper Clyde Shipbuilders, and as she appeared at the end of her Cunard career in 2008. (Drawings by Ian Johnston)*

QE2 - STATISTICS

1969
Length (overall): 963 feet or 293.53 metres
Beam:105 feet or 32.01 metres
Draught: 32 feet 6 inches or 9.9 metres
Gross tonnage: 65,862 grt
Service speed: 28.5 knots
Maximum speed:
Passenger capacity: 2,025 in liner service,
1,700 in cruise service
Crew: 906
Machinery: Four Pametrada/John Brown
Engineering steam turbines
Power output: 110,000 shaft h.p. or 82,060 kW

1972
Gross tonnage: 66,851 grt
Passenger capacity: 1,815

1977
Gross tonnage: 67,140 grt

1987
Gross tonnage: 67,139grt
Service speed: 28.5 knots
Maximum speed: 32.5 knots
Passenger capacity: 1,870
Machinery: Nine MAN/B&W
9-cylinder 58/64 medium speed
turbo-charged diesel-alternator sets,
driving two GEC AC synchronous
electric motors
Power output: 95,615 kW

1994
Gross tonnage: 69,053 grt
Passenger capacity: 1,870

2008
Gross tonnage: 70,327 gt
Passenger capacity: 1,778
Crew: 1,016

GLOSSARY OF TERMS

Araldite: the registered trademark name, originally belonging to Ciba ARL Ltd. for a range of epoxy, acrylic and polyurethane adhesives used for various structural and engineering applications. For QE2 an Araldite fillet along the lapped external joint between the steel hull and alloy superstructure serves to isolate the two metals from direct contact with one another.

beam: the width of a ship, unless otherwise given as beam overall, is the moulded beam, which is the breadth measured inside the hull plating, excluding the overhang of decks, lifeboats, bridge wings, etc.

bilge keel: an external anti-rolling fin fitted amidships at the turn of the bottom plating to the ship's side, called the bilge. Bilge also refers to an internal drainage space along the edges of a ship's double bottom.

bow thruster: also known as a transverse thruster, this is a propeller inside a tube passing from one side to the other of a ship's hull below the waterline providing added manoeuvrability while docking and undocking. Many modern ships have transverse thrusters both at the bow and stern, enabling them to be propelled sideways at low speed towards or away from a dock or quay.

bulkhead: a vertical wall or partition, normally made of steel, and usually being the structures that laterally sub-divide a ship's hull into watertight compartments: used also in reference to insulated fire-screen partitioning of a ship's internal spaces.

bulkhead deck: usually the first deck above the waterline, which is the point below which bulkheads sub-divide the hull into closeable watertight compartments. Passenger ships are usually also divided into larger fire zones above this level.

bunker: compartment or tank aboard ship where fuel is stored: also refers to the fuel itself or to the process of fuelling a ship known as bunkering.

casing / trunking / trunkway: in shipping terminology this generally refers to any enclosed vertical shaft extending through a number of decks to provide access to hold spaces below or to carry ventilation shafts to the ship's interior or uptakes for steam and exhaust gases from the machinery.

cavitation: the formation of air cavities or partial vacuums between solid surfaces and liquids that can occur when a ship's propeller turns rapidly in water, tending to cause vibration within the hull. The design of marine propellers endeavours to avoid this phenomenon at the speeds likely to be used in service.

centre of gravity: the point through which are balanced the various downward forces of a ship's weight and the distribution of her contents.

The QE2 at Malta in July on part of her 'Mediterranean Splendour' cruise. (Ian Collard)

chintz: cloth and fabrics used for upholstery, draperies and other soft furnishings that are printed or *blocked* with coloured patterns, very often of floral designs. Chintzes generally tend to be associated with the charms of a more feminine and sometimes old-world style of decoration than with modern design.

compound steam engine: a development from the earliest single-cylinder reciprocating engines, where the remaining energy in steam exhausted from the primary cylinder was harnessed to power a larger-diameter second cylinder to yield added shaft power.

DM: Deutschmark, the former unit of German currency before the Euro was adopted.

davit: a small fixed or moveable crane that extends beyond the side of a ship and is used for handling cargo or stores, or most commonly used in pairs for handling and lowering lifeboats. Gravity davits lower their payload to the water by gravity upon the release of a holding device.

double bottom: the underside structure of a ship's hull between the bilges, which is plated both below and above the keel and rib frames forming a cellular watertight bottom that provides added strength and protection against flooding of the hull.

deckhead: the ceiling of an internal shipboard space or room.

double-reduction geared turbine: a turbine whose operating speed of rotation is stepped down through two stages of gearing, i.e. two cogs of progressively larger diameters, to drive a propeller or other machinery at a lower running speed.

fin stabiliser: also known as active fin stabilisers or hydrofin stabilisers, these are retractable fins extended from the sides of the hull underwater amidships above the turn of the bilge. They function like horizontally oriented semi-balanced rudders, and are controlled so that as to counteract the ship's tendency to roll by turning in opposite directions on either side of the hull against the sea's tendency to cause rolling.

frames: the vertical structural ribs of a ship known as hull frames that extend from the keel out to the sides of the hull and up to the strength deck atop the hull at intervals usually of about 900 mm (36 inches). In some larger ships, such as QE2, additional web frames are set at longer intervals among the hull frames for added strength and stiffening of the overall structures. In QE2 both the hull and web frames are continued fully up through the alloy superstructure. Ships' decks are also longitudinally framed.

Formica: a registered trademark name of the Formica Corporation for a range of decorative laminates of resin impregnated kraft paper in multiple layers behind a melamine-protected outer decorative layer, compressed and thermal cured to create a durable and easily cared-for surface with various finishes, colours, patterns and textures for wall claddings, furniture and other architectural and decorative products.

freeboard height: generally this is the height of a ship's side from the waterline to the upper edge of the highest complete deck with the means for permanent watertight closure of all openings including portholes, windows, hatches, etc. This is measured vertically amidships downwards from the line of the first open deck to the designated minimum summer load line indicating the underwater depth for which loading of the ship is certified for summer navigation in salt water.

GRP: glass reinforced plastic, widely known also as fibreglass or glass fibre.

GT: **gross tonnage**: also referred to as Gross Registered Tonnage or GRT, this is a measure of a ship's capacity determined by the authority with which the ship is registered, e.g. Lloyd's Register. Having nothing to do with a vessel's actual weight or displacement, this is in broad terms calculated as being a ship's total internal volume in cubic feet divided by 100.

Gurkha: a Rajput soldier or regiment from the Nepal province of Gurkha in the British and Indian armies.

Hessian: From Hessian cloth, a surface with a textured burlap finish.

hull frames: See frames.

knot: a measure of speed in nautical miles per hour: see also nautical mile.

measured mile: used for determining actual speed, this is an offshore location where a ship can run up to speed in a straight line and proceed between two visible points on the shoreline marked by measured mile posts placed one nautical mile apart. For the sake of accuracy there are two posts, one directly behind the other, at either end of the measured mile, with measurement being taken between the points at which the two posts at either end are passed when visually aligned at right-angles to the ship's side.

meth: methane gas.

monocoque: a structure such as an aircraft fuselage in which the outer shell forms an integral part of the load-bearing framework and as in an aircraft, may also be designed to absorb some of the bending and torsion stresses of the whole body's loading and movement.

nautical mile: a measure of distance used in sea and air navigation equalling one minute (one sixtieth of a degree) of longitude of a great circle at the Earth's equator, equivalent to 1,853.2 metres or 6,080 feet.

Plexiglass: a trademark name for an acrylic glass polymer (plastic) among similar products such as Acrylite,™ Perspex,™ Lucite,™ etc. developed by various laboratories around 1928 and at first widely sold in 1933 by the Rohm & Haas Company.

plimsoll mark: named after the nineteenth century British Member of Parliament and shipping reformist, Samuel Plimsoll (1824-98), this is a 300mm-diameter circle intersected by a horizontal line and bearing letters indicating the classification society under which the ship is registered (e.g. L R, for Lloyd's Register) painted amidships on a ship's hull that indicates the location of the summer load line; see also 'freeboard height' above.

port(side): the left-hand side of a ship when facing forward, opposite the starboard (right-hand) side.

Pullman bed: a fold-away berth or bed, usually above a fixed lower bed or seats, originally designed in America during the 1860s by the Pullman Company for railway sleeping accommodation and since also widely adopted for shipboard use.

RFA: Royal Fleet Auxiliary.

shell / shell plating: the steel plating enclosing a ship's hull.

starboard: the right-hand side of a ship when facing forward, opposite the port (left-hand) side.

superstructure: the structural part of a ship or deckhouse enclosing those decks above the hull.

steam excitation: abnormal steam conditions stimulated within a turbine under certain conditions of heat, pressure, rotation speed etc, usually resulting from a design or manufacturing flaw, that can be destructive to the turbine.

tonnage: see GT.

transverse thrusters: see bow thrusters.

triple-expansion steam turbine: exhaust steam is fed from an initial high-pressure turbine to progressively increased-diameter second and third turbine stages of intermediate and low pressure to extract remaining power from the steam as it is spent.

*In her mid-1980s condition, prior to re-engining, an immaculate **Queen Elizabeth 2** steams through the English Channel - the epitome of power and grace at sea. (Fotoflite)*

BIBLIOGRAPHY

Interviews

Interview with Brian Beardsmore, formerly of Dennis Lennon & Partners, by Bruce Peter by telephone, 23 April 2008.

Interview with Tony Benn by Bruce Peter by telephone, 21 April 2008.

Interview with Sir Hugh Casson by Philip Dawson by telephone, 15 September 1982.

Interview with Norman Gilchrist by Ian Johnston by telephone, 3 November 1996.

Interview with Keith Gledhill, former purser of the *Queen Elizabeth*, by Philip Dawson by telephone, 18 January 2008.

Interview with Jim Gordon, formerly of Dennis Lennon & Partners, by Bruce Peter by telephone, 21 May 2008.

Interview with Tony Heaton, formerly of Heaton/Beloe, by Bruce Peter by telephone, 22 April 2008.

Interview with Alan Irvine, formerly of Buzas & Irvine, by Bruce Peter by telephone, 13 May 2008.

Interview with Tom Kameen by Ian Johnston by telephone, 19 November 1996.

Interview with Tom Kameen by Bruce Peter by telephone, 6 June 2008.

Interview with John Lang, President of The Cruise People Ltd, Toronto, by Philip Dawson, 27 September 2007.

Interview with John McNeece by Bruce Peter at his home, 16 May 2008.

Interview with Stephen Payne, Chief Naval Architect of Carnival Corporate Shipbuilding, by Philip Dawson by telephone, 2 June 2008.

Interview with Lady Reilly by Bruce Peter by telephone, 28 May 2008.

Interview with Don Sibebottom, Chairman of Glasdon Group Limited, by Philip Dawson by telephone, 4 May 2008.

Interview with Lord Snowdon by Bruce Peter by telephone, 9 May 2008.

Interview with David Trevor-Jones by Bruce Peter, 12 April 2008.

Interview with Roy Turner by Ian Johnston by telephone, 5 November 1996.

Books

Basie, Count and Murray, Albert, Good Morning Blues, Da Capo, New York, 1985.

Betjeman, John, Ghastly Good Taste, or, a depressing story of the rise and fall of English Architecture, Alan Blond, London, 1933.

Braynard, Frank O., The Big Ship: The story of the ss United States, Mariner's Museum, Newport News, Virginia, 1981.

Broackes, Nigel, A Growing Concern: An Autobiography, Weidenfeld and Nicolson, London, 1979.

Darling, R.F., 40 Years of Progress, A History of the Wallsend Research Station 1945 -85, British Maritime Technology, London, 1985.

Dawson, Philip, British Superliners of the Sixties: A design appreciation of the Oriana, Canberra and QE2, Conway Maritime Press, London 1990.

Dawson, Philip, Cruise Ships: An evolution in design, Conway Maritime Press, London, 2000.

Terry Farrell, Terry Farrell - Life and Work - Early Years to 1981, Laurence King, London, 2004.

Frampton, Kenneth, Modern Architecture: A critical history, Thames and Hudson Ltd, London, 1987.

Gardner, James, Elephants in the Attic, Orbis, London, 1983.

Gardner, James, The ARTful Designer: Ideas off the Drawing Board, Centurion, London, 1993.

Grenville, Anthony (ed), Refugees from the Third Reich in Britain, The Research Centre for German and Austrian Exile Studies, 2002.

Haresnape, Brian, British Rail 1948-1978: A Journey by Design, Ian Allan, Shepperton, 1979.

Haresnape, Brian, Sealink, Ian Allan, Shepperton, 1982.

Harvey, Clive, The Saxonia Sisters, Carmania, London, 2001.

Heskett, John, Industrial Design, Thames & Hudson, London, 1997.

Hicks, Ashley, David Hicks: Designer, Scriptum Editions, London, 2002.

Holland, Ralph, Alan Irvine: Architect Designer, RIBA, London, 1989.

Johnston, Ian, Ships for a Nation: John Brown & Company, Clydebank 1847-1971, West Dumbartonshire Libraries and Museums, 2000.

Kludas, Arnold, Die Großen Passagierschiffe der Welt Band V, Band V, Gerhard Stalling Verlag, Hamburg, 1974.

Long, Philip and Thomas, Jane (eds), Basil Spence: Architect, National Galleries of Scotland, 2008.

Manser, José, Hugh Casson: A Biography, Viking, London, 2000.

Maxtone-Graham, John, Tribute to a Queen: The Rededication of Queen Elizabeth 2, Berlitz, Springfield, NJ, 1987.

The Turboliner Michelangelo of 46,000 g.r.t., Italia Navigazione, Genoa and Ansaldo Shipyard Ltd, Genoa-Sestri, 1965.

Mulchrone, Vincent, 'The World's Finest Ship', Queen Elizabeth 2: Pride of British Industry, Pitkin Pictorials, London, 1969.

Muxworthy, Lt Cdr JL (Ed.) Canberra: The Great While Whale Goes to War, Peninsular & Oriental S.N. Co., London, 1982.

Peter, Bruce, Knud E. Hansen A/S: Ship Design through Seven Decades, Forlaget Nautilus, Copenhagen, 2007.

Potter, Neil and Frost, Jack, The Elizabeth, George G. Harrap, London, 1965.

Potter, Neil and Frost, Jack, QE2: The Authorised Story, George G. Harrap, London, 1969.

Pyatt, Edward C., National Physical Laboratory – A History, Mauve Publications, London, 1983.

Robertson, Bryan, Russell, John and Snowdon, Lord, Private View, Thames Nelson, London, 1965.

Smallpeice, Sir Basil, Of Comets and Queens, Airlife Publishing, Shrewsbury, 1981.

Thatcher, Carol, Flounders, Eric, and Gallagher, Michael, QE2: Forty Years Famous, Simon & Schuster, London, 2007.

Timms, Edward and Hughes, John (eds) Intellectual Migration and Cultural Transformation: Refugees from National Socialism in the English-Speaking World, Springer, Vienna and New York, 2003.

Warwick, Captain Ronald W., QE2: The Cunard Line Flagship, Queen Elizabeth 2, Norton, New York, 1988.

Wealleans, Anne, Designing Liners: A history of interior design afloat, Routledge, London, 2006.

Journal Articles

The Architects' Journal

Baird Dennison, '534 And All That', 25 January 1934, p 156.

Kenneth Agnew, 'QE2: Design for future trends in world travel', 9 April 1969, p 985-996.

The Architectural Review

Arthur J. Davis, 'The Architecture of the Liner', April 1914, pp 87-110.

Ian McCallum, 'Ship Interiors', February 1956, pp 133-140.

The Passenger Ship: Backward or Forward', November 1960, p 367.

Stephen Garrett, 'Amid-Ships', September 1961, pp 155-58.

AR/QE2: Special Issue, June 1969.

Country Life

Guy Oliver, 'The House of Michael Inchbald', No 15, 2003, pp 92-98.

Design

QE2 Special Issue, April 1969.

Designs

Plummer, Russell, 'A New Queen in 179 Days', Designs 87, Shippax, Halmstad, 1987, pp 122-123.

Brogren, Klas, 'An Interview with Lloyd Werft's Chairman Eckart Knoth', Designs 87, Shippax, Halmstad, 1987, p124.

Hansa

Dipl.Ing. Peter Bahr, Dipl.Ing. Anwar Elahi, Dipl.Ing. Dieter Haake, Dipl.Ing. Georg Klinge, Dipl.Ing. Werner Lüken, Dipl.Ing. Klaus Rugel, 'Umbau Queen Elizabeth 2 auf der Lloyd Werft, Bremerhaven, in nur 179 tagen', Nr 12, 1987, pp725-754.

Journal of Design History

Frank Jackson, 'The New Air Age: BOAC and design policy 1945-60', Oxford University Press, Oxford, Volume 4 Number 3, 1991, pp167-85.

The Motor Ship

'Queen Elizabeth 2', January 1969, p 505-510.

Power & Motor Yacht

Diana M. Byrne 'Jon Bannenberg 1929-2002: A look at the rule-breaking originality of the pre-eminent yacht designer', August 2002.

207

Sea Breezes

Letter from E. Armstrong, Slop Chest, February 1969, p159.

Letter from David Simpson, Slop Chest, July 1969, p496.

'Ships in the News', March 1971, p164.

The Shipbuilder and Marine Engine Builder

Canberra Souvenir Number, 1961, p 67.

Transactions of the Institute of Marine Engineers

Presidential Address by Tom Kameen, Volume 87, 1975, pp336-338.

Shipbuilding and Shipping Record

'Queen Elizabeth 2: A ship with a past…and a future', January 31, 1969, pp 146-161.

'QE2 more suited to cruising role', 24 November 1972, pp27-32.

Shipping World and Shipbuilder

'Questionnaire: Sir John Brocklebank – Chairman of Cunard', 28 January 1965, pp282-283.

'A Week at Sea or a Week at Butlins', 28 January 1965, pp390-391.

D. N. Wallace, 'Queen Elizabeth 2: Some design considerations,' January 1969, p 87-88.

Robert Spark, 'Design in Ships of Contrasting Size and Function', October 1969, pp7-11.

Ships Monthly

'Trafalgar House Takeover Bid for P&O', August 1983, pp11-13.

Twentieth Century Architecture

Becky Conekin, 'Fun and Fantasy, Escape and Edification: The Battersea Pleasure Grounds' in Elain Harwood and Alan Powers (eds), No 5: Festival of Britain, Twentieth Century Society, London, 2001, p127.

Newspapers

The Daily Express

'The Uninvited – or how Mr Bannenberg missed the party', Friday 22 September 1967, p2.

The Dumbarton Herald

'Sir Percy Bates at a luncheon for the Institute of Marine Engineers in London', 30 March 1940.

The Glasgow Herald

'New 'Queen' vital to Clydebank', 11 August 1961, p1.

The Independent

Obituary of Dennis Lennon, Architect, no. 1417, May 1991, p27.

International Herald Tribune

Erik Ipsen, 'Kvaerner Is Close to Bidding for Troubled Group: Lifeline for Trafalgar House?', 28 February 1996.

The Scottish Daily Express

'Mammoth order for Clyde is in the offing to replace the two 'Queens' of the Atlantic: Super-liners Ahoy! – and Cunard talks it over with John Brown's,' 9 April 1959, p1.

The Scottish Sunday Express

'What Reliance Can We Place on John Brown Engineering?', 9 February 1969, p1.

The Sunday Times

'Has P&O met its Trafalgar?', 29 May 1983, p63.

'Holed QE2 limps to port after evacuation of passengers', 9 August 1992, p1.

'300 passengers booked for first transatlantic journey on QE2 since refurbishment stranded because of faulty plumbing in cabins', 18 December 1994, pp1 and 24.

Time

'The New Queen', 1 November 1963.

'Hotel at Sea', 16 May 1969.

'Anchor's Awry', 20 November 1972.

President Anwar Sadat, interviewed by telecast by the BBC on 16 July 1974, reported in Time magazine on 29 July 1974.

'The Queen is Hailed', 17 May 1982.

The Times

'Make Q4 British Ambassador', 1 March 1965, p10.

Letter from Sir Hugh Casson, 21 September 1967, p11.

Special QE2 Supplement, 29 April 1969.

'Antilles runs aground in Caribbean; Queen Elizabeth 2 goes to aid passengers', 9 January 1971, p1.

'Extensive security operation launched after mid-Atlantic bomb threat', 19 May 1972, pp1-2.

'QE2: Man charged by FBI', 22 May 1972, p1.

'QE2 – Boiler trouble halts cruise', 3 April 1974, p1.

'Passengers transferred to Norwegian liner', 4 April 1974, p1.

'QE2 turns back after fire in engine room', 24 July 1976, p3.

'Southampton explosives conspiracy: six men face charges; jury told of plan to blow up the QE2', 12 October 1976, p2.

Obituary of Dan Wallace, 29 November 1979, p14.

'QE2 has second refit', 23 July 1983, p2.

'QE2 due in Bremerhaven for two week refit', 28 November 1983, p14.

Trafalgar House buys stake in P&O', 19 May 1983, p17.

'Why Nigel Broackes Stops Laughing', 15 July 1983, p7.

'Trafalgar House to buy Norwegian cruise liners', 12 May 1983, p25.

'Cunard to treble use of Concorde charter', 8 November 1983, p3.

'Concorde makes flight in record time', 15 February 1985, p9.

'QE2 – Widespread problems on first voyage after refit', 1 May 1987, p1.

Bryan Appleyard, 'All at sea on the ocean wave', 4 May 1987, p9.

'QE2 begins celebrations to mark 150th anniversary of Cunard shipping line by cutting 99 minutes off the best time for Atlantic crossing', 23 July 1990, p2.

'Reports that Cunard is to replace remaining British crew members of QE2 with Filipinos spark political dispute', 3 August 1991, p2.

'1,500 pieces of furniture too old or battered for liner undergoing refurbishment spread across NY thrift shops', 21 November 1994, p11.

'Cunard faces further embarrassment after US Coast Guard in NY order safety repairs before vessel allowed to sail', 24 December 1994, p1.

'Passengers onboard unfinished QE2 display Dunkirk spirit but insist voyage no laughing matter', 22 December 1994, p4.

'Kvaerner says it will raise £1 billion from sale of Trafalgar House's non-core assets after company accepts its £904 million takeover bid', 5 March 1996, p25.

'Egyptian Govt demands £16 m in damages from Cunard cruise liner which collided with protected Red Sea coral reef', 11 April 1996, p2.

The Weekend Telegraph Magazine

'The First Colour of the New Cunarder', 7 April 1967.

Welding and Metal Fabrication

Palmer, J.T., 'The Queen Elizabeth II Superstructure: Welded Fabrication of 1,100 tons of Alcan aluminium', January 1968, pp2-19.

Brochures

'Ships Have Been Boring Long Enough', (Cunard brochure, published in 1969).

Pleasure Island (Cunard brochure, published in 1971).

The new Cunard Queen Elizabeth 2 Press Guide, (Cunard, published in 1969).

Unique Ship, Unique Experience: Queen Elizabeth 2 World Cruise 1981, (Cunard brochure, published 1981).

Web Sources

Messages posted by Peter C. Kohler to the Yahoo! Web discussion group Liners List on 14 April 2008. Correspondence by e-mail between Michael Cango and Bruce Peter, April 2008. Prince Charles, in his address to the Royal Institute of British Architects on the occasion of its 150th anniversary Royal Gala Dinner at Hampton Court Palace on 30 May 1984. See http://www.princeofwales.gov.uk/speechesandarticles/a_speech_by_hrh_the_prince_of_wales_at_the_150th_anniversary_1876801621.html. Cunard Line website, www.cunard.co.uk.

Other Documents

John Brown & Co. Ltd, Report and Accounts 1966, Lord Aberconway's statement, p 16, Ian Johnston's collection.

Upper Clyde Shipbuilders documents
UCS 1/107/405, Salholm tender document, 31 May 1963, National Archives of Scotland.
UCS1/5/101. Report of 25 Feb 1966, National Archives of Scotland.
UCS 1/107/405, Draft letter by Robin Williamson dated 31 January 1966, National Archives of Scotland.
UCS 1/5/102, Minutes of John Brown & Company (Shipbuilders) Ltd, 20 December 1967, National Archives of Scotland.
UCS 5/1/5, Executive Committee minutes, 22 April and 27 May 1968, National Archives of Scotland.
UCS 5/1/5, Executive Committee minutes, 2 September 1968, National Archives of Scotland.
UCS 5/1/2 Minutes, 11 September 1968, National Archives of Scotland.
UCS 5/1/2, Minutes, 11 September 1968, National Archives of Scotland.
UCS 1/8/88 and UCS 1/8/89 ///, National Archives of Scotland.

Cunard documents
D42/B10/3, Minutes of Cunard Board, 22 October 1968, University of Liverpool Archives.
D42/B10/3, Minutes of Cunard Board, 27 November 1968, University of Liverpool Archives.
Miscellaneous documents, relating to the career of Dan Wallace, Cunard Archives, University of Liverpool Archives.
Sir John Brocklebank's message to staff, March 1962. Document in QE2 folder, University of Liverpool Archives.

Council of Industrial Design documents
Director's report to the 142nd meeting of Council held on 21 May 1965, Design Archives, Brighton College of Art and Design.

Correspondence, photographs and drawings relating to the QE2 deposited by the estate of James Gardner in the Design Archives, Brighton College of Art and Design.

Lecture notes
Notes for a lecture for the Design History Society entitled 'Plastics to Planes: Gaby Schreiber, Consultant', given on 16 March 2004, provided by Dr Jane Pavitt of the University of Brighton.
Lecture for the Ocean Liner Society's Ship Show entitled 'Ocean Liner Twilight' given on 20 October 2007 by Ted Scull at the National Hotel, Bloomsbury, London on 20 October 2007.

Other sources
'Refurbishment and development proposals for Queen Elizabeth 2', Met Studio/McNeece, February 1994, supplied by Chris Cawle of Met Studio, from the collection of Philip Dawson.
'Marine Accident Investigation Branch report of the investigation into the grounding of the passenger vessel *Queen Elizabeth 2* on 7 August 1992', published in July 1993.
'Project Lifestyle: Refurbishment and development proposals for Queen Elizabeth 2', Met Studio/McNeece, February 1994.
Unpublished and incomplete memoirs of Graham Strachan held by Glasgow University Archives.
Sir Hugh Casson's diaries and personal papers, Victoria & Albert Museum, London.

Letters to the authors
Letter from Lord Aberconway to Ian Johnston, dated 23 September 1998.
Letter from Tom Kameen to Ian Johnston, dated 5 December 1996.
Letter from Roy Turner, formerly Vickers-Armstrong's Naval Architect, to Ian Johnston, dated 5 December 1996.

TV Programmes
'Whicker's World': QE2, BBC TV, 1983.
'QE2: The Last Great Liner', IWC Media/BBC TV, 2007.

*The **Queen Elizabeth 2** at Adelaide in Australia. (Wayne Morris)*

INDEX

NOTE: PAGE NOS IN BOLD, REFER TO ILLUSTRATIONS AND CAPTIONS

A paying off pennant flies from QE2's mast as she sails up the Clyde for the final time on 5 October 2008, just over 41 years after she was launched into the river. (Miles Cowsill)

FAREWELL
CELEBRATION
2008

Queen Elizabeth 2
CUNARD

Southampton,
England

PHOTO CREDIT MILES COWSILL · LILY PUBLICATIONS

Lisbon, Portugal

Gibraltar

QUEEN ELIZABETH 2

Final
Voyage to
Dubai

November 2008

Rome, Italy

CUNARD
THE MOST FAMOUS OCEAN LINERS IN THE WORLD™

FAREWELL
CELEBRATION
2008

Queen Elizabeth 2

CUNARD

Naples, Italy

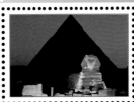

Valletta, Malta

QUEEN ELIZABETH 2

Cairo, Egypt

Dubai

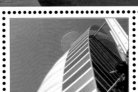

*Final
Voyage to
Dubai*

CUNARD

THE MOST FAMOUS OCEAN LINERS IN THE WORLD™

Isle of Man
Post
Eilan Vannin